All Around the Track

ALSO BY REX WHITE AND ANNE B. JONES
_____

*Gold Thunder: Autobiography
of a NASCAR Champion* (2005)

All Around the Track

*Oral Histories of Drivers,
Mechanics, Officials, Owners,
Journalists and Others in
Motorsports Past and Present*

ANNE B. JONES *and*
REX WHITE

Foreword by Ed Clark

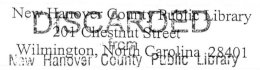

McFarland & Company, Inc., Publishers
Jefferson, North Carolina, and London

LIBRARY OF CONGRESS CATALOGUING-IN-PUBLICATION DATA

Jones, Anne B.
All around the track : oral histories of drivers, mechanics, officials, owners, journalists and others in motorsports past and present / Anne B. Jones and Rex White ; foreword by Ed Clark.
p.   cm.
Includes index.

ISBN-13: 978-0-7864-2988-2
softcover : 50# alkaline paper ∞

1. Stock car racing—History.   2. NASCAR (Association)
I. White, Rex, 1930–   II. Title.
GV1029.9.S74J66   2007   796.72—dc22   2007008335

British Library cataloguing data are available

Cover photograph ©2007 American Spirit Images

Manufactured in the United States of America

McFarland & Company, Inc., Publishers
Box 611, Jefferson, North Carolina 28640
www.mcfarlandpub.com

My work in this book is dedicated
to my mother, Anne "Holly" Barksdale,
who always believed I could do anything,
and to my husband, Sidney Jones,
my best supporter, promoter and friend.

—Anne B. Jones

My work in this book is dedicated
to two wonderful women,
Edith B. White and our daughter Brenda.
They gave me unconditional support,
shared in my early stuggle and
will forever hold a place in my heart.

And to author Greg Fielden whom I commend
as one of the most outstanding contributers
to the preservation of NASCAR history.

—Rex White,
1960 NASCAR Champion

Acknowledgments

We are grateful to everyone who has helped us with this project, and we ask forgiveness for any errors. We did the best we could confirming facts, dates, names, places and events, but time is quickly lowering a veil on racing's past and we're looking at things through the fading light of dusk.

The people who have made this endeavor possible include Sidney Jones, Eddie Samples, Larry Hinson, Eddie Spurling, Rev. Bill Brannon, Darlene Chamlee, Dennis Smith, Mike Bell, Audrey Turner, Bobbie Sanders, members of the Georgia Automobile Racing Hall of Fame, Association members of Living Legends of Auto Racing, Atlanta Motor Speedway, Raceway Ministries, Dale Snyder of www.SnyderVideo.com, the International Motorsports Hall of Fame in Talladega, the Collier Collection Archives, and Appalachian State University. We would especially like to thank all of those who participated in interviews and provided photographs. Without you, this work would have not been possible.

Anne B. Jones
Rex White

Contents

Foreword
by Ed Clark

Like most fans of auto racing, I had a first experience that made a lasting impression.

My love for racing began atop the Ferris wheel at the Virginia State Fair in Richmond, Virginia, when I was eight years old. Each time I rose high into the air I would gaze over the wooden fence separating the midway from the old dirt half-mile fairgrounds speedway and observe the loud mudslinging modified racers roaring at breakneck speed around the oval. The appeal was immediate and powerful.

Now, almost 50 years later, I still get that same rush of exhilaration every time I hear the roar of a powerful racing engine as it comes to life.

I am blessed to have been involved in what my boss, Bruton Smith, calls "the greatest sport in America" for well over 30 years. I've covered events as a journalist and worked with several tracks in public relations and event management positions, including my current job as president and general manager of Atlanta Motor Speedway. For the past several years I've even enjoyed the opportunity to get behind the wheel of a racecar and experience the thrill of driving in competition. None of this has ever felt like a job. Instead, it has been a tremendous labor of love that has resulted in great friendships and many lasting memories.

Auto racing has evolved from simple events played out on dusty dirt tracks carved out on farmers' fields to an industry of epic proportions. The days when drivers competed for the winner's prize of a country ham, a pile of slab wood or an eight-inch tin trophy are gone. Today's winners collect millions of dollars in a single season and garner even more from endorsement deals and investments. Multitudes of new fans flock to speedways each year to watch modern-day heroes compete and see firsthand what the buzz is all about.

One of the genuine appeals of auto racing is the colorful array of personalities who make up what I like to call "the high-powered traveling circus." From the major league of NASCAR to the short tracks dotted across America, racing has attracted many intriguing people who either have in the past made or are currently creating the history of the sport.

The foundation of modern-day auto racing was laid in the 50s, 60s and the 70s—days when winning meant more than the winner's purse. These were times when those in racing's inner circle participated because of their love of the sport and the intense adrenaline rush it provided. Their stories of competition and camaraderie beg to be told and readers will find many of their interesting perspectives herein.

Not all of the people you will read about were big-time winning drivers. Some were or are competitors in racing's minor leagues. Others owned cars driven by these brave and daring racers or worked as mechanics, broadcasters, photographers, event officials, journalists, historians or trophy queens. But they all share a common bond: They felt the same attraction I did years ago at Richmond Fairgrounds Raceway and the thrill of auto racing became a paramount part of their lives.

I'm sure you will feel the same thrill as you explore the life stories found in *All Around the Track*.

Ed Clark is president and general manager of the Atlanta Motor Speedway, which has become one of the highest revenue-producing facilities in Georgia, with millions of dollars going to local charities.

Preface

By the time we had finished our first book, *Gold Thunder*, Rex White and I had built a tremendous writing momentum and a firm friendship. For me, the joy of writing, the thrill of new experiences, and the interesting friends I made were too much to give up.

Even in 1957, racetracks were primitive. This photo shows a mixed convertible and hard top race. Through 1956, promoters held separate races for convertibles, but in 1957, shows were mixed to fill the field. (Courtesy Vaudell Sosebee.)

The grandstands and infield are packed at this early race at Langhorne, Pennsylvania. (Photograph by Bruce Craig. Courtesy Collier Collection Archives.)

In listening to Rex, and in reading and conducting research, I learned things about our nation's history, culture and people I had never known. I gained tremendous respect for the pioneers of motorsports and those who are now fighting to preserve its past.

In the early days of auto racing in the United States, it was a slam-bang, pedal-to-the metal affair. Competitors faced tough times on and off the track. On shoestring budgets, they were forced to improvise. Rarely finding sponsors, they built and repaired their own cars, towed them or drove them to speedways, and then turned around and did the same thing the very next night. As they gradually expanded their territory, they made unanticipated discoveries, broadening their education as they traveled the country.

Exposed to different geographical regions, cultures, dialects, and customs, early racers bonded into a close-knit racing community, a squabbling family helping each other through the hard times while still battling each other. Out of necessity, those who were strong became inventive and ingenious. Through trial and error, they acquired toughness and a knowledge of physics and aerodynamics equal to that of engineering graduates. Many used their experiences as stepping stones, developing people skills, business savvy and a tight-fisted appreciation for the dollar.

This early race in Hillsboro, North Carolina, in 1954 and led by Gober Sosebee shows how close spectators were allowed to get to the track. (Courtesy Eddie Samples Photo Collection.)

The more I learned about the early drivers and their families, the more respect-filled and fascinated I became. Then Rex and I made a horrifying discovery. We found vast voids in the records and historical documentation, and little information about many important early participants... ones whose sacrifices, heroism and determination propelled the sport forward. In addition, we learned that few current NASCAR fans or drivers knew about or appreciated them. Few are aware of how the sport reflects our nation's early culture in its rebellious spirit and rugged individualism, or how racing helped to shape our society through its impact on the auto industry. Many may never know, because, tragically, its history is being lost every day.

Rex and I decided our second book should focus on racing's pioneers and those who are working to preserve racing's legacy. When we began, we were stunned to learn of the deaths of many with whom we had wished to talk and were saddened at the loss of Joe Epton, Bettie Panch and Benny Parsons shortly after their interviews. We realized if we did not act quickly, the book would never and could never be written.

Like *Gold Thunder*, this book was a joy to write. The people we met, the places we went and the experiences we had are irreplaceable. Our interviews were conversations filled with camaraderie and we wish to share them with you. —*A.B.J.*

Introduction

When the *Atlanta Journal-Constitution* reported that Atlanta Motor Speedway was bringing over twice as much money into the state of Georgia as the Atlanta Braves, Falcons, and Hawks teams combined, people took notice. When the projected income reached nearly five billion dollars, people took notice again. These figures are from only one state. Nationally, six million people a year attend Nextel Cup Series races and 200 million more, in bars and at home, watch them on television. This does not include money generated by the zooming popularity of drag racing. Combined with the yearly revenues from licensed promotional materials (over two billion dollars), and radio and television network deals (hundreds of millions of dollars), the totals boggle the mind. Fueled by a passion for power and speed, fans have made racing the second most popular sport in America, next to professional football.

Who were the pioneers who made the sport possible and helped it come as far as it has today? This book provides insider information never before found in racing-related memoirs. Chapters focus on each subject's background and personality with emphasis on parental and geographical influences, life themes, attitudes and decisions which have contributed to their accomplishments, and their insights about this phenomenal sport. These are intimate stories compiled from interviews with and about racing legends. Together they are a wild ride of hysterical and historical tales, carrying readers beyond the cold facts of headlines into the sometimes violent, often courageous hearts of racing's trailblazers and modern-day participants. Readers, start your engines, it's full speed ahead!

CHAPTER 1

Raymond Parks:
Beginning with Liquor Cars

Raymond Parks has been described as an unrivaled pioneer who was the first major car owner to compete in NASCAR-sanctioned races, the moneyman, the ultimate sportsman, and the leader of the "Georgia Gang." It's been said that no one has contributed more to the sport of stock-car racing.

Born on June 5, 1914, in Lumpkin County, Georgia, Parks was one of six children whose mother, Leila, died of leukemia while they were young. They lived in Dawsonville until Parks was two, then moved to Brown's Bridge Road in Hall County. His father, Alfred, next married Leila's sister Ila and sired ten more children in the poverty-stricken North Georgia mountains where they eked out what living they could on the family farm.

By the time Parks was in his teens, he was a major contributor to the family's survival. It was from the hand-to-mouth necessity of feeding the family that he became involved in running liquor cars. For many young men during Prohibition and the Depression, involvement in illegal moonshining meant the difference between sustenance and starvation.

Parks was fascinated with cars and speed right from childhood. As a toddler he pedaled his tricycle as fast he could around a wishing well on the family's front porch, sustaining his first major accident when he crashed head-on into the pump handle.

"That's why I never had sense," he says today, "and I left school in the seventh grade."

Truth be told, according to friends, Parks had to give up a formal education to provide for his struggling family. He ultimately became self-educated and soon applied the life lessons he learned to entrepreneurship, beginning with bootlegging.

"Bootlegging was a way to make a living. My father operated the 'Five Mile Store' [so named because it was five miles from Gainesville] and made liquor. He'd buy his supplies through his store and I remember hauling jars, sugar, and those supplies to the still in a one-mule-drawn wagon. He would transport the finished product in cars.

"I first started driving when I was thirteen or fourteen years old. I'd take my sister to get milk and go so fast the milk jug would be broken by the time we got home." Parks was later promoted to hauling liquor.

"When I was fourteen I was sent to pick up a load and bring it back. I got stopped by the police and when they asked my age I told them I was older, nineteen or twenty. I was arrested, but never charged, and given three months in the Hall County Jail."

The jail housed other inmates from the liquor trade who took an immediate interest in Parks. Soon they talked the young boy into working for them. He left home at the age of fifteen, happy to put the demanding drudgery of farm chores behind him and start his new job. It was a profitable business decision.

During his apprenticeship, Parks made moonshine with a couple of older men near Winder, Georgia, hauled supplies, chopped wood, lit fires, stirred mash and served as lookout. Within a year he was into it big-time and by age sixteen he had purchased his first two cars, a 1926 Model T Roadster and a 1929 Chevrolet two-door sedan.

In 1930, his aunt and uncle, Maude and Miller Parks, located him and convinced him to move to Atlanta, where he could work in his uncle's service station and garage. Parks gave his boss three weeks notice, then headed to the big city in his Ford. He followed his uncle's directions to the Sears and Roebuck building on Ponce de Leon Avenue, met him there and followed him to the station. Later, he went back home for his Chevrolet.

Miller Parks' Northside Auto Service garage and Hemphill Service Station were at Hemphill and Kontz avenues (now Atlantic Drive) in Northwest Atlanta. The work was hard but honest. Raymond, however, had developed a taste for the good life and loathed losing it.

While Uncle Miller was busy training him in auto repair and pumping gas, Aunt Maude tried to teach the young man how to handle his finances. According to Parks, "She thought she'd teach me, but I was always saving my money. Right in my pocket I kept a record of every dollar I spent. I learned to keep careful watch and I've kept a record of all my business transactions, even those from my first house, until recently."

During his early days in Atlanta, Parks saw a market for readily available cheap whiskey. He knew where to get it, how to deliver it, and who would buy it. He immediately re-established his mountain contacts, becoming the middle man in a liquor hauling operation from the foothills of Dawson County to Atlanta. At age seventeen he purchased a house from his aunt and uncle, making $5 payments and beginning his acquisition of real estate. He was working two shifts, the first for his uncle, the second for himself. As evening neared, he'd help lock up his uncle's business, then head for Dawsonville, load sixty gallons of 'shine in his Model T and return down Georgia Highway 5. Before reaching Atlanta he'd stop at a creek and wash the mud off his car, then drive to Marietta where he would blend in with early morning Atlanta traffic.

"I'd leave from Dawsonville to Marietta at school time and ease on through," says Parks. "My 1930 Chevrolet two-door had a trough on each side of the drive shaft. A cover in the upholstery lifted up and there was a trap door under the floorboards. There was a lot of room between the seat and the floorboards.

"During one of my trips I was stopped. The police were coming out of Marietta and signaled me to move over, then pulled up in front of me. I came to a stop, jumped out, took off through a field and hid in a hole. A policeman found me and grabbed me but I broke loose, went across the field and hid until dark, then took a streetcar back to Atlanta.

"I had a two-way radio in my car so I could listen to police calls. Once when I was going through an intersection, I heard them calling my name and saw them turn like they were going after me. When they did, I hit them in the door, then outran them.

"We used to switch the liquor from one car to another in an old wooden three-story parking garage on Ivey Street. Eventually, the police got onto us. I was in one of the cars hiding out with another boy when they opened the door and grabbed him. I jumped out the other side and rolled down the steps to get away."

When other 'shiners would come after him, Parks was armed with a tire iron. Clearing thirty cents a gallon and saving as much as he could, Parks bought out his uncle, then purchased a farm in South Georgia and moved his family there. His goal was to remove them from the harshness of the work and the weather of the mountains. By 1936 he was worn out from his second shift, and his family was running stills around their new home. Parks hired drivers for the cars and mechanics to service them. The most famous of these was Red Vogt. Vogt, well known for souping up moonshiners' trip cars, had a garage on Spring Street about a block from the Varsity restaurant. Soon, Vogt was maintaining all of Parks' cars.

By 1938, Parks was branching out in the entertainment "novelty" industry, renting out juke boxes, slot machines, cigarette machines and pool tables, and was on his way out of the moonshine business. He was also gaining an air of respectability and was known for his gentlemanly bearing, and for his hats. He wore a wide-brimmed straw hat in summer and a felt hat in winter.

Always keeping his eyes and ears open for new ways of making money, he was intrigued when he found out that Vogt was retooling moonshine cars for racing. His curiosity was further piqued when his bootlegging cousins, Lloyd "Flying Blonde Bambino" Seay and Roy Hall, urged him to sponsor a car for Lloyd to run at Lakewood Fairgrounds.*

Lloyd won the first race Parks attended at Lakewood, and racing won Parks' heart. He began buying new cars, usually Ford coupes, and having them delivered to Vogt, who would adjust the springs and change the gears to prepare for the track. The '39 Fords were a good value at $525. They were the first with hydraulic brakes and the last to have the shifter as standard on the floor. The motors could be made to go fast.

Roy Hall and Lloyd Seay, who were in and out of jail, continued to bootleg and race for Parks until the early forties. Sharing their enthusiasm, Parks' love of racing expanded to include Daytona, a wide sandy beach track where Seay managed a victory and Parks' team won five of the seven beach races in which they competed.

Meanwhile, Parks had struck up a friendship with a young man he met in Vogt's garage, Bill France. France and Vogt had known each other from when they both lived in Washington, D.C. Like Vogt, France had come south. He and his family settled in Daytona where, after working several jobs and opening an Amoco station, he began overseeing races on the Daytona Beach and Road Course. Parks and France, who was eventually to found NASCAR, discovered they had mutual interests and became close friends, often appearing together at racing events. At that time, many races were held around Fort Wayne, Indiana; Birmingham, Alabama; Atlanta, Georgia; and High Point, North Carolina.

Before World War II, Parks sponsored Hall and Seay but, because promoters and sponsors always wanted to fill up the field, he carried three cars to the track. Parks would pull in and give up the car to a better driver. On the one time he started a race at Langhorne, he became terrified the other cars would run over him. France was a driver as well as a promoter and would often promote an event, then drive Parks' extra car.

Originally the area of Atlanta's first water plant, built in 1875, Lakewood had become city-owned lake property, encircled by a one-mile horse-track that later became the racetrack known as Lakewood Speedway.

Raymond Parks took the survival skills he had learned in bootlegging and applied them to World War II boot camp and racing. Raymond and his wife Violet stand before a display of his racing souvenirs.

By 1941, France and Parks were having fun. In Daytona, they would get in Parks' Fleetwood Cadillac, hook up a siren and run all over town with it blaring. Then, tragedy struck. During an argument with his hot-tempered cousin Woodall Anderson, the 21-year-old Seay was shot and killed. The next year, Parks was called to war. He immediately took the survival skills he had learned while bootlegging and applied them to boot camp.

"I always kept two cars on the camp, one of them to loan to officers. I never took most of the training or went on the five-mile hikes. Every time they'd have a hike, the sergeant sent me to motor pool. I had my own apartment and would get up and on post in time to be counted, but my bed was already made because I never slept in it."

That easy life came to an abrupt and difficult end when he was shipped to Europe. "I fought in the Battle of the Bulge and was in a foxhole for one hundred and nine days. There were two of us crammed in there. One would sleep while the other pulled guard duty. I would guard at night because I was afraid the other guy would go to sleep." Struggling to endure physically and mentally, the men passed December embedded in snow and were frostbitten despite wearing three pairs of socks. Half of Parks' company was either captured or killed. "I still sometimes have nightmares and remember screams. I helped drag frozen rows of Germans and stacked the bodies." Parks was finally discharged after being honored for his bravery. After the war, he returned to Atlanta and to racing. A first-class sponsor, he always maintained his cars with a showroom finish and never put a damaged car back on the track. His showmanship and style attracted high-quality drivers, such as Red Byron and Bob Flock.

In 1946, Parks bought half interest in a liquor store on Hemphill Avenue. He went in as a business partner, but quickly learned the benefits of a sole proprietorship. Later he bought another liquor store. ("I had to go through a lot to get a license because of my bootlegging background.") At first the county agreed to issue the license, but the city refused. When the county annexed the property, his problem was solved.

By 1947, Parks' Byron-Flock duo was the most powerful racing combination in the country, dominating Daytona. After a horrific crash in October in Spartanburg which temporarily sidelined Bob Flock, Bob's brother Fonty was persuaded to leave his team at E & S Speed Shop and drive for Parks. Fonty Flock had been running second in points to his brother Bob and was a natural to fill the void and finish out the season.

Despite the impressive achievements of drivers such as Byron and the Flocks, racing was gaining national attention for a number of infamous reasons. With its drunkenness, gambling, and wild, chaotic crowds, the sport was out of control. Something had to be done before it was banned. Recognizing the dangers, Bill France called the most influential car owners, drivers, promoters, and their representatives to Daytona Beach. Parks' team members Red Vogt and Red Byron attended. Under France's direction, a national regulatory organization was formed. Vogt suggested it be called the National Association for Stock Car Automobile Racing, and NASCAR was born. In February of 1948, the first NASCAR-sanctioned modified race was held on the Daytona Beach and Road Course and Red Byron won. Parks and his team continued to be a powerful force in racing until the early fifties when he gave up his sponsorship.

"I was spending everything I made in racing," Parks explained. "It cost more to build a car than I could win." It was fun but it was expensive and demanding and, although his love for the sport would never die, Parks decided the time had come to get back to business.

Still a successful entrepreneur, Parks owns prime property in downtown Atlanta and still has his liquor store. Each year, in remembrance of the time he spent with his comrades in World War II, he attends his Ninety-Ninth Infantry reunion. In 1995, accompanied by his wife Violet, he returned to Europe for the Battle of the Bulge 50th Anniversary.

Parks enjoys going to races now as much as he did in the old days and can often be seen with Violet at oldtimers' racing reunions. He promotes the history of racing through personal appearances, is a member of the National Motorsports Press Hall of Fame; Jacksonville's Jax Raceways Hall of Fame; Stock Car Racing Hall of Fame in Daytona Beach, Florida; and Georgia Racing Hall of Fame; and is a recipient of the Smokey Yunick American Racing Pioneer Award. Every June, Parks' legacy is honored when J.B. Day sponsors the renowned Raymond Parks' Birthday Party, attended by hundreds of racing enthusiasts from all over the southeast. The tradition started when J.B. Day learned Parks had never been given a birthday party.

To quote Eddie Samples in *Pioneer Pages*, "Parks has had a stake in many ventures since the old days. Some mentionable, such as beverage stores, service stations, vending services, garages, ice cream parlors, billboards, rental property, music boxes, nightclubs (when they had to wear pasties), nightclubs (when they didn't), and new car dealerships. He has been a race driver, on and off the track, and part owner of a racetrack and a racing magazine. He has a gift for dignity... and common sense."

CHAPTER 2

Chris Economaki:
Editor and Publisher Emeritus
of *National Speed Sport News*

Chris Economaki has been involved in motorsports for over seventy years. Known as "the Dean of American Motorsports Journalism," he has promoted, announced, photographed and written about all forms of racing events. Under his leadership *National Speed Sport News* became the "Bible of the industry" and is one of the most respected racing publications in the nation. Among his many awards and achievements are the 1990 NASCAR Award of Excellence and induction into the Motorsports Hall of Fame of America and the Indianapolis Motor Speedway Hall of Fame.

In the early days, there was a hunger for entertainment and auto racing was built on danger. Publicity was about daredevil drivers coming from far away, risking life and limb, facing death at every turn. The danger element was the principal part of promotion.

From the mid-twenties to the early fifties, racing events were now and then, here and there, and sustained by the agricultural fair. They were typically held around harvest time with only three or four at a racetrack per year. As a consequence, when there was a race, it was important. During the Depression, since the eastern part of the United States was the most densely populated, more fairs were held there.

From the end of June to late September, people who owned racecars towed them from all parts of the country to the East. They lived temporarily in furnished rooms in homes and went from there to fairground races every weekend. East Paterson, New Jersey, where they congregated, was seven miles from where Chris Economaki grew up in Ridgewood. The adjoining town of Hoboken had a dirt track put in at the turn of the century for horse racing. When he was a young boy, Economaki could hear the cars' engines and they drew him like a magnet. Since he didn't have money for a ticket, he climbed over or went through the fence.

East Paterson had a small general interest newspaper called the *Bergen Herald*. One of the racecar mechanics went to the publisher, suggesting auto racing news be carried because so many racers were temporary residents. The publisher said he would if they got advertising to support it. The mechanic sold an ad to Pyroil and the paper's racing news coverage began.

At first, the racing page was only the back of the paper but soon it became so popular it grew to two pages. By 1933, between Easter and Labor Day, almost half of the paper covered racing news. Townspeople became upset because it took priority over politics so when the *Ridgewood News* acquired a rotary press, the publisher of the *Bergen Herald* decided to print his paper there and separate the racing section into a tabloid called *Speed Sport News*. Its first printing was in August of 1934.

"By pure happenstance," says Economaki, "I was walking down Oak Street, looked in the window at the press, saw they were printing the racing paper, and walked in. I got two hundred copies to take to races that weekend. Selling them for a nickel each, I made a penny apiece for a total of two dollars. Later, I worked as a racecar mechanic, but I always sold papers, in addition to any job I had."

Economaki's business ventures were interrupted by four years of service in World War II, ending with the Second Armored Division in Central Europe. When the war was over, he returned home and sold papers again. "One Friday night, in 1948, I went to a race and sold four hundred papers. Saturday, I went to a race fifty miles away and only sold fifty. I couldn't understand the disparity. Why so many sales one night and so few the next? It dawned on me the difference was the announcer. The Friday night announcer was an enthusiast. 'Oh, have you seen the latest *Speed Sport*?' he asked. 'Wow! How 'bout that story on page five? Everybody's talking about it.' The Saturday announcer said, 'The latest *Speed Sport News* is here. It is twenty-five cents. Buy it.' That wasn't the kind of plug that could trigger a sale. I decided to become an announcer to sell my papers."

The first race Economaki announced was at Selinsgrove, Pennsylvania, 165 miles from his home. When he arrived, the sound man was setting up the microphone. "I told him I had never announced a race and asked if he could give me tips on how to be good at it. He said for three dollars he'd tape everything I said and make it into a record. I still have that huge 78 rpm record. Whenever I feel good, I play it and realize how bad I was. Most of it was 'Here they come' and 'There they go.' I had everybody in third place." Despite his inexperience, at the end of the race, the promoter paid him thirty-five dollars and invited him back. Thus began his announcing career. As his reputation spread, he was asked to call races throughout the country.

"I had a certain flair for announcing and would ballyhoo events. I'd get to the fairgrounds at noon and say, 'Good afternoon, ladies and gentlemen. Welcome to this great fair. Today is auto racing day. Daredevil drivers from the world over are unloading their cars in the infield for high speed racing. The governor of this great state has commissioned the Secretary of Agriculture to send the state soil expert here to condition the track for the record speeds we expect to see this afternoon. But, you can't go for practice. Get your tickets now, before all the seats are gone.'"

According to Economaki, in the early days, auto racing was denigrated and looked down upon. It involved people with grease under their fingernails and oily rags in their pockets. The sport was thought to be crazy and meaningless and driver motivation was different. "In August of 1932, during the height of the Depression, I went to a race in Langhorne, Pennsylvania. One hundred and one cars qualified—one hundred and one cars! There was no money, but somehow they got to the next race. Racing people were infected with racing fever and they had to get there.

"The only money a driver received was a percentage of what the car won. There were

Georgia Automobile Racing Hall of Fame Association writers and historians Mike Bell (left) and Eddie Samples (center) discuss old-time racing with *National Speed Sport News* Publisher Emeritus Chris Economaki. Economaki is known as the "Dean of Motorsport Journalism" and *National Speed Sport News* is known as the "Bible of the Industry." Bell founded the Georgia Automobile Racing Hall of Fame Association and Eddie Samples is the son of early racing great Ed Samples. (Courtesy Eddie Samples Photo Collection.)

no salaries, no retainers, no bonuses and no sponsors. When I started announcing, I'd go to a track and say, 'Well, who looks good today? You can forget about Jud Larson. He won last week and he's got money in his pocket. He never goes fast when he's got money. He only runs fast when he's broke.'

"All of the racecars came on an open trailer. In the pits, each driver had one small tool box and maybe two extra wheels, with different tires on them. The fuel was bought at the corner gas station. In the pits, one of the Ambler brothers would put on a pair of gloves and walk around with a can of a thick red liquid called Tetrinet Hyl lead, and a graduated glass measuring tool. He'd say 'How much do you want?' The driver might say, 'There are eight gallons in the gas tank so give me four.' When the four ounces were measured and poured into the tank, they shook the car up and down to mix it. That's how they added lead into gas for the races."

During the early races, cars were harder to handle and driving was rough. Suspensions were rigid and brakes and shock absorbers weren't good. Ninety-five percent of the cars had Model T Ford cylinder blocks with special racing heads. The Model A followed the Model T but a significant change came in 1932 when Ford announced the Model B. It was the same as the Model A, but had pressure lubrication of the main bearings and an electric fuel pump. That was a night and day difference for racers because splash lubrication had caused bearings to burn out and engines to fail.

"Different companies made all kinds of cylinder heads for the Model B Ford Block. From 1933 to the early fifties, ninety percent of all races were won by a Ford-based engine. When I first started going to races, you could tell a car by its sound and some engines would whine. Later racing engines had a deep throaty roar like a lion. They were loud, but their low frequency didn't hurt your hearing. In 1963, Ford came out with an engine for the Indianapolis Speedway that was a screamer. It had a high-pitched '*eeeee*' sound. I'm now totally deaf at high frequency. That's what racing has done for my hearing."

Economaki says racing was dangerous, but to him, that wasn't the main attraction. He was lured by the chance to make a profit, the friendship of the racing community and the opportunity to travel. "It's hard for this generation to understand how huge this country once seemed. I lived ninety-five miles from Philadelphia. In 1932, Philadelphia seemed like a foreign country. Nobody had been to Philadelphia. Nobody went any place in those days. With auto racing, you traveled. When I was a child, I went all over the eastern United States with the father of one of the drivers. I was better traveled than most adults.

"In 1950, I was at a race at Hinchliffe Stadium in New Jersey when Bill France came into the infield looking for me. We knelt down so as not to be in the way of the people watching the race and he asked me to go to Daytona Beach and announce during Speed Week. This was long before the super speedway was built. I drove from New Jersey to Florida and worked for three days. I got fifty dollars a day, with no expenses, and was happy to get it. In 1961, France pushed me onto ABC and I became a television announcer and the rest is history."

There have been a lot of changes since Chris Economaki's early newspaper and announcing days. He purchased what later became known as the *National Speed Sport News* while still a young man. Under his leadership, the paper has become one of the most informative and influential publications in motorsports, and motorsports have become the most influential sport in our nation.

In looking back, Economaki says an enormous number of changes have occurred. "In the old days, there was more respect and courtesy on the track because wrecking cars demanded costly time-consuming repair, but racing was extraordinarily dangerous. Between Easter and Labor Day, almost every issue of my newspaper had a fatality in it.

"Years ago, only the first five or six finishers got paid. Now, drivers have sponsors. They get salaries, bonuses, and retainers. The motivation is no longer how much money you can make by passing another driver, because all of the drivers have money. They don't risk passing someone for an extra hundred dollars because even last place pays well in Nextel today.

"A crew chief used to carry his tool box in his hand. The next thing we knew, cars had sensors and telemetry, and an engineer with a laptop computer. Racing became more expensive than ever and cars went extraordinarily fast. Speed and the setting of track records were the promotional arms of racing, but when technology made cars faster, accidents happened, and parts of cars flew into grandstands.

"As more people were hurt and killed, insurance companies demanded that drivers be slowed. American businesses had begun to sponsor drivers and cars to increase their sales but after a series of major accidents, they decided to pull out. They feared the dangerous side of racing was bad for their image. Today, there are changes in safety and in the sport as a whole, and many of those changes were spurred by the media. People looked at racing differently when television entered the picture. Speed and danger were important in racing in the old days but suddenly, those big promotional facets had to go away. What everybody at the Indianapolis Motor Speedway wanted to hear was 'And it's a new track record!' You don't hear that anymore and you'll never hear it again.

"In the twenties and thirties, drivers were heroic. Auto racing was a mystifying, fascinating sport, with fearless people going fast. I don't admire drivers now as much as drivers back then because their cars are too good and their jobs are too easy, but, I loved racing then and I love it today. Very few of us get to make a living at what started out as a hobby, but that has been my case. I absolutely fell in love with racing."

CHAPTER 3

Ed Samples:
Early Racing Champion

Because early racing was considered an outlaw sport, information about frequent champion Ed Samples' numerous racing achievements has been hard to obtain. We do know he could drive at eight years old and was racing motorcycles before he started racing cars in 1941. A true pioneer, he began when the sport was still deeply embedded in its moonshine origins.

In 1946, Samples won the National Stock Car Racing Circuit Points Championship. In 1947, he finished second to Fonty Flock in Final Point Standings and Carolina journalists called him the finest racecar driver in the United States. The next year he beat Bob Flock to become South Carolina's 1948 Points Champion and in 1949, he won the National Modified Championship. He was Birmingham Racing Club Champion in 1954 and 1955. His competitors included many famous racing figures such as Red Byron, Bob, Tim and Fonty Flock, Roy Hall, Glenn Dunnaway, Marshall Teague, Lee Petty, and Bill France.

NASCAR Champion Tim Flock once described Samples as one of the best Modified drivers he had ever seen and NASCAR Champion Buck Baker was quoted as saying Samples was the driver he emulated. Samples was inducted into the Georgia Racing Hall of Fame in 2003. The following biography is based on recent interviews with members of Samples' family and a rare 1990 interview with Samples, conducted by *Atlanta Journal-Constitution* sportswriter Rick Minter. Samples died June 10, 1991. The interviews have been blended for clarity.

Samples was born on January 31, 1921, in Atlanta, Georgia, and was an entrepreneur at an early age. "If he wanted something done," says his widow Virginia, "he'd figure out a way to do it. He was making money when he was a little fellow. He'd have his mother make five banana sandwiches for his school lunch and then go out and sell them." In those days, the riskiest and most profitable enterprises in which a person could participate were racing cars and transporting moonshine, and as he grew older, Samples did both.

"When I first started racing, everybody knew I was hauling liquor," he said in his 1990 interview. "Promoters would grade out a track in a field, put up a sign, and people

In 1947, Ed Samples was noted as the finest racecar driver in the United States. He is shown here accepting a trophy from Sam Nunis and Joe Epton. According to his nephew Charles Cross, "He only knew one speed and that was wide open." (Photograph by Bruce Craig. Courtesy Collier Collection Archives.)

would come. I always drove fast cars and I raced in the first race I saw. Nobody knew anything about it. I had to tie the doors shut... no two carbs or anything. I drove my first real race for Cannonball Brown in a '32 Ford. That car was so fast, after the first lap, I could run down the front stretch and see cars on the backstretch." Unfortunately, the radiator hose came off, ruining his lead. By 1944, Samples had gained a reputation as a bootlegger and daredevil.

The day he decided to go see the movie *Frenchman's Creek*, a film filled with swashbuckling action, the beautiful Virginia Mullins sat in front of him. The movie was based on a bodice-ripping Daphne du Maurier novel in which a beautiful damsel flees a wimpy husband and lands in the arms of a pirate. No one can say what effect the steamy romance may have had on its audience, but when it ended and they started to leave, Ed grabbed Virginia's arm and asked her name.

"I shook him loose," says Virginia, "but later he located someone who knew me and we double dated. He told me he was Joe Dawson because he was afraid I'd heard his name. I hadn't... but my Mama had."

Virginia's mother warned her daughter to stay away from the dark-sided Samples, but instead of being afraid, Virginia grew more intrigued. "He seemed like quite a catch. He had a car and nobody in our high school had cars. Back then, if I got a box of candy, it was really special. Ed had the money to buy a box of candy and just open it. He was the opposite of me. I'd never met or seen anyone like him and I was fascinated."

After a short courtship, Virginia and Ed were married and that's when Ed's reputation caught up with him. Virginia was shocked to learn that in his past he'd been shot three times and had his throat cut. The shootings occurred when a rival tried to hijack his moonshine and his throat was cut during a scuffle with a man who was later killed by his own wife. Although she was horrified at the dangerous life Samples had led, Virginia stuck by him. Their marriage survived and Ed continued to race.

"He started racing in cow pastures in Georgia and Florida," says Virginia. "There were no restrooms, no drink stands... nothing but dirt tracks. After the cars went into the first turn, you couldn't see who was ahead until they got out of the dust. By the time we started to leave, we were starving, covered with dirt and needed a bathroom. We always had to wait, because the drivers stood in a circle to talk, rerunning the race."

"Racing's the best thing that ever happened to me," said Samples. "You get your anger out of you on the track and it was fun and great financially. I raced the first car I built at Spartanburg. The heat and the feature paid five hundred and fifty dollars and that more than paid for the car. One year, I won a new Oldsmobile."

An early beach racer, Samples ran at Daytona before World War II. "Ed was good on that track," says Virginia. "It was half on the road and half on the beach. They didn't have motels back then and the first time I went with him, we stayed with Bob and Ruby Flock in a beach cottage. He got a trophy, but we nearly froze. We also liked to go to Jacksonville. Ed once got eight hundred dollars and that was a bunch of money."

Racing closed down during World War II, but resumed as soon as it ended. "Greenville, South Carolina, was the first race after the war," said Samples. When over twenty thousand attended, Bill France, the racetrack's promoter, ran out of tickets and let the rest in free.

Samples took off again and so did racing. The late forties saw unprecedented growth but the sport's lack of regulation and unruly crowds made it too dangerous. In 1947, France invited Samples and other influential participants to a gathering in the Streamline Hotel in Daytona Beach, Florida, to establish a regulatory agency. The meeting lasted three days and from it NASCAR was formed. Samples was named chairman of the board and first chairman of technical inspection but, along with several others, he became disenchanted with France's proposal and quit to run the South Carolina circuit. As he continued to race, he gained a large following of fans and got increasing support from his family.

"My Dad had a garage in the West End of Atlanta," said Samples. "When I was racing, we had a notebook where we kept up with what gear I ran and what gear I should have run."

"When I was a small kid in the mid-fifties," says Samples' nephew, Charles Cross, "my mother wouldn't let me go see Ed race. But when I was ten, his father Seth took me to the track. We sat in the grandstands and he had a rolled-up newspaper with him with a pint of whiskey in it and, once in a while, he'd sip on it.

"Ed was driving a number 311 '37 Chevrolet with a Cadillac engine about eight cars down from the start. Seth told me to watch Ed and to watch the flagman. He said, 'Two seconds before that flagman drops his flag, Ed's going to pull out from the pack. He's going to pass three cars before that flag gets down.' Ed did exactly what his Dad said and by the time they made a half lap, he was in first place." Unfortunately, Samples was about ten lengths ahead of everybody when his car died. The track was so full of ruts, the axle broke.

"I didn't have a favorite track," said Samples, "but I always liked Lakewood. The officials didn't appreciate racing and didn't want it, so races in Atlanta were messed up. If you got so much as a speeding ticket, you couldn't race at Lakewood."

In one of his first non-modified races, Samples ran a car for Gober Sosebee at Lakewood while Sosebee drove Red Vogt's Cadillac. "I thought I had lapped Lee Petty and won, but I took second, and since Lee was promoting the race, there was no one to argue with about it."

During the thirties, forties, and fifties, Lakewood was a popular venue—and one of the most dangerous. "At the old tracks," says Virginia, "they had watering trucks to wet the tracks down and we could get water from the trucks for the racecars. The worst thing to happen was for a car to run hot. I always stayed in the infield so if anything happened I could get to the car without crossing the track, but I couldn't do that at Lakewood because of the lake."

As fate would have it, Samples was badly injured at Lakewood in March of 1950, when he lost control of his car on the straightaway. "Back in those days," says Virginia, "you didn't eat peanuts in the pits and the color green was considered taboo. There was no such thing as a green car and Ed didn't wear green. The day he wrecked at Lakewood was the first time, and the only time, I wore green slacks."

"I got my head busted open in qualifying," Samples later explained. "Going into the number one turn, you didn't have to let off, you just slid in. The air got out of the right rear tire. The wheel dug in and the car turned over seven or eight times."

The crowd watched in horror as he hung out the car with every flip. Virginia still recalls the traumatic sight. "They had straps on the doors, but his helmet came off and every time he turned over, his head hit the ground. I went to the gate and told a policeman who I was and he grabbed my arm and we took off. They didn't want me in the ambulance because they thought he was dead, but of course I got in." Meanwhile, the crowd took Samples' helmet and passed it around, collecting money for hospital costs.

"At the hospital," recalls Virginia, "they rolled him into the hall and covered him up. One of the fellows came by, saw the sheet moving and knew he was breathing, so they took him back in and called a neurosurgeon. We didn't know if he would live, but in less than two weeks he was home." Samples had two broken wrists, but was racing before the casts were off.

"I was out for thirty days," said Samples. "They drilled holes in both sides of my head to relieve the blood clots. It was like what Bobby Allison went through. He doesn't remember it. I don't remember it, but I used to catch myself saying the same thing twice. I raced six more years, but I welded the door shut."

In looking back, Samples admitted the sport was unsafe. "Everybody carried fuel in the car. I remember one time Jack Smith put fifty-five gallons of alcohol in a car at Lakewood." One of the track's most horrible accidents occurred in June of 1950 when Skimp Hersey's car crashed, then flipped and burst into flames. Covered in gasoline, he jumped out of the car while on fire, collapsing on the ground in front of the fans.

Samples claimed the most memorable event he won was held in Statesboro, North Carolina. He had a broken valve before the race and the announcer asked the crowd if they wanted to wait on him. To Samples' delight, the crowd screamed *yes*. "The crowd really pumped me up. Marshall Teague sat on the pole and they made me start last."

According to Virginia, the track Samples raced on most often was Birmingham. "Ed could go to Birmingham on a Sunday and not have to travel. At that time, they usually gave prizes instead of trophies and people booed him when he won ten races and he received ten watches."

"I remember, years later," says Samples' son Eddie, "his pit crew member and friend Darrell Downey told how Ed took a watch during the winner's ceremony, walked across the track to the stands and gave it to a crippled child who always attended the races."

"In 1956, Birmingham was my last race," said Samples. "It wasn't a bad decision to make. I ran two or three races most weekends and always ran two times a week. The transmission shop was going good. It started out as a speed shop, but a transmission job paid as much as a hot rod motor and you could do three or four a day. Age will stop you from racing. It won't stop you from the transmission business. I had a boy who wanted to race and I figured if I got out, he wouldn't do it."

Samples' business provided well for his family, but they never knew what to expect. One time a trucker brought his vehicle in for repair and said he didn't have money to pay. When Samples asked him what he did have, the man offered a rattlesnake. Accustomed to taking other things in trade, the fair-minded Samples agreed. The snake soon became a shop attraction, providing entertainment for customers while Samples worked.

"Ed was very independent and being one of the first to work with automatic transmissions gave him an edge," says Virginia. "He was a workaholic and a pioneer. He did what he wanted and did what he loved."

"Ed Samples was a self-made man," adds Cross. "He was the first to advertise on the sides of buses and on the radio and his transmission shop was the talk of Atlanta. His garage was over on Northside Drive in Atlanta, in the middle of Bellwood Mill Village. The people had nothing and knew nothing but going to work in the cotton mills. If Ed saw somebody in need, he was the first one to help him. If he needed money, Ed gave him a job and let him work for it. Nobody gave Ed Samples anything, but he would take somebody people thought was worthless, see good in him and give him an opportunity, when nobody else would have fooled with him."

"Ed had a knack for doing the right thing at the right time," says Virginia. "Whatever he wanted to do, he'd do and whatever he wanted, he went after. He was one to take chances and he wasn't influenced or intimidated by anyone."

"When he started racing, it was an outlet," says Samples' son Eddie. "He probably just got into it because his friends did, but when he won championships and became famous, that was a turnaround. In the next years, it was strictly business."

"Ed Samples was all guts," says his nephew, Charles Cross. "He didn't have but one speed and that was wide open. He was the most inventive man I've ever seen and one of the most successful I've ever known."

At Samples' funeral, Virginia had the organist play *I Did It My Way*.

CHAPTER 4

Frankie Schneider:
The Old Dutch Master

New Jersey driver Frankie Schneider raced over six decades. He is known to have won close to 750 races between 1947 and 1977. In one year alone, he won four track championships. He demonstrated an uncanny ability as a mechanic and a driver with midgets, sprints and late models. Although he ran Grand National, his forte was Modifieds, in which he was often unbeatable.

Frequently racing eight times a week and competing in a variety of divisions, Schneider is reported to have won one hundred races in each of his 1952 and 1958 seasons. In 1957, he drove for the Chevrolet Grand National team. Although he also drove for John Bolander, most of the time he raced his own cars, depending on volunteers to help in the pits. One of those helpers, Rex White, was mentored by Schneider and went on to win the 1960 Grand National Championship. During 1961, Schneider soared to eleven consecutive wins at New York's Orange County Speedway in Middletown, New York, and was victorious thirteen times in both 1961 and 1963. He was the first champion of the All Star Racing League in the sixties. Unfortunately, Schneider began racing before accurate statistical track records were kept. According to many racing historians, it's possible that he was the winningest driver in motorsports history. He is considered the greatest dirt Modified driver of the century.

According to 1960 NASCAR Champion Rex White, Schneider was fast in everything he did. "He was the funniest eater I've ever seen. He ate so quickly, he didn't have time to chew. When he ate bananas, he'd leave on the peels. I first met Frankie at West Lanham Speedway and he was a standout. It was easy to tell the pros from the amateurs. The best drivers knew how to cut corners and were amazing to watch as they bumped and spun and fought their way to the front, shooting flames of methanol alcohol from their exhausts and filling the air with fumes."

Burning with desire to get into the pits, White pried loose a board and let himself in, blending with the crowd. Mingling with mechanics, he offered help and began to hang around Schneider, doing whatever was needed to the driver's maroon and white Ford.

White, who by that time had decided to become a driver, thought he was in Heaven, especially when Schneider invited him out to eat with his wife Dolly and his helper Bo.

When Bo was drafted into the army, White took his place and, with his wife Edith, followed the Schneiders to Florida and stayed in their home. "Frankie taught me to set up a car and I learned about bite and stagger, and wedge, how to increase horsepower, and how to work on a racecar engine. He also trained me to select the right gear ratios and tires, set the chassis, make repairs after wrecks and adapt the car for each track. He was a master at surviving in racing with no money. He used lipstick to draw his number on the side of his car.

"Frankie was an opinionated Dutchman with a short fuse, and sometimes hard to get along with. He was stubborn, thrived on problems and didn't want to be obligated to anybody. Although his racecar had to be perfect, he was always surrounded by junk. He enjoyed working in mud, sometimes up to his ankles. The dirtier and more behind he was, the more pressure he was under, the better he ran. He ran a lot and he won a lot, although he believed it was better to take second or third place, than to risk being hurt.

"To me, Frankie had the most common sense and the most knack for figuring things out of any driver I've seen. That helped his reflexes on the track. He knew where another guy's car was going before the driver did and how to set the guy up and pass him. Frankie loved competition, but to him, racing was a psychological thing. He wanted to beat the other guys by out-driving them, not through better equipment."

"It wasn't what I could buy or who could help me," says Schneider, "it was what I could do. I didn't race for the money; I raced for my own satisfaction... but I'd take the money!"

Frankie Schneider (number 2) races with Pee Wee Pobletts (number 36) at Dorsey Speedway in Elkridge, Maryland, in 1954. (Photograph by Harry Clifton. Courtesy Larry Jendras, Jr.)

"Frankie Schneider raced for the sheer fun of it," says White, "and he always knew his cars. He believed in using his head and feeling what his car was doing. If something broke, he had to know why even if it meant tearing it apart. He used to say it wasn't horse-power that got you around the track, it was the car."

"I was driving a car when I was six years old," says Schneider, "and working on it by the time I was seven. My father had a pig farm outside of Newark, New Jersey, and later a milk and truck farm. We moved all around New Jersey, but my father was always farming. Since I was the oldest of five children, I had to know how to do everything and most of what I knew, I learned on my own.

"From farming I learned how to make a car run when nobody else could. I had to know. Today, kids don't have to know. At seven years old, their parents buy them race-

Frankie Schneider at Reading Fairgrounds in 1962: He raced more than six decades and won close to 750 races. (Photograph by Bill Ader. Courtesy Larry Jendras, Jr.)

cars. Most people don't have enough to do with their life. That's what I think. They've got so much money they don't do anything and their moms and dads do everything. It's not just in racing. People are programming their kids. They want them to be heroes but they teach them by the book. The kids are smart, but they don't have common sense. Everybody wants their kids to be the best but they teach them to be the same." According to Schneider, motorsports serve as a good example. The cars look the same and the drivers look the same. They aren't allowed to say anything bad and spoil their image. When Schneider was growing up, things were different.

"By the time I was sixteen, I knew how to take care of myself. I bought a car for fifteen dollars from my grandmother, and because I worked on the farm, I could get all the gas I wanted during the war. In 1947, I was twenty years old and racing the roads and decided to enter my first Modified race. When I was young, I ran just about everything, sprint cars, midgets, and late models. My fondest memories are of Modified stock car racing. I did crazy things I wasn't supposed to do, especially working on cars. I couldn't just go out and say a car was going to run a certain way. I had to make it run that way, with my gas, my wheels, my steering. I never got the better cars and I did all of the work myself."

When he wasn't racing, Schneider earned money by maintaining a garage and combing junkyards, searching for parts. Residing in New Jersey during the summer and in Florida each winter, he had access to tracks in the north and the south.

"It wasn't the racing I enjoyed so much as the challenge of knowing how to run a car and controlling myself. My strategy was to finish before I crashed so I didn't drive wide open. I never smacked anybody or put them in the wall on purpose. I let other drivers go if they had to and I could size up my competitor by watching his car. I had fun without being a hero or allowing competition to take over my life."

Some of Schneider's most challenging experiences occurred not doing the race, but before it. "Once I went to Williams Grove and the transmission went out in my car during the heat. Meanwhile, another guy's engine blew. I borrowed his transmission, pulled it out, put it in my car and won." Despite such incidents, he claims he never pushed himself. "I tried to be as healthy as I could be, but that's not to say I didn't abuse myself. I'd stay up all night having a party and the next day go race. I might want to beat a guy, and there were guys I was sometimes unhappy with, but when it was over, it was over and we'd party."

Although most of his memories are happy, the worst experience of Schneider's life occurred on the track. "In the mid-fifties, I was running Vineland, New Jersey, when a guy in front of me hit the wall, then came across the track and hit my car and another one, putting us both into the wall. We went down in front of the grandstand and pulled off the brakes, and my car caught on fire." The impact bent the steering wheel against his seat belt, pinning him in. He held his breath to avoid inhaling fumes as the fire burned his legs. Finally, he was able to wriggle loose and get out, but he faced a long painful period of skin grafting. "If the fuel hadn't been alcohol, I wouldn't be here. I never had a broken bone in my body from racing, but I was burned pretty badly."

In 1958, Schneider was scheduled to race in Trenton, New Jersey. Tire manufacturers often gave tires to their test drivers and, although the practice had been recently stopped, Schneider agreed to test tires for Goodyear before the feature. Because the condition of the track was rough, tire wear would be excessive. Schneider knew that if he raced, his tire bill would be outrageous. Because Schneider was a good publicity grabber, the track's promoter promised he would give him free tires if he agreed to participate. Schneider registered and sat on the pole, but was given no tires. Frustrated and angry, he withdrew and left. In retaliation, he was banned from NASCAR and forced to run outlaw tracks the rest of his racing career.

There are many stories about Schneider but the funniest involves Rex White. After a race at Sunbrock Speedway, the two were going home in the Schneider family car while another guy was driving a truck towing the racecar. Hungry and tired, they all decided to stop at a restaurant to get something to eat. When the truck driver pulled into the parking lot, Schneider and White looked behind the truck and saw that the racecar was gone. That night, they searched for the car for three hours, riding up and down the roads looking for tracks. Finally, about 4:00 a.m., they saw a set of tracks leading to a roadside sign. They walked behind it and there was the car, having hit the sign at such speed, it had flipped back in place.

Although he's now in his late seventies, Schneider claims he has never retired. "I raced until last year when I sold my car." Look out, drivers! Frankie Schneider is still cranked up. He's sizing up his competition and may get back in the race.

CHAPTER 5

Julius Timothy "Tim" Flock: Grease Monkey on His Back

Tim Flock has been characterized as a true NASCAR pioneer, one who embodied the spirit and achievements of early racing champions. His first race was North Wilkesboro, at age twenty-four in 1947. He placed fifth in the first NASCAR-sanctioned race on June 19, 1949, at Charlotte Speedway and won the NASCAR Grand National Championship in 1952. He won it again in 1955 with nineteen poles and eighteen victories. His winning percentage is the highest in NASCAR and he finished in the top five in fifty-five percent of his starts. In 1952, Flock was voted *Speed Age Magazine*'s "Driver of the Year" and in 1955, he was voted Most Popular Driver. Flock was a member of the National Motorsports Press Association Hall of Fame, Alabama Racing Pioneers, Old Timers Club, Living Legends of Auto Racing, Talladega-Texaco Walk of Fame, Alabama Sports Hall of Fame, and the Daytona Beach Rotary Club Hall of Fame. In 1998, NASCAR named him one of the Top Fifty Drivers in History.

Pioneer driver Tim Flock was known for his spectacular driving ability and his racing companion "Jocko Flocko." (Photograph by Jack Cansler. Courtesy Bill Chubbuck, Racing Relics, Inc.)

The following is based on interviews with Tim Flock's widow Frances and his competitor Rex White.

One of the most flamboyant drivers in the southeast, Tim Flock was known for his spectacular driving ability and for his constant companion, Jocko Flocko. Jocko was Flock's pet monkey and a familiar figure at the tracks. Wearing his own cloth racing cap and uniform, he sat in a specially designed shoulder harness in a miniature driver's cage in the passenger area. Jocko was a favorite of fans and the hit of the fast-track circuit, until an unfortunate incident took place during a race in Raleigh, North Carolina. Flock was in the lead when Jocko worked his way out of his harness and decided to explore the car. Ungrounded in racing protocol, he pulled the chain that opened the door to the hole in the floor through which Flock checked his tires. A pebble flew up from the track and hit the unfortunate chimp in his head. Terrified, he suddenly bounded upon Flock's back and started screaming. Flock had to make an immediate pit stop to pry the monkey off his back and hand him to a member of his crew. He lost his place in the race and Jocko made his last ride.

According to Flock's widow, Frances, "One year, Tim and Herb Thomas drove from a race in Canada to a Fourth of July race in Spartanburg. Exhausted, they lay down in the infield to catch a quick snooze, propping their heads up on their helmets. The driver of a Champion Sparks Plug truck backed up without seeing them, ran over Tim's arm, backed onto his head, and stopped. Herb Thomas jumped up and grabbed the truck, lifting it off of Tim's head as a state patrolman came running to help. Nobody could believe Herb lifted that truck. He got it off Tim's head, but hurt his hand while he was doing it. Blood was pouring from Tim's head and Herb's hand was so badly injured he had to have it bandaged. Tim was hospitalized for a skull fracture, but Herb raced that night and won."

Born in Fort Payne, Alabama, Flock was one of nine children born to Lee and Maudie "Big Mama" Flock. Nearly all were daredevils, pushing the limits of risk-taking. The oldest, Carl, raced speedboats, and Tim, Bob, Fonty and Ethel raced cars. Fierce competitors, the latter four often raced against each other and Tim was known to be the best.

Flock's father, a Watson salesman and taxi driver, loved tightrope walking and bicycle racing. He died when Tim was only two, leaving Maudie to work in a hosiery mill, struggling to help her family survive.

One by one, her children left to stay with Carl, who was then living in Atlanta helping an uncle in the moonshine business. "I met Tim in 1941 when I was thirteen," says his widow, Frances. "I was at Grant Park with some friends and dancing with a sailor. The guy slung me out and I slipped and Tim caught me. We walked around the lake and he kissed me, and I fell in love. I thought I'd never see him again, but several months later, a girlfriend arranged for me to go to the movies with a blind date. At first, my parents didn't want me to go, but they agreed when I said they could meet him. When my date came, it was Tim. He used to go by Julius, but I called him Tim and it stuck.

"I had an uncle who loved to go to races at Lakewood Speedway. He'd come home covered in red mud and tell me stories about the race, always including Bob and Fonty Flock. After I met Tim, I told my uncle I'd met a young man named Julius Flock. He said, 'Oh my God! Don't tell me it's one of those Flock boys. They're running alcohol. You don't dare tell your Mama and Daddy he's kin to racing people.'

"Six or seven months later, I ran into Tim again and sparks started flying. I was still in school and he was six years older and drove an Orange Crush truck. Each day until I graduated, he rode by my school and left me a drink. In 1944, I married him. We were going to have a big church wedding, but my father was in the Navy and we decided we'd better run off and elope before he got home.

"On weekends, Tim went to the racetracks to help his brothers Bob and Fonty. In 1947, he went with Speedy Thompson to North Wilkesboro and Speedy asked him to test his racecar, a 1939 Ford Coupe. When Tim told him his brothers wouldn't allow it and he didn't have a helmet, Speedy told him, 'They're busy on the track. Here's a helmet.'

When Tim came around the track a second time, his brothers were out of their cars and cheering him on. Before the year was over, he'd won his first race. He actually won the Championship in 1949, but because he'd also run in a non-sanctioned event, Bill France disqualified him."

According to Frances, Tim Flock raced in cars owned by Ted Chester, Karl Kiekhaefer, Bill Stroppe, and Joe Woods. She says that, unlike most drivers, he never had to work on his cars, but the responsibilities placed on his family were overwhelming.

"I did love racing," she says. "That was Tim's career and I supported him all the way. I wanted him to be as great as he could and I was excited about it. It was hard when I had to stay home and couldn't go to the track, but racing was his only income and we raised five children. When I did go, there were no grandstands and since women weren't allowed in the pits, I was stuck in the infield. If I wanted to be with Tim, he had to kiss me through the fence."

To make matters worse, wives weren't the only ones trying to get to the drivers. Even in those days, the sport attracted groupies. Labeled "Pit Lizards" by the men and "Pit Losers" by wives, they trailed drivers from place to place and knew where to find them. "They'd go to their hotels and show up when they went out to eat. No man's perfect, but Tim always said he was faithful." For Frances, and other drivers' wives, life was especially difficult. Today, when there are reunions and stories are swapped... they have tales, too.

CHAPTER 6

Charlie Bagwell:
Good Time Charlie,
"The Levi King"

According to Rex White, "If you're as old as Charlie Bagwell, you can make up your racing career. Most people who saw him race are no longer living." Charlie Bagwell has been involved in racing for over half a century and his orange number U2 car is known throughout Georgia. Bagwell, now seventy-nine, was still racing at seventy-seven and hopes to get back into the sport when he retires from his business. It's been said that if he does he'll need to race at a track with lights, because if he enters a day race it'll be night when he finishes.

Bagwell applied the same energy and dedication he has for racing to entrepreneurship. A successful business and property owner, he now lives a comfortable life as a self-made millionaire. "I love to race," says Charlie Bagwell. "I don't know of anybody who has run races so long or had a better time than I have. I wasn't a great driver, but I've run a bunch of short tracks and I used to win a lot. Now everybody who saw me is dead. I have an old program that shows forty-five drivers and I'm the only one still alive."

Bagwell was born in Waynesboro and raised in the Atlanta area. His father was a heavy equipment operator and his mother ran a dry cleaners. They divorced when Charlie was young, but his mother owned and managed the cleaners until well after Charlie was grown. She passed her knack for entrepreneurship on to her son.

"I grew up in the deep Depression. My family was so poor, my mother had to send me to my Granddaddy's to eat because we didn't have anything. The United States had seventy-five percent unemployment in the thirties and there were soup lines all over town. There was almost no money. My Granddaddy owned a farm and he hired men for fifteen dollars a month and all the food they wanted. As a kid, I worked all day long for fifty cents. When I was ten, I went to work at a ball park selling Coca-Colas. I'd ride a street car for a nickel all the way from Fort McPherson [on the Southside] to Ponce de Leon [in central Atlanta]. The first night, I made thirty-nine cents and was able to get my Social Security card."

Charlie Bagwell stands by the car he drove to win the Daytona World Record. According to Bagwell, "In the old days you 'run what you brung' or picked up rides at the track. Because there weren't any rules, racing was more fun and more unpredictable." (Courtesy Charlie Bagwell Photo Collection.)

Bagwell's early childhood experiences had lasting impact. "I've always worked because I like to make money. If you steal it, you'll go to jail and if somebody gives it to you, you have to pay them back, so I just worked for it."

As a teen, Bagwell tried to combine his need to work with his love of sports, starting out at sixteen as a baseball player. "I signed with the Atlanta Crackers for two hundred dollars a month, then played with six or seven other teams before deciding I wasn't cut out for it."

Next, Bagwell became determined to make his mark on the bowling circuit. "I was a pro bowler for two years, but I didn't make much money. Although I love sports, I've always been fair in everything and not great in anything. Baseball, football, tennis, racing... I love it all.

"In 1949, I had a 1932 Ford B Model hot rod with no fenders and no hood. I averaged 116 miles per hour in a time trial on the Measured Mile at Daytona and broke the world's record for a custom-built hot rod run on the beach. It sounds funny but at that time, the strictly stock record was a hundred. Pace cars run faster now and those cars wouldn't stay on the track at Daytona today. They'd go so slow they'd slide off the banks.

"When I got back to Atlanta, I took the engine out of my hot rod and put it in my '41 Ford. Frank Mundy showed me how to get around Lakewood and I drove my first race there. There were forty-two cars and I finished tenth. "Mundy and I were in Daytona in 1950 when Harold Kite won. Harold was from East Point, Georgia, and traveled in the '49 Lincoln he won the race with. Most of the guys drove their stocks to the races. I remember when drivers towed cars. When they'd go to a small town and have to make tight turns, they'd have to get out and straighten the wheels on the car they were towing.

"I ran Daytona three different times when it was on the beach. If you had a flat during a beach race, you could forget it. Try jacking up a car on beach sand. In 1952, they started one hundred twenty-nine cars and I was running in the top fifteen when I got stuck. The holes were about waist deep and I sunk in the sand.

"The Atlanta Peach Bowl was my favorite track. It produced more race drivers around this part of the country than any other. I ran the first race and the last one they ever ran there. When they opened, every car there was a liquor car except mine. I ran two or three head-to-head races with Tim Flock. In the first race, I won the heat and Bob Flock drove my car to win the feature. I was the Peach Bowl Champion the last time they had a championship. One time, a driver started to run under another driver on a turn and I ran under him. It wasn't wide enough to run three abreast and I wrecked both of them. We were all able to stay on the track but the driver who hit the wall, came up behind me and spun me. He jumped out of his car with a razor, but hit me with his helmet instead. All of his brothers were there and the only reason I didn't get murdered was Jack Smith stopped his car and there was a free-for-all. I was never much of a fighter but that was part of racing. You'd fight with a guy one week and the next week you'd be helping him."

Bagwell continued to race and work for his mother, until 1954, when he decided to open his own business. A general store that specializes in work clothes, it has lasted almost as long as Charlie and become an Atlanta landmark. Known for discounted jeans, it's earned him the title, "King of the Levis."

"When I opened Charlie's Tradin' Post, I had four jobs. I opened the cleaners at six o'clock, went to my store at nine o'clock, ran a dry cleaning route at night, and raced. I started in two old houses, but my mother sold the cleaners, and the man who bought it went broke, so I tore down the cleaners and built a new building."

Despite his hectic schedule, Bagwell found time to sponsor a world championship softball team and teach his son Mike to race. "Mike and I raced twenty-five years and he often won. I ran number U2 and he drove U2-2. If we could find races, we'd run Thursday, Friday, Saturday and Sunday afternoons, and on Sunday night. We took two cars and ran in South Carolina, Alabama and Georgia. "We had a very expensive hobby. Back when I drove in the early days, I had Jones Tire Shop on my car but all I got was four recaps. Another time I ran with a radiator company promotion on my car but all I got was a radiator. For awhile, I drove for Idle Hour Tavern, but how many beers can you drink? When I built my first stock car, I doubt if I had five hundred dollars invested.

"Today, an advertiser pays millions of dollars to have his company name put on a car, but Nextel's just sissy stuff and follow the leader. If you bump somebody, they'll black flag you. If you say a bad word, they'll black flag you. If you look at somebody wrong, they want to suspend you. In the '30s and '40s, if you thought you were going to get whipped by someone, you knocked them out of the way. You didn't worry about following them. If somebody came up behind you, you'd better move. Drivers would wreck you if you got in their way and whip you when it was over. Racing was the dirtiest sport in the world. It used to be said you'd go to a fight and a race would break out."

According to Bagwell, in the old days, you'd "run what you brung" or pick up a ride at the track. Because there weren't any rules, racing was more fun, but was also more unpredictable. "Once, I was running third at Warner Robins, a ⅝-mile dirt track, when my left front wheel came off. I couldn't back off because when I did, the pittman arm dug in the dirt. I kept going and the car ran faster. I completed twenty-nine laps and won the Southeastern Championship."

Back then, racing was more competitive, rougher, and more dangerous. "The better equipment you had, the better you ran but I didn't have good equipment because money was tight. For safety, I used an old airplane seat belt. We didn't have roll bars, so there was no protection, and people hadn't heard of a fire extinguisher. You could always go to a track and find a car, because so many drivers were killed. Lakewood must have killed twenty-five and I once went into the lake. "There are not many places I haven't wrecked one time or another. Once I turned over and hit so hard the motor came out. The car went up in the air and kept flipping, end over end."

Bagwell's last wreck was at Senoia, Georgia, when he was age seventy-five. "The top A frame broke and fell down on the steering wheel while I was going wide open. It didn't turn over; it just went up in the air and came down and hit the inside wall. That's the hardest I've hit a wall in my life. I broke a hunk out of my shoulder blade and all the ribs on one side, but I raced the next Saturday night."

Bagwell and his wife, Dee, live by two lakes on a hundred acres of farmland near Fayetteville, Georgia. He still has "Charlie's Tradin' Post"; he still has his racecars; and he still loves to race.

"I have over $100,000 in my cars and $25,000 in the engines and I want to race as long as I can walk. I don't need to be hitting the wall because my bones aren't as flexible as they used to be, but I have a good time even when I wreck. I've enjoyed every minute of every race I've ever been in. That's why they call me 'Good Time Charlie.'"

CHAPTER 7

Gober Sosebee: Georgia's "Wild Injun"

Gober Sosebee was one of the most well-known and successful drivers of the forties and fifties. He wowed crowds with his floor-it-and-go style while he racked up wins throughout the southeast. Sosebee, who won the Daytona Beach and Road Course three times, was as good on sand as he was on dirt. He was the first driver in NASCAR history to enter a "Strictly Stock" race. Other accomplishments include the 1950 "Most Popular Driver" Award, Peach Bowl Speedway, Atlanta, Georgia; 1950 NASCAR Sportsman Division Champion Peach Bowl Speedway; 1951 National Points Champion/NASCAR Sportsman Division; 1955 Southern Racing Enterprises Points Championship; and the 1960 NASCAR Georgia State Champion/Peach Bowl Sportsman Champion; Jacksonville Raceway Hall of Fame; and North Georgia History Center Sports Hall of Fame. In 2002, he was inducted into the Georgia Racing Hall of Fame. Although he has been dead for many years, his legend lives on, especially in the hills of north Georgia. The following is based on research and a 2006 interview with his widow, Vaudell Sosebee.

Known as the "Wild Injun" from Georgia, Gober Sosebee was known for spinning dirt, winning races and his Cherokee garage. (Photograph by Jack Cansler. Courtesy Bill Chubbuck, Racing Relics, Inc.)

Gober Sosebee (in car) with Harold Kite at Lakewood Speedway in Atlanta, Georgia. (Courtesy Vaudell Sosebee Photo Collection.)

Part Cherokee Indian, Gober Sosebee was born in the foothills of the Cherokee (now called Appalachian) Mountains in Dawson County, Georgia. He lived for many years in Atlanta, where he worked out of the Cherokee Garage, before returning to his roots in Dawsonville.

Sosebee attended his first race in the summer of 1939 at Atlanta's Lakewood Speedway and was thrilled by the roughness and action. He vowed not to return until he could bring his own car. That Thanksgiving, he returned with a 1940 Ford with its bumpers off and a soap box derby helmet with sponge rubber in the top and a throat latch. Despite his lack of experience, he came in third to Lloyd Seay and Roy Hall. With the exception of the period during World War II, he raced from that day onward, the excitement never leaving him for over four decades.

Fond of spinning dirt, his flat-out go or blow style combined with a high-speed temper to earn him the nickname "Wild Injun." According to Sosebee's widow, Vaudell, "Gober worked hard on his motors and racing, and auto mechanics came naturally. He was the first to put in a roll bar. Some of the guys laughed at him and said if he was good enough he wouldn't need a roll bar.

"In the old days, drivers beat on each other. They respected each other but they wouldn't give. When one bumped another one's car they'd talk it out but if that didn't work, fists would fly. Gober was a gentle guy, but not to be messed with. During a race at the Peach Bowl, Jim Reed kept beating on him and he got tired of it. Gober hit him but didn't think he'd done enough damage, so he put his car in reverse and backed into him. Jim jumped out of his car ready to fight."

Sosebee drove all over the country to race in "the big ones" (Langhorne, Darlington, Detroit and Daytona), but when he ran for NASCAR, he preferred to stay close to home. His biggest wins were at Daytona Beach where he won the Modified race in 1950 and 1951. In the 1949 race, he'd run first in stocks, but was sidelined on the last lap by a bad tire. He finished fifth in the Daytona 500 when the new super speedway opened.

In 1950, Sosebee qualified on the Daytona Measured Mile at a then-sizzling 114.43 miles per hour. That same year, he sat on the outside pole in the first Darlington Southern 500 and wowed the crowd by leading the first four laps. In 1955 he was chasing points in Grand National and ARCA when he was temporarily banned from NASCAR for running on an unsanctioned track.

"Back then," says Vaudell, "he didn't win a lot of money and drivers raced because they enjoyed it. Usually they'd get a trophy and when Gober drove someone else's car, he'd let the owner have it. He was always a quiet person so when he won he didn't talk much about it, but I could always see a sparkle in his eye. He just loved to get out and go and built his motors to 'floorboard it.' Go, blow, or spin, he put on a show. Once, he spun and crossed the Winner's Circle backwards."

Sosebee learned how to race on the backroads and hills of Dawson County. Famous for his daredevilry as well as his wins, he prepared his cars in the garage and then proved his driving ability and courage by driving up Stone Mountain. Known as the largest mass of exposed granite in the world, it stretched a steep mile to its summit. He was known as a fan-thriller, but his biggest supporter was his wife. Although she didn't always get to go, Vaudell attended races whenever she could. She preferred to be at the "scene" rather than stay at home where she found it terrible "just to wonder what was happening." She especially liked Daytona because she loved the beach.

According to Vaudell, she and her husband were both superstitious. She used to carry a buckeye for good luck and wouldn't allow his helmet to be placed on their bed. Gober wouldn't wear green or race in a green car. He also stayed away from black cats. Although his favorite racecar was his '39 Standard Ford, he was also famous for driving Oldsmobiles and was well recognized for his wins in a Studebaker. He had a picture of a Cherokee Indian on the side of his car.

Once considered one of the most talented drivers in the country, Sosebee drove his last race in Charlotte's 1964 World 600, citing a need to retire because his insurance company was threatening to cancel his policy. He had over 200 wins in the NASCAR and ARCA circuits. Inheriting their father's love of speed, his sons David and Brian also raced. David ran NASCAR and Brian still runs Lanier National Speedway and Senoia Speedway. Vaudell and Gober Sosebee were married and in love for fifty-one years.

CHAPTER 8

T. Taylor Warren: Picture This!

According to Rex White, "T. Taylor Warren is a NASCAR legend. Familiar to everyone on the track, he, more than any other single individual, is responsible for the recording of NASCAR history. I bet 90 percent of the pictures you see related to NASCAR in the fifties, sixties and seventies were taken by T. Taylor."

Thomas "T. Taylor" Warren risks life and limb, not as a stuntman, but as a racetrack photographer. The nationally famous cameraman was recently hit but uninjured after an ARCA car slid through the pit gate. Once at a track in Lynchburg, Virginia, a car flew out of the pits and bore down on him. The driver was gunning it coming down a hill and focusing on the track instead of what was ahead. T. Taylor, who was also facing the track, couldn't hear the car's approach, due to speedway noise. Suddenly, Martinsville Speedway President Clay Earles saw what was happening and screamed out a warning. T. Taylor jumped to the side in the nick of time and his life was saved.

During a race at Langhorne, Pennsylvania, a car flipped and sped on its side toward T. Taylor. Backed up to a flag-stand, he couldn't move. Faithful to his calling, he took what he thought was his last shot as it zoomed toward him. The car finally came to stop a few feet away, but his valiant attempt at a picture was just a blur.

Racing is wild enough without adding drama, but T. Taylor goes to all lengths, heights and speeds to get his shots. Fireball Roberts took him on "shoots" in his racecar, roaring down the straightaway, and he has been in the Goodyear blimp, flown in helicopters, and gone up with the Navy's Blue Angels. His brother, who was a pilot, buzzed him over a race on the old Daytona Beach and Road Course so low they were almost arrested. The result was a collection of the first aerial racing photographs made.

Although he is quiet and soft-spoken, T. Taylor has been one of the most recognizable faces at NASCAR events for fifty years. He is known to wear brightly colored outfits to avoid getting hit and uses a thousand roles of films per year. In the old days, he had a panel truck that served as a darkroom on wheels. It enabled him to develop his film within hours and produce over twenty thousand pictures a year.

According to T. Taylor, some drivers were reticent about having pictures made at certain times, just before rolling out to qualify, or at the start of a race. Some held back

T. Taylor Warren goes to great lengths to get his shots. He is one of the most recognizable figures at NASCAR events and wears bright colors to avoid being hit. (Courtesy T. Taylor Warren Photo Collection.)

because of racing superstitions. Those superstitions soon bit the dust, when they saw the power of pictures in gaining publicity.

"I've always been involved in photography," says T. Taylor. "I've been interested since I was a kid. My parents allowed me to play with their box camera. They didn't use it much and I took it and pretended to make pictures."

The first time he knew he wanted to be a professional photographer was when he visited a local studio. He found its old-fashioned camera fascinating and the whole operation impressive. As a teenager, he joined his high school's camera club and was elected president.

"One year our school had a play and since our town didn't have a portrait photographer, I persuaded the guy in the next town to come. After he developed the pictures, I peddled them. I became friendly with him and hung out at his studio. I didn't do any work. I just visited. He had graduated from the Rochester Institute of Technology and said if I was interested in photography, I ought to study it. One summer, he took me to RIT and introduced me to the people there. That was a big deal for me. Rochester, New York, is the home of Eastman Kodak."

After high school, T. Taylor was unable to join the service because of high blood pressure so he accepted a job in the medical division of Dupont, giving exams to potential employees. When the summer was over, he enrolled in RIT. There he became friends with another student who persuaded him, after graduation, to join him taking pictures for the Northwest Color Lab in Chicago.

"We were doing what was called 'kidnapping.' We went to drugstores or other stores that would let us run ads and arrange to take pictures of children. Of course, we had to give a percentage of our earnings back to the store. In the mid-forties, a lot of people came in and we'd spend two or three days. After we finished shooting, we'd go back to our lab and make prints. I didn't sell them, I just did photography and lab work."

While at Rochester, T. Taylor had met an attractive retail major named Virginia Young. They dated until he left for Chicago, and then corresponded. "I rode back to Rochester to see her and, during the summer, I visited her home. We married in 1947 and she began showing the proofs and taking orders, sorting the prints and filing the negatives.

"I had moved to Milwaukee to work for a color lab when my brother Frank, who lived in Manassas, Virginia, wrote he was building and driving racecars. They called them 'Roarin' Roadsters' back then. I'd always looked up to my brother so it wasn't long before I went to the Milwaukee Fairgrounds to see what racing was all about. "When I went back to the lab, one of the photographers said he could get me in free. The next event was a midget race and he took me and I took my camera. He signed us in the back gate and I shot two or three pictures. He told me if I made prints, and took them back, I could sign myself in. That began my racing photography career.

"I didn't try to sell the prints at first, just gave them to people so I could get in. Since there were all kinds of racing [competitions], I shot a little of everything. There were Indy cars, roadsters, sprint cars and midgets. It didn't cost as much as it does today. A guy who had a good garage could build a car and race it. If he didn't want to race, he could always find someone to drive it.

"Later, I worked in Chicago again, going back and forth from Milwaukee to Chicago events, photographing at the track at Blue Island where they ran midgets and stock cars, and at Soldier's Field, where Grannetelli promoted stocks and roadsters. By that time, a lot of guys could afford late models and race them.

"In 1952, I moved to Kansas City, to run a one-hour lab, became friendly with two or three drivers and hung out at their garages. There was a lot of racing out there, but more backyard stuff than organized. I hooked up with a guy who owned a service station and a racecar his son was driving. His son ran all summer, but in the fall he wanted to quit. His Dad told me 'If you'll drive it, I'll fix the car.'

"If I'd accepted, I would have become a driver instead of shooting pictures, but I had a job offer from Highpoint, North Carolina, near Greensboro. That was about the time Big Bill France was organizing the National Association for Stock Car Automobile Racing and those NASCAR drivers were hotshots. All of them were professional because they had been racing so long. I made out pretty good and could get into the races, so I kept taking pictures rather than driving."

Back then, there were only a few track photographers, so T. Taylor was able to bring in a little bit of extra income. His main job was working at Alderman Studios, where he established their first color department.

"Forty years ago, color photography involved dye transfer which was very technical. I took pictures of commercial products and furniture when needed but my primary duty was running the color lab. You have to be an artist if you're going to sell prints. You take into account lighting, composition and perspective. I studied all of that at RIT, but the main thing was the technical part, the basic chemistry and processes. You had to study how to do it because it was involved. In those days we mixed our own chemicals and everything was done by hand. It wasn't mechanical and computerized like today. I'm into digital now, not because I like it; it's a requirement."

T. Taylor kept his day job, but his joy was at the track. "I would leave on a Friday night or Saturday morning. It wasn't a steady income, or very profitable, because the only people you could sell to were drivers and car owners. I only sold a few prints per race.

"I rode to the track with a driver or mechanic. There were two or three of us guys in a car and I'd sell prints for a dollar apiece for an 8 × 10. When I moved to Highpoint, I started going to races around that area taking shots. I'd spend a couple of nights in the darkroom after work printing them. Often the guys I'd photographed decided they didn't want their pictures or couldn't afford them. They didn't have the money to spend and I'd have to eat it.

"There weren't many sponsors and the cars didn't have many signs on them. A gas station might give a fellow a tank of gas. If you'd give him the print, he'd take it, but he wasn't going to spend a dollar. He gave that money to the driver to sponsor the car. The biggest year I had, I made a thousand dollars."

Much later T. Taylor was able to shoot pictures for sponsors like Champion Spark Plugs and Firestone Tires. The few sponsors there were only bought prints if their drivers won and they wanted a setup rather than an action shot to show their driver with their decal.

"I wasn't in it for the money. I enjoyed taking pictures and hanging around people. I related to the racers because they were independent and I've always done what I wanted to do. In photography, you have to push ahead. You can't stop and say, 'Should I do it this way or that?' Right or wrong, you've got to do it. If the consequence turns out bad, you figure out what you did wrong and do it right next time. The mechanics and drivers were like that too. They knew what they were going to do and did it, not depending on somebody else. If they wanted to build a car, they might call for help, but they did it their way.

"Race drivers were forceful and they meant what they said. If one said he was going to beat the hell out of you, you knew you were going to be beaten. If he said, 'Hey, you're my buddy, let's go out for a hot dog,' that's what you did." For T. Taylor the most enjoyable aspect of racing was its sense of community. The most fun was its unpredictability.

"You never knew who was going to win. There were certain ones I wanted to do well. Back then, there was more finesse, not aerodynamics and super horsepower. Drivers had to manipulate the race, pay attention to little things, and have lots of skill. They were an entirely different group of people than those today. I was a mixture of Milwaukee, Chicago, New Jersey and New York. I didn't have a drawl, but they accepted me, took me in, and I was their friend. It wasn't because I was making pictures. That was just something they put up with."

Soon, T. Taylor was into eating Southern cooking and discovering grits. To expand his business, he visited NASCAR's head, Bill France, in his office in Greensboro. "That was when Bill was promoting different tracks around the southeast and he was connected with Hillsboro, Wilkesboro, Martinsville, and Bowman Gray. Houston Lawing worked in public relations and he used my prints for programs and publicity. I'd work all day at Alderman's, then grab dinner, run over to Greensboro and work in the darkroom. I worked at Bowman Gray every Saturday night for two or three summers. When I began going off with the drivers on weekends and didn't get back on time for work Monday, Alderman fired me." T. Taylor was soon rehired.

"The next summer, Houston Lawing hired me to work for NASCAR full-time. I made enough money to work at Bowman Gray and different tracks during the summer, have a month off and go to Daytona. I went down to Florida when France started the big track and worked as a full-time photographer there until '71. Sometimes I took off and went back to Greensboro to shoot prints for their national program."

T. Taylor's favorite Daytona picture decided the controversial Lee Petty versus Johnny Beauchamp dead-heat finish of the inaugural Daytona 500. Using a 4x5 graphic with a 15-inch telephoto lens, so heavy he had to brace it on the pit wall, he captured the cars forever in time, before they crossed the finish line. At that moment, Beauchamp was declared the winner but after more film studies the victory was given to Petty.

The most tragic and best-known picture in T. Taylor's collection is an award-winning shot of the fire that burned Fireball Roberts. It's one he regrets having had to take. He's thankful for safety changes that have made it unlikely he'll take such a shot again.

T. Taylor's strongest supporter over the years has been his wife. "When we lived in Chicago and Milwaukee, Virginia sometimes accompanied me to the tracks, but women weren't allowed in the pits. She got a case of lonesome sitting in the grandstand or car, and at Highpoint women didn't go." T. Taylor's hearing disorder, two children, and the travel involved made attending difficult. He eventually bought a studio in Martinsville, but still freelances at races. The Warrens alternate between a home there and one in Florence.

Beloved for his generosity, T. Taylor Warren is described as the most famous photographer in NASCAR. "The most famous photographer?" he modestly asks, dismissing the compliment, "I've just been at it so long, they can't get rid of me."

CHAPTER 9

Roby Combs:
Pioneer NASCAR Flagman

Roby Combs began his involvement in auto racing in 1950 when he, Ike Kiser and two-time National Champion Buck Baker began promoting races at the Charlotte Fairgrounds Speedway in Charlotte, North Carolina. This lasted only a year before they sold their lease to Charlotte Motor Speedway president Bruton Smith. Combs then went to work for NASCAR where he became chief steward.

Combs was one of NASCAR's first flagmen and his job took him all over the United States. Beginning in 1952 and working into 1972, he was dedicated to his job and the sport and was well known to all its participants. A popular track personality, he was selected to explain the NASCAR flagging system on the 1968 album *Gentlemen Start Your Engines*. The following is based on a recent interview with his son, Phil Combs.

Roby Combs literally lived a Mayberry life. He was born and raised in Mt. Airy, the town on which the Andy Griffith television series was based.

"My Dad and Andy Griffith were close in age," says his son, Phil. "His sister was in Andy's class and they became close friends. When Andy made it big time and moved his parents to California, they basically gave away everything in their house. I have their old milk pitcher which I got from my aunt and still treasure.

"The first auto race my father and mother attended was in North Wilkesboro in 1949. Later, my Dad became best friends with Enoch Stanley, who was the track's manager and one of its owners. Dad had a sign shop and he eventually decided to expand into the racing business. He partnered with a fellow named Ike Kiser from Charlotte. Ike owned a garage and wrecker service and they fixed up a racecar Buck Baker drove. Since my father held partial ownership of the car, he worked on it and did all of the lettering. Baker ran the car in 1951 and had so much success, it became one of his favorites. He used to tell stories about how hard it was to outrun him when he was in that car and he won an unbelievable number of consecutive races at the old Charlotte Fairgrounds Speedway.

"Back then, drivers didn't have trailers. They towed the racecar all over the country, traveling up and down two-lane roads, using a tow bar attached to Dad's sign truck. When the car was wrecked, they had to fix it before they could tow it home. "In 1952, Dad was given an opportunity to work as flagman for NASCAR. He worked at his sign business during the week and then on Thursdays he'd go to Columbia, South Carolina. On Fridays, he'd go to Asheville's McCormick Field. It was one of the most historic and unusual racetracks in the country, because it encircled an old baseball field.

"My Dad was a starter but his official title was chief steward and he was more or less an overseer of the race. He made sure inspection rules were followed and the race was run under NASCAR's format.

"My mother Irma worked as track steward. She sold membership forms to all of the drivers and made sure they had insurance by selling them pit passes. She was also in charge of mailing race reports to Daytona to keep drivers' points up to date. Since there were no computers or fax machines, everything was done through the postal service. The race reports were prepared on Sundays to make sure they got in the morning's mail for Daytona. As a kid, I thought my parents' involvement in racing was neat. My Dad dealt with drivers such as the Pettys and the Bakers, Jack Smith and Rex White. They came to our house on a regular basis.

"My brother sold *National Speed Sport News* and, as he got older, I picked up where he left off. When I was six, my Dad put me in business for myself, selling *Southern Motor Racing, Southern Motor Journals* and *Racing Pictorial* magazines. I paid six other kids to work for me, giving them five cents a copy to sell them and keeping two cents each for myself. Dad told me to sell them to drivers so I'd get to know them and they would know me. I was called 'Little Roby' and I look back and cherish the moments."

Many of those special moments were at Charlotte Motor Speedway. In 1959, Bruton Smith and Curtis Turner formed a partnership to build the track. Its first race was on June 19, 1960.

"Dad flagged the first Charlotte Motor Speedway World 600 and it was amazing to hear him tell about how long it was and how tiresome. The track was one and a half miles long and, since it was before they had two-way communication, my Dad had to keep up with what was going on all over the track."

According to Phil, Charlotte was his Dad's favorite track because of his relationship with Bruton Smith. "Everybody knows Bruton owns tracks in Atlanta, Charlotte and Bristol. What most people don't know is how my father helped get him involved in racing. Dad had been working for NASCAR for a short while when he began partnering with Buck Baker and a couple of other fellows to promote races at the old Charlotte Fairgrounds Speedway. Bruton Smith wanted to lease the track from them. Doc Dorton, a guy from Shelby, North Carolina, owned the track and when Dad and Buck went to see him on Bruton's behalf, he'd only agree if Dad handled the money. It's hard to realize that Bruton, who has so much money now in so many states, started at a little dirt track in North Carolina.

"Dad had such good judgment, he was trusted with everything, and when the track at Charlotte was built, he was superintendent. My Mom has a copy of the original plat and lots of pictures of Bruton." Smith left in 1962 to pursue other interests and then returned in the mid-seventies as majority stockholder, regaining control of the track and hiring Humpy Wheeler as general manager. The multi-million dollar facility, now called Lowe's Motor Speedway, is a Charlotte landmark and has provided the setting for numerous movies. *Days of Thunder, Speedway,* and *Stoker Ace* were all filmed there. "Elvis Presley's 1967 filming of *Speedway* was a highlight. I stayed out of school so my Mom could take me to watch. The movie is still played on TV and I can see my Dad flagging."

Although most of Phil's memories are happy, there are some that haunt him. The worst is of his father flagging the race the day of the wreck that burned Fireball Roberts. "Dad was a good friend of Fireball and he had a premonition before the race something bad would happen. He was on the flag stand, looking directly at Fireball, Junior Johnson and Ned Jarrett when they wrecked." According to Phil, it was one of the worst events his father experienced.

Another terrible wreck occurred at Charlotte. "Jimmy Purdue was testing tires when my Dad heard one blow out and the car crash through a guardrail. My father was the first to get to him and found him dead. The toughest part of racing for him was having friends get killed. He saw those guys every week, got close to them; then they were gone. I know it had an impact on him and I think that's part of why he got out of it."

Roby Combs flagged during NASCAR's formative years. He also drove the pace car at Daytona. Since there weren't any interstates, he finally got burned out from traveling and formed a successful real estate company.

"Dad could flag right-handed or left-handed and he could write both ways too. Anything he could do with one hand, he could do just as well with the other. In 1968, an album was made about NASCAR, called *Gentlemen Start Your Engines*. Ten top drivers were selected to talk on it and my Dad was picked to explain the flags. Twenty years after my father died, I ran into a friend who had a copy." Today, Phil Combs turns on that tape and still hears his Dad's voice. He is very proud that his Dad was a small part in the huge puzzle that, when pieced together, became the most successful racing organization in history.

CHAPTER 10

Frank Mundy: Hell Driver

If anyone grew up hard, it was Frank Mundy. It is unbelievable what he was willing to risk to accomplish his goals. A "Hell Driver," "Death Charger" and stock car driver, he went from having nothing to having it all. Of all the early daredevils, he is among those most remembered, most successful and most talented.

"Mundy is my racing name. I had to change my real name, Franco Eduardo Menendez, because nobody could pronounce it. Eighty percent of the people in show business use a 'show name.' I told them everybody could say, 'Here comes Mundy. He started a race on Sunday and finished it on Monday' but everybody called me Tuesday."

Frank Mundy was born in Atlanta in 1919 to a Spanish father and Irish mother. When he was a teenager, his father, a cigar store owner, died. His mother, unable to support him, was forced to put him in an orphanage in Macon, Georgia. It's been said if a child has a role model in his life, no matter how hard the circumstances, he can be successful. For young Mundy, that role model was boxing champion William Stribling.

Stribling's home was near the orphanage and across the street from the young boy's school. Mundy milked cows before leaving in the morning and as he walked barefoot to class, he'd see Stribling run past him as part of his training, and sometimes join him.

Watching from a distance, the barefoot teen viewed Stribling's life and possessions as if they were a part of another world. He was fascinated by the boxer's private plane and bright yellow convertible. Vowing he would someday have the money to have those things too, he focused on achieving that goal.

As soon as he could, Mundy returned to Atlanta and earned money caddying at the Bobby Jones Golf Course, saving every cent he could to buy a motorcycle. He then switched jobs and sped through the streets delivering telegrams. Wild and willing to take a dare, he became skilled at performing tricks, challenging other cyclists to drag races and thrilling them with stunts.

At eighteen, Mundy found a demand for his risk-taking behavior in Lucky Teeter's Hell Drivers. A friend suggested he apply for the job after one of Teeter's cyclists broke his leg. Bursting through flames and crashing through walls of burning boards became routine.

"The Hell Drivers and Death Dodgers started at fairs. Teeter had a Lucky Teeter

Hell Driver coin he sold in the grandstands and that coin helped make him a millionaire. Every fair had a racetrack. Some were for horses, but they ran cars and motorcycles on them too. During the show, I'd slide my motorcycle off the back of a car in front of the grandstands at seventy miles an hour. I'd jump from ramp to ramp, sometimes over twenty cars. They also had walls to ride around and the tremendous speed and geophysical force would keep you on the wall."

According to Mundy, the drivers were called daredevils, but the term was used only for those taking a chance. Although there was risk, the experts knew what they were doing and were very precise. The key was a combination of precision, coordination and timing and to Mundy all three came naturally.

"I would stand on the motorcycle, in front of the grandstand, going thirty-five miles per hour and leaning against the wind to keep my balance. The only time I was hurt on a motorcycle was at a night show at a fair in Pennsylvania. It was raining and the track was slippery. I was short on the ramp-to-ramp jump with ten cars in between. The front wheel hit on the ramp and the back wheel knocked it out from under me. I cut my nose. It wasn't bad."

Later, Mundy went to the New York World's Fair, where he encountered the Jimmy Lynch Death Dodgers at the Goodrich exhibit. Since they needed another driver, he applied for the job. "We put on seven to ten shows a day for over ten million people. We would go over ramps and cut in front of each other. I cut a little early one day and found I could balance a car on two wheels. It was fun and I could keep the car up as long as I wanted or until I turned."

Disaster finally occurred during a show at the Charlotte Fairgrounds. Mundy was thrilling the crowds with his two-wheel driving when his left arm hit the door release. With his weight on that side of the car, the door swung open and Mundy was thrown onto the track. Seeing the car falling on top of him, he threw up his hands and feet. The action may have saved him, although the car crushed his pelvis. He was in a body cast for five months, a broomstick between his knees to keep his legs apart. All he could move was an arm and his head. The 200-pound contraption was so cumbersome, it took five people to turn him.

Stock car racing began to get big after the war and Mundy decided to forego his daredeviltry and give it a try. Involved in the founding of NASCAR, he met with Bill France, other promoters, car owners and drivers at their first meeting at Daytona's Streamline Hotel. There they hashed out the rules for the new organization.

"I ran the first night race in history. The track was in Columbia, South Carolina and owned by Perry Smith, who also owned the Studebaker dealership. I also ran the first race at Darlington. At that time, stock car racing wasn't paying the kind of money it's paying today. Darlington was the first super speedway built in America and that was nine years before Daytona's. I ran a Studebaker and one hundred twenty cars tried to enter. They took nine days to qualify and we finally started with eighty-two cars. That meant thirty-eight cars had to go back home. They were from all over the United States. With nine days of qualifying, their hotel bills had run up, but they didn't get a dime.

"Our biggest obstacle in racing was money. When we went to races, my wife Mae and I had to sleep in our car most of the time because we didn't have money for a motel. "Racing wasn't big-time back then and I had to work on my car, tow it, and drive it. Since we didn't have sponsors, I would arrive in a town two or three days before a race, go to

Frank Mundy was a "Hell Driver" and a "Death Charger" who also drove for Karl Kiekhaefer. Considered a high roller, he was good at investing and believed the best money to be made was through buying land. (Photograph by Bruce Craig. Used by permission of Collier Collection Archives. Courtesy Eddie Samples Photo Collection.)

the promoter, and offer to be interviewed for radio, television, or newspaper for a couple of hundred dollars to pay to stay in a hotel. At that time, it was hard to get on TV, but radio always wanted somebody."

In the mid–1950s, Mundy's big break came. Karl Kiekhaefer, the wealthy owner of Mercury Outboard, was looking for publicity, and formed his own racing team. Bringing businesslike professionalism to the sport, he dressed his pit crew in uniforms, hauled cars inside trucks, paid high salaries and provided good tools and Chrysler cars. A first-class operator, he provided backup parts and extra engines.

When Mundy was recommended as a possible driver, Kiekhaefer jumped at the chance. He called Mundy from Wisconsin and invited him to fly up to meet him, all expenses paid. "He offered me $1100 a month as a retainer fee, plus all the money I won. He paid the pit crew, but I gave them ten percent. I enjoyed two really lucrative years with him." The head of the Ford racing team tried to lure Mundy away with double his salary but, appreciative and loyal to Kiekhaefer, Mundy refused.

When Kiekhaefer decided to get out of racing, he offered Mundy a job with Mercury Outboard as sales manager of the South, including the Carolinas, Georgia, and Florida, working out of Atlanta. "I took him up on it, stayed with him ten years, and then retired."

Mundy and his wife Mae still live in the house he bought while working for Kiekhae-fer, located on a prime piece of property in Atlanta near the Georgia governor's mansion. A snappy dresser who has traveled the world, Mundy credits his successful retirement to good real estate investments.

CHAPTER 11

Louis Jerome "Red" Vogt: Pioneer Master Mechanic

In 1947, Bill France met with the most influential race drivers, mechanics, promoters and car owners in Daytona Beach. Convening on December 14 at the Streamline Hotel, the men talked about the future of racing for three days. France and his colleagues put forth ideas related to their concerns about increasing track safety, promoting events, and issues of fairness and track regulation. France proposed the formation of a national regulatory organization and a national series. The group agreed, voted him president and formed a board of directors. Board members included drivers Buddy Shuman, Marshall Teague, Red Byron, and Red Vogt. Vogt, who at that time was car owner Raymond Parks' chief mechanic, recommended the organization be called the National Association for Stock Car Automobile Racing, and NASCAR was born.

The Vogt-Parks operation dominated NASCAR's early days, especially at Daytona, and sponsored such greats as Tim, Bob, and Fonty Flock, Lloyd Seay and Roy Hall. Vogt was a mentor to the later famous car builder Smokey Yunick and, in addition to his work for Parks and other well-known racers, Vogt advised and helped any who asked, regardless of their racing status.

In the middle fifties, Vogt accepted a job with Pete Depaolo's Ford team and moved to Charlotte. He also worked as crew chief for Karl Kiekhaefer and Fish Carburetor. He was inducted into the Darlington National Motorsports Press Association Hall of Fame and the TRW/NASCAR Mechanics Hall of Fame.

The following is based on research and interviews, primarily with "Red" Vogt's daughter, June Vogt Wendt.

Vogt, who was born in Washington, D.C., in 1904, found employment at age 10 at a Cadillac dealership. By the time he was sixteen, he had become shop foreman, but the older workers resented such a young man giving orders. When he was in his early twenties, he moved south and set up a shop in Atlanta. Known as the infamous Red Vogt garage, the business was located on what is now prime big-city property, the corner of Spring Street and Linden Avenue.

Known for his bright red hair and his preferred uniform of white pants and shirt, Vogt originally got into racing while working for Raymond Parks, souping up bootleggers' cars.

51

A master mechanic, he became famous for his skill and the speed of the cars he worked on, especially those of Red Byron.

In 1947, concerned about unscrupulous promoters and bad working conditions, racing promoter and driver Bill France invited the most influential people involved in racing to the aforementioned meeting in Daytona Beach. The next year, Vogt's mechanical expertise enabled Red Byron to win the first three NASCAR sanctioned beach races and the 1948 National Championship.

According to his daughter, June Vogt Wendt, "He was interested in cars from an early age when the industry wasn't that old. When I think of him, I think of Henry Ford. Dad thought he was wonderful and his assembly line was fantastic. Once I went to a banquet where Henry Ford was honored. I wanted to tell Mr. Ford's family my Dad thought he was the most wonderful man in the world. "Dad admired Henry Ford and Franklin Roosevelt because they were public figures with great accomplishments. It was important to him to feel useful and he considered work to be a privilege."

As a child, Vogt visited his grandparents, who lived in Eustis, Florida. He admired the early beach racers and went to Daytona to watch them compete. He became quite an expert in flathead engines and is considered by many to have been an engineering genius.

"When he was young, he raced motorcycles," says Wendt. "In the old days, fairs had round buildings where drivers could race them on walls. Motorcycle stunts were similar to, and as dangerous as, skateboarding stunts are today. He lost his teeth at a very young age, because he ran into a post.

"I'm sure he finished high school and he was good at doing math in his head, but his education came chiefly through hands-on work with automobiles. He insisted book learning could not replace experience. When he had his shop on Spring Street, Georgia Tech engineering students frequently challenged him because their books said one thing and he told them something else. He said it was what really worked that mattered, not what the book said. They could get him riled and the conversations were hilarious. Some of those men are still alive and attended his funeral.

"I remember my Dad as thoughtful, introspective and Victorian in his thinking. A child in a generation that didn't show emotions, he worked all the time and was a strict disciplinarian, shaped by the events of his day. Because he lived through the Depression, he had very little desire for worldly possessions. He confessed to delivering illegal whiskey to the White House when he lived in D.C., but it was more as a lark than a desire to make money.

"Dad was slow to answer a question or offer an opinion, but when he did, it was with certainty he was right. He could be very insistent when it came to doing things correctly and his way was always the right way. He worked on his own clock and you could not make him hurry. However, I wouldn't say he was difficult as he was always willing to learn something new."

An example of this relates to his attempts to please June's mother, whom he met when she was working as hostess in an Atlanta restaurant. "He courted her with long drives out to the country in the wee hours of the morning when she got off work. Mom was a social person who enjoyed people, dancing and travel. They had marital problems stemming from his desire to work all the time and his lack of time with his family. Dad was very self-reliant and worked in his 24-hour Atlanta garage seven days a week. He didn't require much rest and in the middle of the night, he'd curl up in the back of a car and go to sleep. I remember him going three or four days without sleeping and then sleeping for eighteen hours. When he planned to go to a race, he worked at the shop until time to leave. After the race, he'd turn around and come back that night, then get up and work the next day. I don't know how my mom withstood it. She was his second marriage. My father had two sons from his first marriage, named Jerry and Tom. I was his stepchild, but he was a big influence on me and later adopted me."

In retrospect, June says racing has always been difficult for families. "I know it's hard on women and children today, but it was much harder back then. There was never a nice place to stay, never enough restaurants, never a normal life by any means. The sport was rough. Drivers had bad reputations, didn't get any respect, and when they finished one race, they were always planning for the next. They worked on their cars in their spare time, when they weren't at their regular jobs. My mother didn't want me to become involved with anyone in racing. She had very little education, but was an amazing person who always had books. My parents both loved learning, but their life was hard.

"The biggest problem was Dad's work. Mom wanted to have some social life. Dad finally began to understand and respond to my mom's needs after they were divorced the first time."

It took two divorces and three marriages to June's mom for Vogt to get the message.

"He took a Dale Carnegie public speaking course with her, and dance lessons. Although he appeared to enjoy them, it was obvious to me they were for her. He loved her very much and always tried to please her. She thought he would make a great teacher and they talked about having a trade school for mechanics. They had great ideas but they never transpired."

One of the little-known facts about Vogt was his passion for watching wrestling and his great physique. "In today's world, he would have been called a body builder. He took pleasure in physical things like lifting heavy weights. He was so strong he could pick up an engine block with one hand."

According to June, Vogt was also superstitious. Once when the family went up to the Carolinas for a race, Vogt turned onto the wrong dirt road. It was twilight and suddenly a black cat shot out of the darkness in front of them. "He would not go where that cat crossed the street, and started cursing and backing up. He backed all the way up the block while towing the racecar. One time when we were going to a race, my mother bought a beautiful new dress. My Dad made her take it off, because it was green."

In the fifties, Vogt moved to Florida to be in Daytona and went to work for Fish Carburetor. He left them to accept an offer from the famous car owner and entrepreneur, Karl Kiekhaefer.

Kiekhaefer's venture into racing was short and his relationship with Vogt was even shorter. "Dad had trouble with Kiekhaefer because Karl was a pusher and very regimented. Dad, like many of the drivers, couldn't fit into that mold." Afterwards Vogt worked briefly for Smokey Yunick before opening his own garage. "He had a shop right behind the speedway, behind the airport."

Although he raced some in the forties and fifties, June recalls Vogt as primarily an engine builder who made his living from his garage. "Everybody knew him because, back then, mechanics got more attention and were considered more critical. He was a very trusting person, but he had a bad temper and would cuss people out. Because he believed people should always do the right thing, when someone he cared about didn't, it was crushing.

"Dad used the best equipment and if somebody asked what it would cost for him to build an engine, his question was always, 'How fast do you want to go?' He was very competitive and was documented as having the first recorded shortest pit stop that enabled a car to win a race."

June says that, despite his accomplishments, there is little to be found in racing records about Vogt. "He was modest and not a person who boasted. I remember when he was inducted into the Hall of Fame, I gave him a shirt with his name and new title printed on it, but he was too modest to wear it. He did not believe in self-promotion. Don O'Reilly once told me he was such a quiet man, little was known about him."

Vogt finally retired when he reached his late sixties, when engines were becoming computerized. "Things were changing faster than he could keep up with them. I think that is a common story among older people and, sooner or later, it happens to all of us."

CHAPTER 12

Joe and Juanita Epton:
A NASCAR Tradition

In the early days of NASCAR, individual scorers kept up with the placement of cars in a race. If the event was a hundred-miler, NASCAR would provide a scorer; if it was a smaller event, drivers had to provide their own. Many used their wives or girlfriends to assure no lap was lost. A scorer was assigned to every racecar and marked cards containing small squares for each lap completed and the time their car crossed the finish line. Each scorer was required to record their times by referring to an electronically operated clock, which was directly in front of the scoring stand. The clock flipped a numbered card each second (from one to 9999) beginning when the race started. The numbers were referred to at the end of the race and included pit stop delays.

Racing was adrenaline-fueled and emotional. Controversies over scoring were frequent, some of them lasting for days and sometimes changing the winner. Joe Epton was NASCAR's first, and most famous, racetrack scorer. It was the driver's responsibility to cross the finish line, but it was up to Joe to declare the winner.

Joe's wife, Juanita "Lightnin" Epton, has worked in the Daytona International Speedway ticket office since it was built. A member of "Annie's Army," named after Bill France's wife, Anne, she is the oldest and longest employee in track history.

"When I started scoring," says Joe Epton, "I had two pieces of equipment... a pencil and a yellow pad." Raised in Cherokee Springs, South Carolina, Epton was a teenager when he went to his first race at the Piedmont Interstate Fairgrounds. A country boy, the son of a carpenter, Epton spent most of his childhood picking cotton. By age sixteen, he had acquired his father's woodworking skills and moved closer to Spartanburg where he soon became friends with track promoter Joe Littlejohn and was persuaded to score.

"With dark clouds over Europe, I decided to join forces with J.A. Jones Construction Company, which was engaged in building defense projects. My first job was in Grenada, Mississippi, where we built Camp McCain which was an army camp and a triangle air base. It was there I met my soon-to-be wife, Juanita, at a skating rink."

Joe nicknamed her Lightnin because he "never knew where she would strike." She was also his soon-to-be racetrack companion, a role she did not anticipate.

"From Grenada, I was deployed to Greensboro, North Carolina, then to Panama

City, Florida and from there to Knoxville where we built the famous plant at Oak Ridge that would develop atomic energy. I was a foreman on the K-25 project; however, while at Oak Ridge, I received my draft notice to report to Fort Jackson, South Carolina, to be inducted into the armed services. Due to an injury to my spinal area, I was termed 4-F and returned to the Oak Ridge area where I remained until the war was over."

After his time in the service, Joe returned to Spartanburg, South Carolina, to work again with his father in construction. "I didn't realize it then, but 1945 was to be an eventful year. The first stock car race was held in Charlotte and I scored my first [race] of a long career.

"Lightnin's first race experience was not a pleasant one. The race was held in Charlotte at a dirt track that had been watered down all night to keep down the dust. After a dozen laps, that red dust was flying. I had parked our car on the fourth turn on the top of a hill and she sat inside with our three-month-old baby. Every time those cars came around that turn, red dust hit the top of the car. The car was a convertible and the dust sifted through the cloth. It was too hot to roll up the windows and by the time the race was over, their clothing was covered with dust."

"I told him if I ever got home, I wasn't going to another race," says Lightnin today.

Through Littlejohn, Joe met Bill France, who would soon found NASCAR. France was already promoting races throughout the southeast and needed someone familiar with racing to handle the scoring. Joe jumped at the opportunity.

According to Joe, racing became like alcohol. Once it got in his blood, it took over his life. Fortunately, his wife became involved in it too, becoming a part of France's all-encompassing racing community.

As Lightnin puts it, "Big Bill used to say we were just one family and we were. It wasn't like it is today. Nobody had anything and if anyone got into trouble, everybody was willing to help. One of the things I liked about Bill was, no matter how big or little a person was in racing, they were all equal to him. He spoke to and shook hands with everybody. Once he met you he could recall your name, when and where he met you, and under what circumstances. He always had something good to say about somebody or he didn't say anything at all. His wife Anne was the same. She never belittled anybody or put anybody down."

The Eptons made numerous racetrack friends among fellow employees, drivers, pit crews and fans. Two of the drivers Lightnin remembers best are Curtis Turner and Wendell Scott. "Back then, Curtis was our favorite. I have a son and daughter and no matter how big a figure Curtis was sports-wise, he was always kind to the children. When we worked a race at Winston-Salem, our kids sat in the grandstands and Curtis would lean over and talk to them. He'd hand them each a dollar and make them feel like big shots.

"Wendell Scott came to the races with his family, his tires, and everything, inside his car. Those kids were so well behaved. You never saw them acting up and everybody loved Wendell."

"Most of the other drivers did anything they could to help Wendell," adds Joe. "If he busted a radiator, they would give him one if they had it. Race wasn't such a big issue because people weren't trying to push themselves on each other. All of the drivers were attempting to do the same thing. When people are working for the same goal, they cooperate."

When NASCAR was formed, Joe became France's chief timer and scorer. A few years later, wanting to improve the racecar scoring process, officials sent him to Philadelphia to learn how motorcycle races were scored. "We drove all night going up and all night coming back, because that was the night before the Grand National race in Charlotte."

Joe was fascinated by the new system which he quickly put into effect in NASCAR. "There was a big scoring clock out front, with numbers that changed every second and individual scorers each had a card for their motorcycle. When a scorer's motorcycle came by, he'd write down the time and the lap number. He could see how many seconds it took for his motorcycle to finish each lap and have a record of each lap completed. To us, that was automated." Soon, the new system was in place throughout the circuit.

Meanwhile, Joe's job took him from speedway to speedway and life was hard. "Joe used to score the races every weekend," says Lightnin "If the weather was bad and the race was cancelled, we didn't get paid, but that didn't stop us. We kept on because we knew eventually they would race and we would get paid. There were many times we didn't have much, but Joe loved the sport. He could score races with the placement of cars in his head. He'd write down their laps and hardly look back at the cards. At the end of the race, he knew where every car finished."

At that time, Bill France was running the old Daytona Beach and Road course, offering time trials as well as races to drivers and fans. The track was the most unusual the Eptons had seen. Its backstretch consisted of a temporarily closed-down portion of A1A, bordered by houses, and its front stretch was sand.

"The drivers raced down the back stretch wide open and came up the beach," says Lightnin. "There were a lot of holes and they tried to dodge them as much as possible. If they didn't get around them, they had to bump through them. It was so much fun to watch. Many a time they went in the ocean, flipped, just kept on rolling, and that was something to see. One time a spark caught a rabbit on fire. The poor thing ran through the bushes and they caught on fire and that caused a lot of excitement. There were ticket salesmen at intervals, but people always tried to go through the palmetto bushes. They used to say anybody brave enough to get through the rattlesnakes needed to get in anyway."

Because of the difficulty in warding off freeloaders and the ire of residents temporarily blocked from their homes, France decided the time had come for a change and dreamed of a super speedway. Since Joe Epton had construction experience, France asked him to help.

France had a dream, but when Joe arrived at the site, all he saw was woods. He immediately went to work with the construction crew. "Bill France was probably the greatest man I've ever known," says Joe. "When he first started he was broke, but I believed in him. I built the ticket booths and helped install the guardrails and then helped out with the grandstands. I helped operate the track for over thirty years."

"Joe worked on the speedway while we were still living in North Carolina," says Lightnin. "He was a carpenter, and a carpenter can do anything. He helped build that speedway. It was just a swamp back then and he worked hard. The workers killed rattlesnakes so big they stretched across the hood of a Jeep. When he came home he'd say, 'You won't believe that track' and when I saw it, I knew he was right. Daytona International Speedway wasn't just another racetrack. It was a one-of-a-kind. It was unbelievable to see how they had taken dirt out to make the lake and made the high banks. The track's opening was thrilling to me and I thought it was awesome.

When the track finally opened, Joe became head scorer and Lightnin took a job in ticket sales. During the first race, she and the other ticket sellers had a ledger in which they recorded each ticket sold. They wrote down each person's name, address, and ticket information to begin compiling a mailing list. That was not an easy feat, as over forty thousand people attended. "Now, of course, we're all on computer and have an automatic renewal system."

"You can't beat a die-hard race fan," says Lightnin. "Fans will come in any kind of weather and they'll sit through anything as long as their favorite driver is there. I'll never forget the time we had a rain delay. The people left the grandstands and some of them went to the laundromat, dried their clothes, and came back. They were so dedicated, they didn't dare go home. They knew something was going to happen."

Added together, the Eptons dedicated over one hundred years to racing. They are a symbol of the sport's tenacity and their contributions are recognized by thousands of fans. Joe Epton died shortly after this interview at age eighty-five. He is survived by his loving wife Lightnin, his daughter Joan, and son, Joe Epton, Jr. Joe and Lightnin were married sixty-one years. His death was a great loss to racing and a traumatic loss for his family and friends. He will be sorely missed by the racing community.

CHAPTER 13

Morris Metcalfe:
NASCAR Scorer

Racing's early events were often scenes of controversy without modern technology to determine who won. Scorers, assigned to each car, were usually volunteers and friends, fans, or relatives of the drivers. The mixture was a time bomb set to explode at the wave of the checkered flag. When protests occurred, they could end in fights and last for days.

NASCAR measured lap times with an electric box clock, placed in front of a scoring stand. Set to begin at the start of a race, the clock flipped a card each second, beginning with number one and ending with 9999.

Scorers were given smaller cards with squares on which to note their drivers' laps completed and pit stop delays. Relying on the clock, they recorded the time each driver crossed the finish line.

At the big races, NASCAR also provided time checkers in the pits, clocking drivers as they came in for stops. Darlington had the first scoreboard, but it just listed the top five cars and was changed only after every ten laps. Drivers could think they were winning while they were *losing* the race, and confusion ran rampant.

Joe Epton was NASCAR's first official scorer and Morris Metcalfe came shortly thereafter. Known to have the memory of a calculator, Metcalfe could determine a car's place by watching the scorers in the stands hold up their cards. An engineer by trade and a whiz at math, he could score a race by himself. Easily recognized by fans, he always wore a white shirt and tie, and carried fourteen sharpened pencils in his pocket. Starting in 1952, he was involved in the sport for over fifty years.

"I have a love for figures," says Metcalfe. "I wasn't interested in the cars. I just liked the challenge of scoring. In the old days, there weren't many people who could score races accurately because of the lack of equipment, and the number of volunteers were few. Some drivers used their wives. Buck Baker and Herb Thomas's wives scored for them and Lee Petty started out with Elizabeth who also scored for Richard. Rex White once had a scorer named Robin Peters who was twelve years old."

Metcalfe's career had its start with a seventh grade teacher named Mrs. Maddox. She taught her students to calculate math through memory.

"You had to have a fast mind. She would have us add, divide, subtract, add again and multiply. Only then could we write our answer."

Metcalfe, who began going to races in 1952, learned motorsports were less predictable than mathematics. During a race at Darlington, Johnny Allen's car soared over a guardrail, knocking down half of the scoring stand on which Metcalfe was standing. Through the grace of God, no one was seriously injured.

Metcalfe was born in Tennessee and moved to Miami when his father took a job as a traveling salesman. When his dad became seriously ill, his parents moved back to their native Tennessee, buying a grocery store in Morristown. Metcalfe worked at a bowling alley and at Western Union before enlisting in the Navy in World War II.

"I enlisted in the Navy as a signalman. Back then, a signalman stood on the bridge of the ship and sent messages to other boats by flashing lights and waving flags. Afterwards, because my father was in the hospital, I helped my mother run the family business. When she became ill, we decided to sell it.

"After selling the grocery store, I married and went to the University of Miami where I majored in engineering and industrial management. When I graduated I had three job offers. One was in Virginia and one was in Saudi Arabia. I went to work for Western Electric in Winston-Salem, North Carolina."

He first got involved in motorsports at Bowman Gray when officials let him watch for free if he'd score. According to Metcalfe, Bowman Gray is the oldest continuously running track in NASCAR and was a football field when it wasn't being used for racing. At one time, all the high schools in the city used it.

"If you paid your way in and scored for a team, they gave your money back at the end of the race. I didn't make any money, but I certainly didn't lose any. After the race they said they had another event coming up in two or three weeks at Hillsboro. I went down there and scored and got my money back again. There were races all around so I scored twice a month. After a year, NASCAR hired me as a minor official."

Two years later, while still working full time as an engineer, Metcalfe was assigned to his first pole race and soon became a chief scorer. Because of the organization's strict rules, he only scored at tracks on the NASCAR circuit.

"By 1960, I was working part-time somewhere in the United States every weekend. It didn't interfere with my job and I had a boss who worked with me. If I had to leave a few hours early, I put in extra time to make up for it. In a typical week, I might go down to Columbia on a Thursday night, come home and take off for Richmond on Friday and stop in South Boston on Saturday. That way, I might get in three races in a weekend. Before I went full time, the least year I had was eighty events. I was also in the Air Force Reserve.

"In the mid-seventies, Western Electric sent me to school during four summers at Texas Tech University. I received a Masters degree in industrial engineering and biomechanics, which is the study of the effect of a workplace on its workers. In 1982, after thirty years of working for Western Electric, I retired at age fifty-five.

"My last two weeks were spent on vacation. At that time, my NASCAR boss was Bill Gazaway, and I was assigned to a race in North Wilkesboro. He told me to bring along an extra set of clothes to fly down to Daytona. While I was there he threw a set of car keys to me and said they were mine if I went to work full time. If I didn't, he'd give me a ride to the bus station so I could get home. I took the keys!"

CHAPTER 14

Ray Fox: Master Mechanic and Car Builder

Ray Fox is known as one of the greatest car builders of all time. His racecars won hundreds of Sportsman, Modified and Grand National races. Fox was the first to have cars win on every super speedway and is responsible for jumpstarting the careers of Buddy Baker, Junior Johnson, and David Pearson. Other drivers included Fireball Roberts, Herb Thomas, Paul Goldsmith, Cale Yarborough, and Tiny Lund. Fox is a member of the National Motorsports Press Association Stock Car Racing Hall of Fame, an original member of Daytona Speedway's Checkered Flag Committee, a member of the TRW/Western Auto Mechanics Hall of Fame, Jax Raceways Hall of Fame and the International Motorsports Hall of Fame of Talladega, Alabama. He was 1957 NASCAR Mechanic of the Year, has a car on display in the Smithsonian Museum, and is president of Florida's Living Legends of Auto Racing.

Raised in Salem, New Hampshire, Fox became interested in cars at the age of seven when he went to his first race event at a local "board track." The board tracks were made of two-by-fours turned up edgewise and Indianapolis cars came to race on them every year.

As Fox grew up, his fascination with the cars grew too. As a teenager, he worked on engines and made money by selling parts to a local junkyard. By his twenties, Fox and his best friend, Bob McFee, were building and racing midget cars run by outboard motors. Fox was also a skilled mechanic.

Fox heard about the daring speeds of racers recorded at Daytona Beach's Measured Mile because "I listened to everything that happened at Daytona when the racers were running, guys like Barney Oldfield and Malcolm Campbell. They were doing some awfully fast things on the beach and it was talked about so much, I thought the best place in the world was Florida."

After serving in the military, Fox decided he didn't want to live back home. Still interested in racing, and wanting to strike out on his own, he felt compelled to go to Daytona.

"I drove down in an old '35 Ford with a cracked block and had to put water in it all the way. When I arrived, I was pooped. I didn't have money for a place to stay so I lay down on the beach. I fell asleep, got horribly sunburned, and ended up in the hospital."

Author Anne B. Jones, Living Legends secretary Paulette Mandala, Ray Fox and Gerry Fox Ajlani at the International Motorsports Hall of Fame Banquet, Talladega Super Speedway, Talladega, Alabama.

Fox was burned so badly, he was there two weeks. When he was released, he found a job in a Chevrolet dealership and rented a room in a home. Later, he changed to a Studebaker dealership.

"A guy who owned a gas station would come down to see me and when I wasn't working on other things; he'd have me fix carburetors. Finally, he asked me to work at his station and said I could stay there." Fox worked there for awhile, gaining experience, before hiring on with Fish Carburetor where he was mentored by master mechanic Red Vogt.

By the early fifties, Fox was heavily involved in racing, honing his skills as a driver with Glenn "Fireball" Roberts and Marshall Teague as he traveled the dirt track circuit. "I had a Hollywood supercharged Graham when I started out and that was a beautiful car. It went fast, but it fell apart, so I started building engines for Fireball." In the mid-fifties, he served as chief mechanic for Karl Kiekhaefer and was named 1957 NASCAR Mechanic of the Year. When Kiekhaefer got out of racing, Fox decided to open a garage.

In 1959, Bob Fish, owner of Fish Carburetor, died, leaving his shop to Fox, along with money to encourage him to keep building racecars. The next year, Fox found out that local Daytona Kennel Club owner John Masoni wanted a car to run in the second annual Daytona 500 so Fox went in with some other fellows to build a Chevrolet for Junior Johnson to drive.

Held on Valentine's Day, the 1960 Daytona 500 was a wreck-strewn affair. High gusting winds caused severe problems for the souped-up cars attempting to travel at high speeds. Driver Bobby Johns' rear window was sucked out by a wind pocket; Tommy Herbert crashed his T-Bird into the guard rail; and Tom Pistone lost control of his car. Damages and injuries were so high, NASCAR cancelled two Grand National events planned for the next week. To everyone's surprise, the Kennel car won.

"It had a little 348 Chevy engine," says Fox. "Most of the other contenders had big Pontiacs. We built the car in eight days. I told Masoni we couldn't build a car that fast, but he offered me double what I usually made. I got together with a bunch of boys and we worked day and night. I had no idea we could win. It was my most exciting moment in racing."

Another exciting race for Fox was the 1961 Charlotte 600. "The next year, I built a Pontiac for Masoni. I had a great car, but no driver, so someone recommended a young man named David Pearson." Just starting in racing, Pearson was the 1960 Grand National Rookie of the Year.

"He was putting a roof on a house when I called him. I asked him if he would like to race for me and he came and tested my Pontiac. When he got out of the car, I asked him what he thought. He said he wasn't sure as he had never driven anything that fast. During the race, he had a four-lap lead when a tire went flat. We were afraid he would come into the pits, but he limped around the track and won. He won two more super speedway races for me that year, Atlanta and a race at Daytona."

Fox retired in 1972 when he turned his business over to his son and decided to open a tire store. A few years later, NASCAR asked Fox to return to racing as an engine inspector. His new career lasted until 1996 when he retired again, this time to devote his energy to "Living Legends." The purpose of Living Legends of Auto Racing is to promote the history of auto racing and honor the pioneers of the sport. Located in Daytona Beach, the organization sponsors a yearly beach parade and banquet honoring drivers, mechanics, teams, and others who have made significant contributions to stock car racing. It also houses motorsports memorabilia and documents in a non-profit racing museum.

Fox says his purpose in life now is to keep the history of stock car racing alive. In pursuit of this goal, he has served as president of Living Legends for the last eight years.

"I've been a lucky person. Racing was my life. Taking care of people's cars, building racecars... that's all I've known, but I've had many great experiences and have many great memories. I've met wonderful people I'm sure I would not have met otherwise."

Today, Fox's racing legacy is carried on by his grandson, Raymond Lee Fox III, who works as a crew chief with the Robert Yates Racing Team.

CHAPTER 15

Rex White: Flat-Out
and Belly to the Ground

In the fifties, Chevrolet fans prayed for a savior and *v-a-r-o-o-m*, Rex White answered. Within years, shocked drivers and spectators watched White become one of the winningest drivers in NASCAR history. In 1960, he won the Grand National Championship, nearly 4000 points ahead of second place winner Richard Petty in Final Point Standings.

Rex White (left), 1960 NASCAR Champion, with friend and former driver Eddie Spurling. Rex White ran "southern style," flat out and belly to the ground, hard and wide open. (Courtesy Harlow Reynolds Photo Collection.)

Rex White and #22 Johnny Cramblitt battle it out in 1954 at the Marlboro Raceway in Marlboro, Maryland. (Photograph by John Ward. Courtesy Larry Jendras, Jr.)

He scored six wins and thirty-five top tens and was named Most Popular Driver and Stock Car Driver of the Year. In 1961, he was chosen as Motor Life's Man of the Year.

NASCAR has designated White one of its Top Fifty Drivers. He is in the National Motorsports Press Association Hall of Fame and the Georgia Racing Hall of Fame. He was selected for the Living Legends of Auto Racing Pioneer Racing award and the Smokey Yunick Pioneer Racing Award. Nicknamed "The Little King" and "Mr. Chevrolet," White is credited with developing racing chassis designs still used in racing today and was the first to use jack screws on a stock car. He is also known for his generosity—even to racers who were competing against him. A two-time driver for Chevrolet's racing team, White raced from 1954–1965. From 1959 through 1963, he won more races than any other driver while competing among the best. He has been described as Chevrolet's best driver in the early sixties and one of the most consistent NASCAR drivers ever. His gold and white number four Chevrolet is equally famous.

As a small boy working on his parents' Model T, White had no idea that the mechanical skills he was learning would change his life. He was too young to know that the car on which he worked represented hope to people around him and frustration to those trying to stop the transporting of moonshine. To White, automobiles were merely transportation, faster than the horse-drawn wagon. A half-century would pass before they were symbols of a billion-dollar sport.

"I knew drivers who made quick mountain turns and modified their cars to run at high speed," he says today. "They were a source of pride to teenage boys, racing through the valley, impressing their girls." As a youth, fish and deer were his hobbies rather than girls, but the screeching of tires interrupted his dreams. At midnight, he'd lie in bed listening as liquor-laden cars raced by. Their sound would start low in the distance and grow to a roar, a throbbing rolling thunder, echoing through the hills and piercing the night.

White was born in Taylorsville, North Carolina, during the Depression. Like other mountain boys who lived on a farm, his childhood was hard. "Some people say our family survived on luck, but if we did, we created our own. You make yourself available for luck to work for you. My father believed in working from can to can't, 'from morning when you can, 'til dark when you can't.' He said, 'Hard work ain't never killed nobody.'"

White says he was a naughty child, avoiding chores when he could and sneaking away. His main chore was plowing fields. Trudging behind the mule, he learned perseverance. Their movement was slow; one walked in the furrow just plowed, and the other walked the new ground. White would find a groove, set a pace, and follow along, understanding that if he just hung in there, he'd eventually finish the job.

"I learned that before I ever raced, and it was on the farm I fell in love with speed. I was always working to make things go fast, whether it was a mule, a buggy, or washing machine. I used to run wild on our horses chasing Indians. The first vehicle I ever raced was an old wagon. I had a couple I'd run off a bank and a hill near our church. My best friend 'Nom' and I attached wheels to a homemade wooden axle, added a seat, tied a rope to the wheels for steering and were ready for action. I finally got a bicycle and liked to speed through the woods and the roads."

When his parents got cars on the farm, they caught his attention immediately. "I helped keep them running, always improvising, especially with tools. We used what we had available, and I served as a tool myself. My hand was so small I could reach right in the transmission. I'd sit in our old Model T and my mind would go wild. I'd play with the wheels, press the pedals and pretend I was driving."

When he was ten years old, White was diagnosed with polio. It was a frightening experience for a child. The illness left him with a damaged right leg and a limp. Relieved he wasn't dead, he decided not to let it to become a handicap.

At age fifteen, White stole some of his mama's chickens to sell, ran away from home with a friend and headed for Washington. He found a bed on a park bench and a job at the Toddle House Restaurant. Lying about his age, he became a short-order cook.

"Later, after I was married and working in a gas station in Maryland, a man came by with a racing sign. He asked if he could put it in the window. I stared at that sign for weeks, saving my pennies. The race finally came and my wife and I were there. When I saw the first car coming out of the turn, I turned to Edith and said, 'I'm going to be a race driver.'"

It was hard to talk to drivers or get near the pits. When White saw a few loose boards on a fence, he let himself in. Volunteering to help, he worked himself into a job. He moved quickly from mechanic to driver. Only 5'4" and having to adjust the car to his foot, he was an unlikely candidate, but he hung around the tracks until he was taken seriously.

In the early days, he raced without a sponsor and life was tough. He'd sometimes pool his money with his crew, sleep in his car, and bathe in streams. He soon learned to cut corners, adapt his car for each track, and add innovations. When a sponsor came along, it was Chevrolet. Drawing on his knack for modification, and his natural driving skills, he raised the car's performance to its highest level.

"I wanted a nice shiny gold," says White. "My mechanic, Louie Clements, made a mixture of clear lacquer and gold dust. That car was magic." The "magic car" enabled White to win the only super speedway race won with a 409 engine.

Rex White (left) with his former sponsor, Max Welborn, during a recent presentation at Appalachian State University in Boone, North Carolina.

Today, at 76, White is in great physical health. He lives in Fayetteville, Georgia, near Atlanta Motor Speedway and spends time watching races, attending driver reunions and giving presentations and interviews. "Communities should embrace NASCAR," he says. "It's a home-grown, home-based industry, bringing in billions of dollars." As NASCAR's oldest living champion, he offers a unique view of the sport.

"When I was racing, I ran 'southern style,' flat-out and belly to the ground, hard and wide open. Back then, drivers usually built their own cars, a six-man volunteer pit crew was considered big and we had little special equipment. Our toolbox consisted of a hammer, a tire iron, a few wrenches, a welding torch and, if we could afford them, replacement parts. Our hammer and tire iron worked double duty, repairing cars and adjusting attitudes. They were known to be instruments of change before psychotherapy.

"Most drivers were poor and drove from race to race towing their cars. Some rented cars because they couldn't afford them or drove cars they'd bought on installment, putting tape on the headlights and grill to help prevent damage. There would have been no racing without our fans and they didn't have much either. Thousands of them raised money for tickets by turning in return-deposit Coca-Cola bottles they found by the side of the road.

"There were no fancy facilities at tracks, and spectators frequently stood or sat on their cars. Few tracks had rest rooms. A little track in Starky, Virginia, was considered upscale because it had one grandstand on the straightaway and drivers and fans could take a leak behind boards and hide from the crowd. I remember racing there, then heading back to Maryland with Bill and Satch Steel. We were filthy as could be, all covered in grime. When I saw a creek running under a bridge, we stopped, threw off our clothes and bathed in it.

"Looking back, it all seems crazy, but we were always stepping out of the rule box, in our lives and on the track. Some people called it cheating, we called it creative engineering. For example, people usually made roll bars out of exhaust pipes, but Tim Flock made one out of a 2 × 4. NASCAR outlawed that after the race, making the rule if it didn't hold a magnet, it wasn't legal.

"The more we could do with a carburetor, the more horsepower we'd get. Since we ran stock, there was plenty of room for innovation and a guy could hide a 'cheater carburetor' in his heating compartment. He'd let the inspector look at the legal carburetor, and then when the inspector told him to mount it, he'd switch it. If the seal wasn't broken at the end of the race, they wouldn't inspect it again. If a driver had to tear down his engine for some reason and the car had already been inspected, the inspector usually sat the carburetor aside and later resealed it.

"It was common practice to run an illegal cylinder head on the left side of the engine and a legal one on the right. Ninety-nine percent of the time, inspectors only looked at the right one and cars picked up horsepower without losing balance."

Drivers also fudged on their gas tanks, mounting them and then blowing them up with air to stretch them to hold more gas. They used fuel additives, mounted an extra fuel tank underneath the dash, put fuel in the roll bars, enlarged fuel lines and wound fuel lines under the car to hold an extra gallon. A few squirted laughing gas in their engines, blowing it into their intake manifolds. It worked to increase horsepower.

"Some ran locked rear ends to stop them from spinning. I've known drivers to narrow their car bodies, taking two to three inches out of the middle and lowering them on the frames. People pushed the rules, and then NASCAR changed them, but drivers always found ways to get around regulations. I won't name names, because people who live in glass houses shouldn't throw stones. Everybody did it; we just couldn't admit it. We'd make our cars go faster, and as soon as NASCAR found out, they'd hold our feet to the fire. People claim things happen by accident, but they're usually hoping to get away with it. Body work isn't done without someone knowing. Today, it's almost impossible to get stuff by inspectors because there are so many of them, but it's always happened and always will. Sometimes it's intentional and sometimes not.

"In 1961, an hour before the Darlington Southern 500, my car was disqualified over the way the engine was mounted. It had come that way from Chevrolet and I'd raced with it all along, [and I was] never told to change it. If I'd been told earlier, I could have fixed it, but there was no time. When Jack Smith found out, he loaned me a Pontiac, but it wasn't set up right. I managed to drag in tenth, which was the best I could do.

"Drivers and their crews are always complaining about NASCAR, but they have been forever. The rule book is one way racing has changed, but still stays the same."

CHAPTER 16

Louis and Crawford Clements: Crackerjack Racing Mechanics

During the fifties and sixties, brothers Louis and Crawford Clements earned reputations as mechanical geniuses. Their knowledge and ability came naturally and their cars were easily identifiable by their reliability and speed. Both were innovative, quick to figure out problems and offer solutions, and known to think out of the box. Those who were fortunate enough to have them work on their cars had "the racer's edge." When the Clements applied their magic to an engine or chassis, the car would fly.

Having taught themselves mechanical engineering, the two were on the Chevrolet factory team and Chrysler's Nichols' Engineering team, and they served as automakers' consultants. Among the men they worked for were Frankie Schneider, Buck Baker, Paul Goldsmith, Cotton Owens, "Junior" Johnson, Bud Moore, Bobby Issac, A. J. Foyt, J.T. Putney, Sam McQuaig, Joe Frasson, and Rex White. Louie worked for Gene White Firestone on cars driven by Lloyd Ruby and Sam Sessions at Indianapolis and built pace cars that ran at Indianapolis and Daytona.

Louie Clements' wife, Magdalene, held the first meeting of the Grand National Racing Wives Auxiliary, which was begun by Bettie Panch, in their home in Spartanburg.

The following is based on interviews with Rex White, Louis' son Mike and Crawford's son Gary.

As his son Gary Clements tells it, "Crawford Clements was probably the cockiest son of a gun who ever lived. That man thought nobody could do anything better than him except one person and that was his brother. Louis was his hero; he thought Louis was the smartest guy he'd ever seen. He used to say that you could give Uncle Louie a piece of sheet metal and a hammer and he could make anything you wanted out of it. Today they have shrinkers and stretchers, but back then, they worked with their hands and they showed us how. My dad was more of a motor guy and Louie was more of a chassis guy. They worked on things together but each had his specialty.

"Louie and Crawford got into racing when they were in Owensboro, Kentucky. My dad Crawford was a crazy wild teenager flying through town in his hot rod. My mom, Dottie, worked in a drive-in restaurant and that's where she met him. He'd speed through the parking lot wide open in an old Desoto without any mufflers. Her girlfriends told her not to get involved with those Clements boys, because they were out racing cars. They told her to leave them alone." Shortly thereafter, Dottie and Crawford married.

"My Mom was a stabilizing force," says Gary, "and my dad was a very loving person. He had as big a heart as anybody and he'd give you the shirt off his back. By the time he and Uncle Louie were in their mid-twenties, they had established Clements Brothers' Garage and were sponsoring a racecar."

Their "Flying Saucer," driven by G.C. Spencer, dominated the tracks in Kentucky, Tennessee and Ohio. At that time, most drivers ran Flathead Ford engines but, thinking out of the box as usual, the Clements wanted to be different. Their car was a 302-six cylinder GMC with a Wayne cylinder head on it.

According to Gary, his father never turned down an opportunity to race. "Once he was coming from Spartanburg, driving a '57 Chevrolet with a fuel injected 283 engine. He raced some guy coming through the mountains and hung his left front fender on a rock. He tore it off and just kept going. One morning I came to work and asked him if he'd seen a guy down in a ditch. He told me yes, he'd spun him out and put him there."

"Louie and Crawford had different personalities, "says Louie's son Mike. "Louie was conservative and Crawford was flamboyant. Louie was a slow driver on the highway and Crawford was wild. Crawford had a lot of ability to work on engines and carburetion. Louie's talent was from bumper to bumper, engine, body, frame, chassis and front end settings. They complimented each other but Louie was more versatile. They loved to race, but they both had big families and they knew they had to survive.

"Louie had five children and Crawford had four, and we were like traveling gypsies. I grew up on my mother's lap watching old dirt track modifieds, midgets and sprint cars. I remember when Dad and Uncle Crawford first worked for Chevrolet. A driver named Jack Smith had recommended them so, while they were in Florida at the 1957 Daytona Beach race, they went over to the Chevy garage. They watched the guys working on motors and noticed they were having problems. The mechanics had head gaskets for the old 265 engine and were trying to use them on the new 283. They had just torn an engine apart and thrown the gasket into the trash. My dad walked over to the trash can and pulled it out and then walked over to the Chevy engineer. He told him the gaskets couldn't be made to work. When the engineer asked him how he knew, he told him the head gasket was hanging into the bore of the motor and tearing up the piston. He explained that if the cylinder and pistons were bigger, he'd have to go with a bigger hole in the head gasket. They hired them both on the spot."

"Louie was a metal man," says Rex White. "He'd work on a rear-end housing by putting a weld on it and then taking a cold wet rag and a torch and line up that sucker perfectly. When we were working on the gold paint for my car, Louie and I experimented with a lot of different colors. Finally we bought some Venus Gold Dust at the paint store. He mixed enamel with the gold dust until it was the right thickness and sprayed it onto the car. Then, he went over the top of it with lacquer, making it sparkle."

According to Louie's son, Mike, it didn't go quite that easily. "After Chevrolet pulled out of racing, Dad went to work for Rex. Back then, there were no racing radios, so when drivers and pit crews needed to communicate they used sign boards and hand signals. For example, when the racecar was overheating, Rex would drive by and hold his nose like something smelled bad. They knew immediately he smelled boiling coolant.

"Since they needed to be able to recognize the car anywhere on the track quickly, they decided to paint it gold with white up the center. Once when they were going to

Daytona, they finished the paint job and covered the car in a plastic bubble so it wouldn't get dirty. It rained on the way and formed moisture underneath the bubble, and then, the sun came out and baked it. By the time they got to Daytona, the paint had turned green. Since green was a bad luck color, the situation was heartbreaking but humorous."

According to Mike, there was always something going on with racecars. "In the old days, NASCAR had rules about how cars looked. They wanted the dings all out and the paint to look good. Ralph Earnhardt was the king of dirty drivers. He drove a beat-up, torn-up racecar and he'd just as soon crash you as drive on by. My dad Louie became angry with Ralph because he was always banging into Rex, trying to slam him and crash him, or run over him and take him out. Every time Ralph was near Rex, he put a wheel to him and tore up the racecar.

"Each time he tore up the car, my dad had to go down to the shop at night and put on new fenders. He'd have to knock out the dents, put on a new door and repaint it before the next week. Finally, he had enough. He said it was taking his family time and he didn't like that. One night, after Ralph beat in Rex's racecar, Ralph pulled in the pits where my dad was waiting. Dad jumped in the car, grabbed him by the neck and told him if he continued, he was going to 'level his clock.' In those days, a lot of things were resolved by the threat of a tire iron or hammer, and they often went past the threat stage."

On a funnier note, driver Eddie Skinner was prone to pull pranks. "One night when we were at a race," says Mike, "he came flying into the pits. He jumped out of the car and threw up the hood as the pit crew came out to help. 'What's the matter? What's the matter?' they cried. Skinner answered. 'I've got to slow this thing down before somebody gets hurt.'" Another time when a driver didn't qualify in Charlotte due to lack of horsepower, he walked back over to his car in a raging fit and beat it to death with a jack handle.

"My mom was named Magdalene," says Mike Clements, "but everybody called her Maggie. She took us to races in her old station wagon and we'd have fun in the infield with the other kids. That wagon had everything from band-aids to pencils. She'd carry five kids, our pet chihuahua and a parakeet. Once after we'd moved to Spartanburg and my dad and Crawford were working for the Bud Moore factory team, we were on our way to Asheville-Weaverville when everyone realized Cotton Owens had forgotten his helmet. One of the guys on the team had a '58 Pontiac lowered down with Glaspak mufflers and hopped-up racing parts, so he roared back to the garage wide open. I bet he didn't see under 100 mph on his way back to get that helmet. My mom had brought fried chicken, potato salad, drinks, and a homemade prune cake. Cotton Owens had a sweet tooth so before the race he came down to our car and ate half of Mom's cake. Cotton won and lapped back around, but instead of going to the winner's circle he jumped out and ran into the port-a-john. We decided any time we wanted Cotton to win, we'd just bring him prune cake."

"Uncle Louis was pretty much a one-man guy," says Gary Clements, "but my Dad, Crawford, would go wherever he could make the dollars. When he worked for Holly Farms, my mom would pick up my brother Tony and me after school and take us to the race shop. My dad worked for Rex and Fred Lovett, who owned Holly Farms Poultry, and they would give us each a coat hanger, straightened out with the hook on the end. While they were working on the cars, we ran out into the yard and caught chickens. They paid us a quarter for each and sent what we caught to the processing plant."

"Both of them worked hard," says Mike, "and they were perfectionists, but they always enjoyed themselves and, sometimes, a drink. Neither had a drinking problem, but they liked their spirits."

"Every time they won," says Gary, "Daddy drank Ol' Forrester with Seven-Up and Uncle Louis drank Southern Comfort. Once, he got some Cherry Bounce, which was moonshine with white liquor and cherries. Rex White got two jars from him and took them to a Ford Motor Company Christmas party. Everyone liked the cherries but nobody realized their power. Everybody in the plant got drunk."

"Both stepped out of the innovation box," says Mike, "and sometimes stepped out of the rule book. Uncle Crawford was more susceptible to 'superior rule interpretation' but they were good at what they did, worked with the tools they had and made everything better and better.

"Louie was smart and well-liked by everybody," says Rex White. "He could handle the engine, chassis or parts and was always figuring out how to make things work. Together, we were a force to be reckoned with." While working for White, Louie was a winner in the "Golden Lug Wrench" pit crew contest in Charlotte. They shared *Motor Life*'s Men of the Year racing award, and White won the 1960 NASCAR Grand National Championship with Louie as his crew chief.

To this day, the Clements brothers are considered two of the best racing mechanics and car builders in NASCAR history and their talent is legendary.

"Louie and Crawford both had ability and craftsmanship," says Gary. "They probably forgot more about racing than most people know. Today, guys are whining because they have to run thirty-six races a season. Louie and Crawford were the best guys on the circuit and ran over fifty races per year. In the old days when they only had one racecar, they learned how to go down the road with a flatbed trailer and work on the car while another guy towed it. They never got the recognition they deserved, but they paved the way for the crew chiefs of today."

CHAPTER 17

Charles "Slick" Owens:
From the "Golden Glove" to
the "Golden Lug Wrench"

Known affectionately by his friends as "Slick," Charles Owens was a driver's dream. An ace pit crew mechanic, the former Golden Gloves boxer and paratrooper was an integral part of Rex White's 1960 NASCAR championship. He helped in the testing of cars at the Chevrolet proving grounds and later worked for Holman-Moody.

White first became involved with Owens when he hired him as a bookkeeper. Joining Louie Clements, Sonny Steel, James Hylton, Wes Roark and Ken Miller, Owens proved to be a great addition to the team. According to White, "Slick is known to hold his money so tight, it squeals as it passes through his fingers. He'd been a helper for Cotton Owens and had a lot of racing knowledge. He was also a former Korean paratrooper and Golden Glove boxer. It was said he could knock you out three times before you knew he'd swung." That quick footwork was responsible for more then success in the ring: He soon became one of racing's fastest jackmen. When White's team entered a pit crew time competition, they won a "Golden Lug Wrench."

According to friends, Owens had a business side and a lighter side and was always up to his ears in shenanigans. "Once he pretended he was me on a date," says White. "The next day when I came in first, his date heard the announcement and ran up to Slick saying 'Rex White, Rex White, you won the race.' Another time at Daytona, he called himself Cotton Owens.

"My crew chief was never a hard drinker," says White, "but he loved a good shot of moonshine. Once he had a half-gallon that was especially good and he dearly loved it. One night when we were working hard, he'd go to the jar every so often and take a sip. Slick noticed and the devil got into him. He found a similar jar and 'accidentally' dropped it, and then let him suffer an hour, before bringing the real jar out again.

"Slick was a picky eater and would turn down a steak for a green bean or peanut butter sandwich. He'd fill his car trunk with crackers and, if we went to a steakhouse, he'd order tomato juice, fill it with crumbled saltines and eat it like soup."

When Owens was a child, his granddaddy ran a store. "Candy was rationed during

73

Charles "Slick" Owens (right) and Johnny Allen at J.B. Day's annual driver reunion at the Raymond Parks Birthday Party in Easley, South Carolina, June 5, 2005.

World War II," says Owens, "but Granddad would allow me to have a little extra. There was an army camp nearby and when the troop train stopped near my grandparents' house, I sold candy for a dime, which was a lot of money in those days. I also sold candy and shined shoes at a nearby army camp.

"I worked from the age of seven. At thirteen, I got a paper route and then began hopping cars at a drive-in. We didn't have menus and I had to remember what was offered. I can tell you what it was today."

Owens became interested in racing when he discovered Cotton Owens' garage was not far from his Spartanburg home. "The first race that stands out in my mind was at the Spartanburg racetrack and I think Buck Baker won. He had an Oldsmobile and I never will forget it. The car had Hell's-a-Poppin' on the side of it.

"I loved racing and wanted to get involved so when I was nine I started going up to Cotton's to hang around, wash and go get parts, or get hot dogs and hamburgers for him, or clean the garage. He'd pay me and buy me a hot dog and Coke now and then. There were only a couple of us guys working there and when I reached fifteen, I went with the cars to the track. We'd tow them on the ground since we didn't have trailers back then. All kids like cars and I was fortunate. I especially liked working for Cotton, because we were second cousins on my mother's side and my name was Owens, too. Later, when Joe Eubanks came along, I helped him. Darlington was the first big racing event I went to and probably had 30,000 people or more.

"Although Darlington is my favorite, I liked fast short racetracks because I could see the races from the pits. Working a short track was harder than working at super speedways because, most of the time, we only had a day to get ready. We had one car so if we broke something, we had to fix it quickly to race that night."

One year when Slick was working at Cotton's garage, Cotton told him to be on the lookout for a little fellow with a limp at the track. "He said, 'I'll tell you one thing; Rex White's little but he can drive a racecar. Everybody needs to get their best hold on the short track when he gets here, because he can drive.'" Of the two, Slick says Cotton had the edge on soft dirt and Rex had the edge on asphalt. "Rex often outsmarted other drivers. He had a low left tire and when the dirt got hard he could outrun anybody. It may have been the way he set his car up, but Rex was a lot stronger than most people thought."

Slick continues, "Back then, the drivers were a lot tougher. Everybody did their own jobs and didn't leave them for somebody else. Drivers had to be tough, but they also had to have endurance. There wasn't any way to keep cool, except for the windows being out of the car, and drivers kept a bottle of water in the back with a tube running to it."

Owens says he had his most memorable racing experiences when he was working for White. "He was the first driver I went with who actually made money. He did a heck of a good job driving a racecar and I felt important. I felt like I was really doing something. There weren't but one or two teams that bothered us, teams like the Pettys, Smokey Yunick's and Holman-Moody. They had more money but we had the better mechanics and Rex worked on the car and did most of the welding. He could chew your butt out, but we were like family. Everybody worked together; we were all involved in decision-making and we were rewarded for extras.

"When Rex won the Grand National Championship [now Nextel Cup], we went to the Daytona banquet in tuxedoes and that was a big deal. It meant as much to us back then as it does today and nobody could have enjoyed it more than I did. Our later super speedway win at Atlanta was my most memorable moment in racing.

"When I got on with Holman-Moody, there were two hundred employees. It was different working there than when I'd been with such a small team, but I spent most of my time, as I did with Rex, ordering parts. With Rex, we didn't seem to have a lot of money problems, but at Holman-Moody, there were never any. Ford was behind us 100 percent."

While he was working for White, Owens accompanied several members of the team to Chevrolet's secret Arizona proving grounds. There, tightly guarded from competitors' view, engineers tested and experimented with tires and engines. Since it was part of the research and development division, no unauthorized people or cameras were allowed and its thousands of desert acres were surrounded by a circular fence.

According to Owens, the team had been competing against more powerful cars with only a 409 engine. A formidable force on drag strips, it was unsuitable for oval racing. "The reason we had been running so well with it was due to the car's handling and Rex's driving. The Fords and Pontiacs had a lot more horsepower. The 409 ran well on short tracks coming off corners, but we didn't have much chance on super speedways. After two laps, the engine got hot and slowed down by two or three miles an hour. I remember hoping for cautions, so we could catch up.

"When we went to Arizona, Chevrolet had just come out with their mystery engine. What made it special was the increase in airflow through the intake manifold that gave it more horsepower. Talk about being excited. I said, 'Oh boy! We can run any place now.'

But, we didn't get the benefit of the thing because the other teams demanded the engine and Chevrolet soon quit making it."

Working with a race team was challenging, but also dangerous. Cars didn't have the safety features of today, nor did the tracks. It wasn't unusual for a car to spin into the grandstands or pits, and the rowdiness of fans made life unpredictable. Owens witnessed several horrific accidents and bizarre events and the fact that his family often accompanied him made things scary.

Once when the team was racing at Asheville-Weaverville, the track broke up and the race was cancelled. Angry fans rioted and blocked the exits. When the drivers sent a spokesperson to calm them down, they greeted him with angry remarks and threw him into a lake. A man who tried to leave through the racetrack fence was grabbed and beaten and others were attacked and stabbed. Neither the local police nor State Patrol could break up the crowd.

"That was frightening," says Owens, "because we didn't know what was going to happen. The gates were blocked so we couldn't get out and we were in there for hours." Finally, the teams held hostage had enough and Maurice "Pop" Eargle tried to talk to the mob. Suddenly, a man swung a two-by-four at him. Pop, who weighed two hundred fifty-three pounds, grabbed the two-by-four, slammed it against its owner, stared at the crowd and asked who was next. Needless to say, the crowd dispersed.

Today, Owens is retired from Holman-Moody. He credits his racing and career success to the time he spent and the experience he gained with Cotton Owens and Rex White. "Being around Cotton and Rex, being involved in their racing and enjoying it... I was very fortunate."

CHAPTER 18

Hubert Platt: Dragster Showman of the South

Known for his funny cars, his extraordinary and sometimes humorous showmanship and his phenomenal racing ability, Hubert Platt was a flamboyant champion. Platt, who once defeated Richard Petty in a drag race, drove for Ford's Holman Moody racing team and won championships throughout the nation. He has been inducted into the National Hot Rod Association Hall of Fame, the Super Stock & Drag Illustrated Hall of Fame, the East Coast Drag Times Hall of Fame, the Old Drag Racers Reunion Hall of Fame, and the Georgia Racing Hall of Fame.

During the Depression, things were tough. Many families depended on their children for help and Platt's was one of them. Born in 1931, he was raised in the Myrtle Beach area where his father, Clarence, was a carpenter and his mother, Elizabeth, stayed at home with six children until she had to find work from necessity. When the family still struggled to make ends meet, Platt quit school while in the sixth grade and went to work too. "I started as a bag boy at an A&P and worked up to assistant manager." Later, he learned welding as a trade while gambling and running liquor in his free time.

"My first car was a 1939 Ford, wrecked on one side, with no oil pressure. I bought it for two hundred dollars when I was fifteen. I asked a mechanic how much he'd charge me to fix it and he said two hundred seventy-five dollars. Since I'd only paid two hundred, I decided to pull the oil pan off and repair it myself. That started my interest in fixing up cars."

By the early fifties, Platt was known as a moonshine tripper. "The cops always ate at the same restaurant, at the same time, like clockwork. They would stay an hour to an hour and ten minutes and it was always the same. When they went in to eat, we'd run to Hell Hole Swamp and get a load of liquor. We'd come back and have it unloaded before they finished their meal. We had a once-a-week route. We'd put it out on a Sunday or Monday night and collect our money the following Saturday. Back then, we sold it for forty dollars a case on credit or twenty dollars a case for cash.

"In those days, we drove old Chryslers and we'd run them wide open. I could blow the doors off of those Chryslers and still keep the rods in them, running thirty or forty miles with my foot on the floor. I'd reach over into the back, pull up a half gallon and take a drink, put it back and keep on knocking."

Dragster showman Hubert Platt at J.B. Day's Raymond Parks Birthday Party in Easley, South Carolina, June 5, 2005. Platt was known to pour beer into his carburetor to thrill the crowd.

After Platt married and had children, his responsibilities increased, but so did his racing passion. In the mid-fifties, he went into the army where he became a demolition expert. While he was in the service, he bought a "real hot" '57 Chevrolet with a 270 horsepower engine and raced it at a dragstrip in Manassas, Virginia. The experience was so thrilling, he continued to race. "When I got out of the service, a buddy and I bought a 1937 Ford from Banjo Matthews and tried stock car racing, but that was not for me."

Platt soon sold the Ford but his interest in racing continued. When his enlistment time was up, Platt returned to South Carolina. He intended to reenlist but was sidetracked by a twist of fate. "I was at my buddy's home when he asked me if I could get him liquor. I told him yes and he asked me to get him ten cases. I got eleven instead of ten, as I wanted to take one to a friend for Christmas. When I returned to his house, a fellow was there who didn't like me. He pointed out the remaining case and when I didn't give it to them, he reported me to the sheriff." Platt ended up paying three hundred dollars, losing his car, and going to jail. When he was released, he bought an old police car and headed to Atlanta to see relatives. "I had planned to re-enlist but my aunts and uncles talked me out of it and I went back into welding." After several months, he had earned enough money to open a service station.

"I moved my whole family there from South Carolina. I moved my brothers first, putting several of them to work for me, and then moved my mother and father. It was in the late fifties and I was messing around with cars at the station. When I bought a 1938 Chevrolet and started running it, I realized I had a knack for building engines. One thing led to another and before long I was setting records at Covington and went on to Florida.

"The hardest thing was trying to race and support a family. I worked up to eighty hours, seven days a week, welding, hauling liquor, playing poker and racing. Once I was in a house in South Carolina, where I drank and played poker until I fell asleep. The next morning when I woke up, I found I'd slept through a hurricane. It had blown off the end of the house and washed the whole beach out.

"Back then, we ran a race for $18.75. That's the cash value we got on a savings bond. Since I needed money, I'd take my trophies and sell them for $2.00 apiece. I kept setting records and pretty soon I was known around the country. People thought everybody in California was bad, but when they came our way, they got their ass kicked."

Platt's success caught the eye of fans and corporate sponsors. "When Triple Transport offered me a job, I took it. They paid me a weekly salary, gave me part of my winnings, two people to help me, a tractor and trailer, and two cars. They called them the Double T Specials. I liked to go out, have a good time, and show what I could do. I'd put on a show no matter what. I'd make a hole in the exhaust and make a flame come out or set a tool box on the front of the car and pretend I forgot it. Once in California, the promoter offered a set of wheels to the man that did the highest wheel spin. I put my tool box on the back and kept it on the rear wheel so long it lost all of its pressure. When I set the car back down, the wheel bounced and the tool box went through the bottom and scattered tools all over the track. I got out of the car and went over to the fence, grabbed a girl and kissed her and the crowd went wild. We did all kinds of things to make people laugh and we outran everybody."

Tracks were not the only place Platt practiced his skills. For over seventy-five years, Atlanta has been known as the "Home of the Varsity." One of the first fast-food restaurants, its "nekked dogs" and onion rings are traditions for natives and tourists. During the fifties, one of Platt's favorite pastimes was screeching through the parking lot in his '55 Chevrolet with its 283 fuel-injected engine.

"That thing would go a hundred and three!"

In the early sixties, Atlanta's Nalley Chevrolet opened a racing shop. "They called it the Nalley Nicholson Dyno Shop and hired my brother Houston and me to race for them. We stayed with them a couple of years.

"When I started racing Chevrolets, everybody called them Shakers. Since I was from Georgia, they called me the Georgia Shaker. My other nickname was 'Hube Baby.' Once when we were in Columbia, South Carolina, we blew our engine. The next day, we were due in Savannah, Georgia, and since they paid a $500 show fee, we decided to go. When we arrived, I told my buddy I'd go talk to the promoter and while I was talking to come over and say, 'Hey, I fired the car up awhile ago and it made a heck of a lot of noise.' I'd tell him to go back and check it out and I'd be there later. When I went back with the promoter to look, he told us he'd pulled the head off and it had dropped a valve. Hell, that thing hadn't even had a head on it. The man told us to just unload the car and he'd give us our guarantee money." Platt saw the man again five years ago and finally confessed.

Platt became one of drag racing's wildest competitors and also one of its best. In the mid-sixties, the Ford Motor Company offered him a job with their East Coast Racing Team. "I went to Dearborn, Michigan, where I tested cars for them. They gave me a salary, an expense account, two cars, a truck, a trailer, all the parts I needed and two people to help me. We gave two or three seminars during weekdays and raced on weekends. We called the seminars 'Ford Drag Team Clinics.' A program generally ran an hour or an hour and fifteen minutes, but sometimes we took a lot longer. We stayed for the people to ask questions and were never in a hurry to leave. We'd just shoot the bull about the cars. The biggest ones were in Detroit, Michigan, and Providence, Rhode Island and they were so successful we were put on [TV's] *60 Minutes.*

"I got paid $50,000 apiece for the decals on my cars, was given a cost of living raise every year, kept all of my winnings, and received cars for myself and my wife. I could fly anywhere I wanted to go and at the end of the year, they gave me my cars to sell. You never saw me dirty at the racetrack. They bought our clothes and I wore fifty dollar pants with alligator shoes. In those times, that was high dollar and people were impressed with the way I dressed.

"Back then, everybody accused me of cheating, but I never had an illegal engine in my life. It wasn't the fastest car that won the race, it was the best driver. A dragster has to be quick out of the cage and do the same thing every time. He has to know how to drive a car, how to feel a track to know where the bumps are and how to concentrate. He's got to keep his eye on the light or the flagman, watch the rpm gauge, be sure not to over-rev the engine, and not miss a gear. I used to grind my transmission off slick. I'd grind this off, and then I'd grind that off, leaving out anything to make it shift faster. A dragster also has to know how many rpms his engine will take. If he runs too tight, he'll hurt his engine and start slowing down. I believed in W.A.O., running 'wide ass open.' When I left the start light, I'd put the pedal to the bottom and leave it there. I blew a lot of engines, but I won a lot of races."

Despite his upbeat tales, he can't deny racing was dangerous. "I was thrown out of the car once in Riverside. Back then, if you ran super stock too fast, it could throw you. I was smoking the front tires and dragging the brakes. I wore the tires flat, but I survived and won the race."

Platt finally called it quits in 1977. He still loved racing but was tired of the traveling. When he was offered a high-paying job in welding, he took it and stayed in the field for ten years. When he tired of that, he bought a restaurant and became a partner in a tree surgeon business. Today, he enjoys real retirement, going to car shows where he rehashes old times with his friends.

"Today, drag racing has changed. In the old days, you had to make everything yourself. Today, if you've got money, you can race and buy anything. I made a lot of money in racing, more than anybody would think, probably as much in the early seventies as the guys are today. I didn't have to win a race, because I won money shooting crap. Sometimes, I'd walk around with almost four thousand dollars in my pocket. I was known as a high roller because I would go into a bar, throw five hundred dollars on the counter and tell them, 'When this runs out, run us out.' It didn't bother me a bit to make it and spend it."

A heck of a driver, Platt was as well known for his entertaining and partying. "My favorite saying was 'Let's party!' When I went to a race, I went to party. There were three things at which no one could beat me. Number one was shooting craps; number two was chasing women; and number three was drinking liquor."

Fans still remember his antics. Larry Hinson recalls Platt "feeding beer to his Ford." He did it to clean the carbon off of his pistons but spectators went wild.

"My shows were all packed and the whole crowd roared. I had a hell of a life and a lot of fun. They called me the 'Showman of the South.'"

CHAPTER 19

Robert Glenn "Junior" Johnson:
Win, Wreck or Blow

Robert Glenn "Junior" Johnson was one of the most dynamic racecar drivers in the sport. Johnson was one of the few drivers who bridged the pioneer days of racing and the modern era. By the end of his career, he had become a cult hero and the subject of two books (*The Last American Hero* by Thomas Wolfe and *Brave in Life* by Tom Higgins and Steve Waid). *The Last American Hero* was made into a popular movie.

Johnson raced for over a decade, racking up fifty Winston Cup wins before becoming a successful entrepreneur. In 1966, he stopped driving and became a car owner, sponsoring such hot dogs as Cale Yarborough and Darrell Waltrip and winning six NASCAR Winston Cup Championships. After retiring from car owning, he went into the pork business.

In 1998, *Sports Illustrated* named Johnson the greatest NASCAR driver of all time and NASCAR named him as one of their all-time Top Fifty Drivers. He is a member of the National Motorsports Press Association Hall of Fame at Darlington, the International Motorsports Hall of Fame in Talladega, the Charlotte Motor Speedway's Court of Legends, and Bristol Motor Speedway's Heroes of Bristol Hall of Fame.

If anyone in American history pulled himself up by his bootstraps, it was Robert Glenn "Junior" Johnson. Johnson was raised in the backwoods of the North Carolina foothills, in the community of Ingle Hollow near Wilkesboro, and his colorful life is a rags-to-riches story. The region was in the heart of moonshine country and he learned to drive at an early age, delivering "lightnin'" for his bootlegging father. At that time, making illegal whiskey was a matter of economic survival for residents of the poverty-stricken area.

Because of the necessity of evading the law, "shiners" spent part of their profits souping up their cars, and Johnson applied his natural mechanical ability to increasing horsepower. According to Johnson, "There's no better learning than trial and error and I learned a lot through that teaching method." His modified cars outran and outmaneuvered both police and competition. He became famous for his "bootleg turn," which swung a fast-moving car 180 degrees, to face in the opposite direction.

In the early fifties, Johnson decided to apply his racing prowess to the dirt track. He

(Front) Writer Tom Higgins (left) and "Junior" Johnson, at the annual Moonshine Festival in Dawsonville, Georgia (fall, 2005). At center is 1960 NASCAR Champion Rex White. Behind White is racing enthusiast Dale Cosby and at rear right is former driver Eddie Mac-Donald. Known for his "pedal to the metal" style and "bootleg turn," Johnson learned his driving skills while transporting moonshine.

was an up-and-coming driver when years of eluding the law caught up with him. Found at his father's still, he was arrested and incarcerated. After his release, he decided that the racetrack was a better way to make a living and took NASCAR by storm. He amazed other drivers with his aggressive, wide-open style, pushing his car to the limit.

"I was going to be a Major League [Baseball] pitcher," says Johnson. "I was very good as a youngster, but I turned our tractor over and broke my arm. I think I could have done well at any kind of sport. I grew up running moonshine and racing attracted me because I like fast cars, although in those days, racing was tough and it was hard to make money, because there were so many dominant competitors. I raced against Buck Baker, Fireball Roberts, Marvin Panch, Curtis Turner and Herb Thomas. There were a lot of good guys in NASCAR. Some people thought I was crazy, but I was good at setting up my car and that helped me a lot.

"I had to learn the safety side of racing quickly, because I wanted a well-built car and a safe one, but I knew the combination to get my car controllable. If a driver didn't have a good motor and a good driving car, he had lots of trouble. I worked on my own cars, even when I was winning, and that's what later made my owning cars successful. I knew what I had done when I was driving and adapted it to those who drove for me. Cale Yarborough, Darrell Waltrip, and Bobby Allison were consistent winners."

Johnson says if he were to describe the sound of a racing engine, it would be like describing music. "If you've worked on motors awhile, you can tell who's got a good motor by the way it sounds."

Fine-tuning motors was one of Johnson's specialties. He was also adept at adjusting his car to a track. "Darlington was one of my favorite racetracks because it was a challenge and you had to prepare. They had the Southern 500s there and those were the biggest races in the country. You didn't go to Darlington to race competitors; you went to Darlington to race the track. I'd start months ahead, checking my car's springs, changing the tires, and finding the right combination. We educated ourselves about how to make our cars run and the drivability of the car was crucial. Darlington would take you out, if you let your guard down.

"The most memorable race I ran there was in 1953 when they had a two hundred mile modified race. I was a youngster at the time and didn't know anything about racing, but I had the fastest car in the moonshine industry. I said, 'It's faster than anything on the highway. Why don't I take it to Darlington?' and I wound up winning the race. I'd done a little dirt track racing but it was the first super speedway I'd ever run. My car was a '39 standard Ford coupe, which was a very famous car at that time.

"The most unusual thing I've ever had happen to me on a track was when they first opened Charlotte Motor Speedway. In the first race they held there, the track tore up and a hunk of asphalt the size of a bowling ball came through my windshield and landed in the back of the car."

Although Johnson could run any model, he was best known for Chevrolets. "Chevrolet was my favorite engine because of its options. You could improve it so many ways. The 350 was best because it was easy to work on and you could make more horsepower."

Johnson says if he were giving advice to drivers today, he would tell them to get a lot of experience, be honest, and have patience. "The most important skill a race driver needs is patience. If he gets over-eager, he's going to hurt himself or somebody else."

Johnson has seen tremendous change in the sport over the years, from individual effort to joint competition. He thinks the reason the sport is so popular is its high visibility. "Racing is one of the most visual sports; it's so competitive; and teams may have three or four hundred people involved. If a guy's not competitive, he takes his whole team out."

In looking back, he says racing has been a huge part of his life and had a positive impact. "When I was running a racecar, I learned every aspect of the sport. Travel was part of it. I was in a different environment at different tracks and none of them were the same. Because I traveled, I met a lot of different types of people. I gained a wider perspective on life and a better outlook. I had a great adventure in the sport and it broadened my world tremendously."

Johnson, who resides in North Carolina near his roots, has a profitable country ham and pork skin business. He is still connected to racing, attending events and meeting with former competitors. One of his favorite pastimes is cooking big breakfasts for his friends, workers, and family.

CHAPTER 20

Bobby and Socrates "Shorty" Johns: Racing's Premier Father-Son Team

Bobby Johns raced in NASCAR Grand Nationals from 1956–1969. During that time, he had 141 starts, two wins, twenty-one top fives, thirty-six top tens and sat on two poles. In 1960, he finished third in Final Points Standings. His total Grand National earnings exceeded $145,000.

Believing the only way to be successful was through physical fitness, Johns was a

Wanda Tallent, Sidney Jones (center) and Bobby Johns at the Living Legends of Auto Racing Annual Banquet. Johns and his father, Socrates, formed a unique father-son racing team. Bobby Johns believes a key to driving skill is keeping physically fit.

driver-athlete who spent much of his time swimming and exercising. The rest of the time, he concentrated on building a topnotch racing program with the help of his father. Bobby and "Shorty," as his dad Socrates Johns was called, lived together and worked together, forming a close-knit team. Racing as independents was hard, but their loyalty was strong. Bobby once turned down a factory ride when his father wasn't included. As Rex White says, "Bobby and Shorty Johns were special and there will never be a race team like them."

Bobby Johns' mother died when he was young, leaving him and his sister Angeline with their father. Socrates "Shorty" Johns, a mechanic and midget racer, exerted tremendous influence on their lives. He had faith in his son's race driving ability and helped steer him into the sport.

"I was born in Miami in 1932," says Bobby, "and, working for my dad, I became a grease monkey before starting grade school. He liked to joke around but had a strong work ethic he passed on to me. When it came to accomplishing what he was after, time meant nothing. At three o'clock in the morning, he'd be working on an engine, a differential or frame. For us, the five o'clock whistle never blew.

"In the mid-thirties, when midgets were starting to catch on, my dad built a unique one to race. It had a four-cylinder Continental engine, dual sparkplugs in the cylinders, a quick change gear box and a quick change rear end. He didn't have to fight to change gears at the track and had plenty of room on the bottom."

In the old days, participants called their cars "junkies and roadsters," but the roadsters were just jalopies with their tops cut off. They called their competitions dirt track racing, but, "if you've ever been to Florida, you know it was sand."

Bobby continues, "In later years, my dad changed to a straight up and down overhead-valve four-cylinder Chevrolet. That was a strong machine, but rough, and it was good for breaking axles and tearing up gears. In the late thirties, Ford came out with an eight-cylinder 60 engine. At first, the price was prohibitive, but when they hit the junkyards they took off like bandits. Everything became open wheel and Ford.

"By the time I was seven, my dad was letting me race kids who were thirteen and fourteen, and when I was twelve, I worked on his pit crew. The first car I ran was a 1929 Pontiac. It didn't look like anything because it didn't have a body, but it had open wheels and roll bars, which were uncommon. I also raced a Model T and a Willis Overland. We didn't have crash helmets and money was hard to come by. Because there were no go-karts or racetracks, we had to race real cars in cow pastures.

"When we had midgets, my dad and I sometimes ran locally against each other and, as I got older, we decided to leave the garage during the summers to race. World War II curtailed competition, but we picked up where we left off when the war was over. When I was seventeen, I started racing short track, not just for fun, but in a professional manner."

In the late forties, Bobby built his first stock car. "Midgets and open wheels were one thing and stocks were another. The cars were 180 degrees apart, but after I built the car, Dad liked it and he started driving it. When we raced stocks, we ran Ford coupes, especially '34 and '37, and I probably had twelve or more. The '34 Ford with a flat-head engine was 'A-1.'

Bobby and Shorty competed against each other for the last time in a race at Opa Locka, Florida where Shorty wrecked and got "banged up bad." After that, he told his son to take over the driving. "In the early fifties, I was in the army and took a couple of our cars to Fort Jackson to race Charlotte and Spartanburg. I also ran for the first time on the Daytona Beach and Road Course. Because I had to leave from Fort Jackson, I got there late, but Bill France let me start last. There was plenty of room on the beach, but the north turn was sharp. I slid off the turn and down to the fence and had to work my way back on the track.

"My dad and I still did garage work after I got out of the army, but racing was more of a full-time affair. By then, Ford had the overhead engine, but I got to Grand Nationals through Chevrolet. A local Miami track owner had a '56 Chevrolet he'd gotten from Red Farmer. He used it to run a few races and then stored it in a barn. We bought it and it financed our racing program. Later, we built a '57 Chevrolet and stayed with it until the end of its life.

"I was known as a 'Ford Person' before I switched to Chevrolet, but I've also driven Plymouths and Pontiacs. We were hooked on Pontiac because it was the first car I drove and we ran well with it."

Racing provided opportunities for travel as well as entrepreneurship. "We could have been classified as gypsies because we were going from one town to another like a circus, putting on shows three to four times a week. Some people were kings at their local tracks and didn't leave, but those who moved around expanded their knowledge and friendships. Racing was a good stepping stone for me and it opened a lot of doors. I learned about our country and met different people, and we made fine friends who helped us in business ventures.

"Back then there was more fun and less friction. Everybody knew what the other guy had and we respected each other. We protected our equipment and that helped protect the other guys'. Now, if a driver runs into someone else's car and hurts his own, he just jumps in another one. He doesn't have to go in his shop and work on it. Of course, when we were with our racing friends, there was no telling what to expect and every time we turned around, jokes were being pulled."

Johns says of all the tracks he ran, his favorite was West Palm Beach, a half-mile track where the key to success wasn't horsepower. "The track was similar to Darlington in that you had to have a car that handled well. A driver could drive into a corner thinking he should back off, but knowing he didn't have to, or think he was over-driving and not drive hard enough. I really liked any racetrack, unless it wore out my car. I loved to drive Martinsville, but stepping on the brakes a thousand times was wear and tear. Lakewood Speedway was fun, but its washboard dirt was rough and tore my racecar to pieces."

Occasionally, Johns' sister Angeline got in on their act. "She didn't go to many races but she enjoyed them. In 1956 she went with us to the first Darlington late model I ran. We started 44th and placed tenth. After the race was over, instead of going back to Miami, she went to Montgomery and became part of our pit crew, changing our tires."

Johns became famous running stocks in Grand Nationals, but his most exciting moment was at Indianapolis in a pace lap, running down the back straightaway in a Lotus Ford. "At that time, the exhaust pipes came up the rear of the cars and, since we burned nitro and alcohol, the flames shot out. I looked around and wondered what I was doing there but when we moved from twenty-second to seventh, I thought, 'This is something.' Taking the green flag at Indianapolis was one of the biggest thrills of my life."

Today, Johns owns a tire and wheel export company and his office has pictures of him and his Dad at the racetracks they loved. "I admired my father and I miss him. We made a lot of friends and we had a good time. Shorty was a great inspiration, the best father a person could have, and always a part of my life. Wherever we went, we were just two guys working together, and, there was never a better feeling than when we were leading the field."

CHAPTER 21

Phillip "Pee Wee" Jones:
King of the Carolina Piedmont

Phillip "Pee Wee" Jones ran all the Piedmont tracks (Raleigh, Bowman Gray, Greensboro, Victory, Champion, etc.), plus most of the Southern tracks from Daytona to Martinsville. He was track champion at many, including six years at Bowman Gray. At one point, he was running two different cars in two different classes per night and he was one of the first to run a Corvette in stock car races.

Jones describes himself in his youth as a half-wild teenager. None of his family was involved in racing, although they lived only six blocks from Bowman Gray Stadium. The track is the oldest venue of continuous weekly NASCAR-sanctioned racing.

"It's a little quarter mile track in a stadium," says Jones. "It used to be an aggravating track because drivers had to have patience to get around it and there were so many wrecks, it became a show. That's where NASCAR got its feet on the ground."

The track was built during the Depression as a 17,000-seat football stadium and named for a famous Winston-Salem businessman. It was faithful to its original purpose until a promotional group from the north introduced midget racing. Later, a man named Alvin Hawkins, aware of the growing popularity of stock cars, envisioned it as a NASCAR facility.

Hawkins was a former driver who had become a flagman for Bill France and he flagged Bowman Gray for years. At that time, races were flagged from the ground. During one race, Hawkins was hit by a car and suffered a broken back. But his love of the sport continued and he became the site's most passionate promoter. Under his leadership, the track's popularity soared and Jones came under its spell. Lured by its showmanship and high speed excitement, he was soon itching to drive.

"I feel like I grew up with NASCAR. I ran four races the year before NASCAR was formed and full-time thereafter. Mr. France lived in North Carolina when I started racing. He had a panel truck and during the week we rode all over the country putting out posters. We put them anywhere we could, on the sides of barns and telephone poles. Service stations let us tack them on standup signs in return for free passes.

"The first car I drove was a '39 coupe. It was owned by three guys who wanted a driver to run it at the Greensboro Fairgrounds. I told them I could handle the job; it wasn't a problem." It wasn't. Jones finished fifth in his inaugural race. "I must have gotten somebody's attention. From then on, I never had trouble getting a ride." He eventually won six championships at Bowman Gray and it became his favorite track. 'I enjoyed racing at Bowman Gray and had fun doing it."

One of the racers Jones most admired was championship driver Tim Flock. "When I went to my first race, I didn't have a helmet and he loaned me one. Tim helped me as much as anyone did in racing. There weren't but about thirty drivers back then. Most were out of Atlanta and I knew almost all of them, Roy Hall, Ed Samples, and the Flock boys. One driver, whose name you never hear, was Bill Snowden from St Augustine, Florida. He was as good as there was."

Jones was primarily a driver and not an engine builder. "I never worked on a car. I never turned a bolt on one. All I did was go to the tracks, get in the cars, get out and go home. Whoever owned the car I drove did the work on it. We didn't have trailers or trucks and we towed our cars everywhere, but there were good people backing me and I always had good equipment. Bringing money home was the name of the game and that was my favorite part."

Jones says that in order to be a consistent winner, he relied on brainpower as much as horsepower. "If you don't use your head, you're not going to get anywhere."

He says he did a lot of things to help him win races and admits some were devious. "I was at Bowman Gray Stadium on a Saturday night with Billy Myers sitting on the pole and me on the outside. Glen Wood started right behind me and Johnny Bruner was flagging. Johnny always smoked a long cigar and when he was ready to drop the flag he'd bite down on it. I had a wadded paper Coca-Cola cup the size of my fist. We started jumping around the track to finish and when Johnny started to bite that cigar, I pitched the Coca-Cola cup across Billy's hood. He looked to see what it was and I jumped the flag. Glen and I both ran past him that night and he never got over it. In those days, something was going on everywhere you went. Now, drivers have cleaned up their act."

There were a lot of shenanigans and also a lot of wrecks. "I had a bad wreck in 1971 that came close to putting my lights out. During a race at Bowman Gray, I was passing another car in the turn and ran as deep as I could. The brake shoes and the brake system were on the front and when I came down on the brake, the pedal came loose. The brake jumped up and locked the right wheel. The side of the racetrack was barricaded by two 55-gallon drums, full of concrete, buried halfway in the ground. The car slid into one of them, breaking the frame in two and bursting into flames." Jones had broken ribs, but survived the inferno.

After ten years, Jones began driving for the Steelman Motor Company, running five or six times a week. "I'd go to Greenville, South Carolina, on Wednesday night, leave there and go to Fayetteville, North Carolina, on Thursday, go to Raleigh and race Friday and then on to Bowman Gray Stadium for Saturday night. On Sunday, I'd run a dirt track. At that time, I had two cars. I'd run one and leave the other at home to be worked on. By the time I got to Raleigh, the guys with fresh cars could beat me. In 1961, I didn't have a shop or any help so I made a deal with Jimmy and Ruby Scearce. Later, after driving for T. L. Neal, I took a job in sales for Chevrolet and got out of racing."

Jones says the most important lesson he learned from racing was how to handle people and some of those people were spectators. "I met a lot of fine people and many fine fans."

Today, he enjoys reminiscing with other oldtimers. "I like to get together with them in High Point and also in Danville, Virginia. We meet every year, get to see different drivers, hang out and shoot the bull."

CHAPTER 22

"Tiger" Tom Pistone: Racing's Little Giant

Tom Pistone began racing in the early fifties in the Chicago area. He won the Soldier's Field Track Championship in 1954 and 1955 (and eventually captured the championship five times). He started competing in NASCAR in 1955 and drove on the 1957 Chevrolet racing team. During his eleven years in NASCAR, he recorded 130 starts, five poles, two wins, 29 top-fives and 53 top tens. One of the smallest competitors, he earned respect for his racing skills and his sense of humor. After retiring as a driver, he returned as a car owner and sponsored racers such as Tighe Scott. He is the owner of Tiger Tom Pistone Racecars and Parts, which has supplied parts and built cars for NASCAR for almost fifty years.

A full-blooded Italian, Pistone was born and raised in Chicago where he started working at five years old for his father, a fruit and vegetable peddler. At sixteen he bought his first car and when he was seventeen, he took the money he'd saved, pooled it with his buddies' and opened a garage. "When I was twenty-one, I knew a guy who had a hot-rod Mercury. He told me races were going to be held at Soldier's Field, so my friends and I decided to build a racecar. In 1950, we got a 1941 Ford. When we heard Andy Granatelli had a speed shop, we got him to soup up the engine." Pistone had a winning streak at Soldier's Field and won the championship. In 1955, he won it again and, with his confidence soaring, headed south to compete in NASCAR.

"NASCAR was big and when you beat one of those southern guys, you beat the best. Curtis Turner, Junior Johnson, and Joe Weatherly knew how to plow up dirt."

Pistone was anxious to start the circuit, but encountered an obstacle he didn't expect. "The first thing southern racing taught me was I was a Yankee. When people called me Yankee, I didn't know what that meant.

"Bill France was the first man I met. He liked me because he was from the north and always called me 'son.' He said, 'Where are you going, son?' I told him I was going to Martinsville, Virginia to race. He said 'Son, that race was last week. You're a week too late.' Then he said, 'Son, what you want to do is paint a Rebel Flag on the hood of your car. Write *I saw the light* and sign it *A Converted Yankee*. After I did that, the southern people took a liking to me.

Pistone quickly earned the respect of his new southern brethren, traveling from track to track enjoying competition and camaraderie. "Junior Johnson was one of the top drivers in those days. He could drive on dirt or asphalt and he was very supportive of me. I could go to Junior's shop and do anything. He'd give a driver the shirt off his back. Whenever I needed something, he'd give it to me and he'd go to the racetrack and help me.

"Rex White was another driver who supported me. He was a southerner who had lived in Maryland, and although Maryland is south of the Mason-Dixon line, he caught a lot of ribbing. Rex was small and I used to tease I was bigger than him. I found out he used to wear elevated shoes, so I still say I'm taller, although I believe I am shorter."

The two were the brunt of many jokes because of their size and Tiny Lund was their main harasser. So huge he could barely fit in a racecar, Lund would pick them up and throw them over his shoulder like they were flour sacks. He was known to turn Pistone upside down and shake him until the change fell out of his pockets.

Lund's most outrageous prank occurred at the beginning of a race in Macon, Georgia, when he handcuffed Pistone to a fence. "It was good there was a policeman who could unbuckle me. When I ran to my car and grabbed my helmet, he'd put ice water in it. He pulled so many pranks it's hard to remember them all. Tiny was a hard-charging driver. When you drove against him, he'd slam you all over the place."

After particularly brutal races, Lund would seek out Pistone to apologize. "He'd say 'Look-a-here, I got no brakes. I didn't mean to hit you.' He was so likable you couldn't get mad, but he still won the race.

"There are a lot of NASCAR stories. Joe Weatherly was the biggest jokester on the circuit and he used to play jokes on everybody. In those days, we had ignition switches with keys in them. During one race, Joe took all of the keys from the cars. The race was about to start and we couldn't find them. Another time, he took all of our gas caps.'

Pistone's first NASCAR race was at North Wilkesboro, where he drove a Chevrolet. His first win occurred the next year in the NASCAR Convertible Division. In 1957, he worked briefly for Southern Engineering which was the pseudonym for the Chevrolet team. He continued to drive Chevrolet throughout his career until he became a car builder.

"When I began running NASCAR, I'd go back to Chicago every week towing my car, then come back and race the next weekend. Each trip took sixteen hours. Finally, Bill France showed me a shop space and gave me enough money to race and survive. If it hadn't been for him, I would never have stayed south all these years. Every time I went broke, he gave me money to feed my family. In 1968, he financed my shop when I opened it."

Pistone learned driving skills through trial and error, but held his own with the hot dogs. "I didn't know what racing strategy was in those days. All I knew was flat out. I didn't have common sense and I didn't have a teacher to teach me. I didn't know to wait until the end of the race before punishing the car.

"I loved every track, but of all of them, I liked Daytona. Daytona was the first super speedway I ran and, in 1959, I had the fastest T-Bird there. We had to run with the windows closed and those cars were well-sealed. During the first qualifier, Tommy Irwin spun out of control, across the grass and into Lake Lloyd. He stayed down so long we feared he'd drowned. The window handle had come off and he was looking all over for it. He finally found it, lowered the window and, unable to swim, climbed onto the roof. That's when I decided to wear a life jacket and take an aqua lung when I raced there.

"The biggest scare of my life was during a race when I saw Lee Petty and Johnny

Beauchamp go through the guardrail and three or four more cars go over the wall. I stopped to see what happened and that was a big mistake. Seeing Lee all crumpled up upset me so much, when I got back in my car, I couldn't buckle the seat belt. Bill France Jr. was standing nearby. He said, 'Get in that car, boy. Drive that car.' I got back in the race and finished sixth, but that was the race that got Lee. He didn't drive much after that.

"The hardest thing that happened to me was in a 1957 race at Martinsville. It started drizzling and Billy Myers, who was driving a Mercury, came up behind me out of the straightaway. Myers' car hit the rear of mine and jumped over my car. We hit the wall and went into the grandstand and I thought we'd killed a little boy." Although the child survived, Pistone, who had children of his own, was so overcome with grief, he took time off from racing.

"The most difficult part of my life was driving and raising eight kids. It was hard because racing didn't pay much back then. In order to make money, I had to start building racecars. When I started my shop, Harry Gant was my biggest supporter. Gant was the strongest driver I've ever seen. He'd drive a Busch car 300 laps and then jump into a Winston Cup car and drive a 500-miler. He was the toughest man alive in those days. I gave him my chassis and he won over 200 races. I served on his pit crew and he drove the car."

Over half a century has passed since his first race at Soldier's Field, but Pistone is as in love with racing as ever. "Racing was my whole life and it's all I think about. The one thing I regret is never getting a chance to win a NASCAR championship. That was the greatest thing I wanted to accomplish." Today, he lives in Charlotte with his wife Crystal, whom he met in high school. He still has his shop and is still involved in racing, now helping his grandchildren.

CHAPTER 23

Marvin Panch:
West Coast Marvel

Known affectionately by his friends as "Pancho," Marvin Panch made his mark on racing with speedway finesse. Originally from Oakland, California, Panch won the 1950 and 1951 Late Model Crown. He was the first West Coast NASCAR Champion to succeed on the Eastern circuit, winning 17 of his 216 starts.

Virtually unknown in the East, Panch took drivers and fans by surprise by becoming a consistent winner in the fifties and sixties. In 1957, he finished second to Buck Baker in Grand National Final Point Standings, ranking less than a thousand points behind the two-time champion.

Panch, known as a pragmatic thinker, adapted his style to different cars and tracks. He raced Fords, Chevrolets, Dodges, Pontiacs, convertibles and sports cars. Among his sponsors were Ray Fox, Ray Nichels, Smokey Yunick, Holman-Moody, and the Wood brothers. His most famous win was the 1961 Daytona 500 in which he drove a 1960 Yunick Pontiac to victory. He battled a knockout list of contenders including Joe Weatherly, Fireball Roberts, Fred Lorenzen and Cotton Owens.

Marvin Panch is a member of the National Motorsports Press Association Hall of Fame. In 1998, NASCAR designated him one of their Top Fifty Drivers. He serves on the board of directors of Living Legends of Auto Racing.

"I was a car nut," says Panch, "and always interested in driving. I grew up on my uncle's dairy farm, learned to drive on tractors, then graduated from tractors to trucks. I was so young, I had to stand and grab hold of the steering wheel and put both feet on the clutch. I used to spend every day I could, until dark, out in the field. When my uncle bought a John Deere Model A tractor with headlights, my aunt brought me lunch because I'd stay 'til midnight, without going in."

As if already in training for NASCAR, the child plowed in circles. "My uncle had eighty acres and set the tractors to go to the end of a row, where we'd turn them around to come back, making a ring. The arm of each tractor went down in a furrow. When I'd get one tractor going, I'd put the arm down, jump out and let it steer itself. I'd start another tractor behind it and plow with two at a time. I usually rode in the rear one in case something happened and I needed to shut it down."

Panch was born in rural Chippewa Falls, Wisconsin. When he was three, his father died and his mother had to work in the city, leaving the care of their child to relatives. Panch played baseball and football in high school before having to support his mother and attempting a boxing career. His biggest regret is being unable to finish his education.

"My advice to up-and-coming drivers is always to get their education first. A smart, educated driver will do a lot better than one who is uneducated. I didn't go far enough and I miss that more than anything. I got through high school and that was it. Not going to college hurt me down the line. A lot of people have common sense and a man with common sense will outdo the man who's educated in the long run, but if you have an educated man with common sense, then you have a good man."

In the late forties, Panch bought the car of a friend who'd joined the Merchant Marines. While home on leave, he persuaded Panch to go to San Francisco with him. When he reached California, Panch labored in a shipyard before getting a job in a brake and wheel alignment firm. A fast learner, he was soon moving from shop to shop, training employees.

Since California was a racing hotspot and Panch loved cars, the sport quickly caught his attention. By 1949, he was spending his weekends at Oakland Speedway. Oakland was unusual in that it had a short track, surrounded by a larger track on its perimeter.

One of the frequent racers was a short-track driver named Lloyd Reagan who drove a six-cylinder roadster and consistently won against the V8s. His success caught Panch's eye and when the announcer said a stock car race was going to be held on the big track, Panch had a sudden idea. "I figured I could use my Mercury, which was a pretty good car, so I went down to the pit area after the race to talk with Lloyd. I asked if he would drive my car and he agreed to run it in several races." Things went so well, they decided to build a Flathead Ford hardtop.

"There were a bunch of amateurs at the first race Lloyd won and the guy who came in second spun him so hard he crossed the finish line backwards. After the race, he told me he didn't want to run any more because the guys were so amateur. I told him I'd let him decide but he agreed to come back the next week. Next week came and he didn't show up, so I drove."

West Coast NASCAR representative Margo Burke saw Panch's first race and suggested he become his car's regular driver, keeping all the money he won for himself. A shrewd businessman, Panch took her advice. "That worked out better because I didn't have to split the cash."

Panch drove his "weekly runner" on the short track until he heard of a NASCAR late model race in Bay Meadows. He entered his Mercury and placed third. Continuing to run on the West Coast, he won the 1950 and 1951 California NASCAR Late-Model Crown. He briefly experimented with midget racing, but the lure of the stock car stayed strong.

In 1953, Panch's career was interrupted by two years in the army. He took basic training at Fort Ord, then while waiting to be shipped overseas ended up in a motor pool at Fort MacArthur in San Pedro. The base had a brake and alignment shop, but no real mechanics, and a bunch of cars with deadlines. Detailed out to the garage, he began working in maintenance.

The sergeant in charge had been given a staff car for a brake job, but he didn't know what he was doing and had brake fluid all over the floor. While he was working, Panch was sweeping and he began moving closer to him. When Panch asked, "Can I help you with that?" the sergeant threw down his tools and walked away.

"I ended up doing the brake job and when I finished I took it out in the yard to test it. When it stopped straight, I drove it back in. He ran out of his office, looked at me and the tools on the floor, and said, 'You're not finished with that.' When I told him it was all done, he got in and drove to the parking lot, where I could hear him sliding the wheels. After awhile, he came back in. He asked me, 'Where are you slated for?' When I told him overseas, he took my serial number and told me to stay.

"I was very fortunate. I had a good friend in Gardena who had a garage and let me keep my car there. He would take in cars during the day and hold them so when I'd get off from work at the base I could fix them and earn extra money. I was still able to race, but not every weekend. When my company commander brought his car into the base garage, we got to know each other. He ended up on my pit crew and tried to schedule my duties on weekdays when I wasn't racing."

While still in Gardena, Panch met his future wife Bettie and, with her support, after the service, began racing full-time again. Fascinated by stories about Darlington, they headed for the Eastern NASCAR circuit. "Darlington was the Indianapolis of stock car racing. My wife and I drove an old burned-out Oldsmobile across country with our tools in the back and cans with holes in them on the ends of our exhaust pipes to quiet it down." They settled in Charlotte where Panch set up a new brake alignment business.

"Our first race was in Langhorne, Pennsylvania. After the race, when I pulled into the pits, the front fender dropped over the tire. An Oldsmobile dealer who owned a race-car walked over and asked me if I'd run his car and that's how I got back into driving. I ran Darlington for a man name Dick Myers and then later the factory picked me up and I went on from there."

In 1957, Panch took the racing community by storm, driving a Ford. As an unknown rookie on the eastern circuit, he won six races, finished in the Top Ten 27 times, and tallied 9,956 Final Point Standings in the Grand National Division. He shocked drivers and fans alike, coming in second to champion Buck Baker. Panch took his winnings and moved his family to Daytona Beach. There, he switched to NASCAR's convertible division, began selling go-karts and purchased a farm.

"In 1961, Smokey Yunick was building a new 1961 Pontiac for Fireball Roberts and the old '60 Pontiac that Fireball had wrecked was still in the shop. One of the mechanics working on the new car said, 'Smoke, why don't we run that one?'

"Smokey said it was too old, too big and too wide. He told them if they wanted to work on it on their own time, they could take it out back and he'd furnish the parts." Panch drove the car against Fireball in the Daytona 500 and won. His average speed was 149.6 miles per hour, shattering the track's previous record.

"I needed to win as money was scarce and at that time, that paycheck looked big. I was in an original Fireball Roberts #22 car, racing as #20 and painted black and gold. It was a beautiful car and one of my favorites."

Daytona remains special to Panch, along with Atlanta and Charlotte. "I can't really put one ahead of the other. Charlotte and Daytona were good to me but any track I won on became my favorite. My strategy depended on equipment, but I never pushed the throttle too early. At the beginning of a race, if I had a hard time keeping up, by the end of the race I'd catch up. At Daytona, you couldn't hang back so I'd get a good drafting partner.

Panch says of all the tracks, he found Darlington the most difficult. "I always liked Darlington because it was the most challenging track and many drivers couldn't get around it. I ran second a couple of times, but I never won there. Darlington was the trickiest track

Marvin Panch, 1961 Daytona 500 winner, on the hood of his car with two unidentified trophy girls. Daytona remains special to Panch, along with Atlanta and Charlotte. (Courtesy Bill Chubbuck, Racing Relics, Inc.)

because it had two different corners. If a driver set his car to handle good in one turn, it didn't handle well in the other one. Martinsville was a dragstrip off each corner and a brake contest at the end. That track was rough on equipment and brakes."

Panch says when he was preparing to race, he'd attach a Fiberglas seat to a steering wheel linked to a steering gear, hooked to a shock. At night, he'd set the shock on stiff and watch TV while he worked his arms. "A lot of the drivers were flying to the tracks in planes, but I drove. I'd disconnect my power steering belt, keep the windows rolled up and turn the heater on.

"When I raced, we had to wait to go to a track. We couldn't go weeks and months prior, and when we arrived we'd go through inspection and then into practice. We'd go out and shake it down to see what we had. It didn't make a lot of difference which type of car I drove, as long as I could win races with it. If General Motors was the hot item, I enjoyed driving GM. If Ford was winning the majority of races, I drove a Ford. During the race, I concentrated all the time and tried different grooves. Since we didn't have radios, we depended on sign boards we passed in the infield. Toward the end of a race, I'd listen for different car sounds and hope everything stayed glued together."

He was also alert for new smells. "The mechanics used a stinking grease on the rear of the car. If a driver could smell it, he knew it wouldn't be long before he lost his rear end.

"I tried to get along with everybody and if somebody was running better than I was, I didn't fight them. We usually worked well together, especially when drivers owned their cars. If somebody needed parts and didn't have them, we'd help them. When we were with the factory teams, our mechanics helped independents. If somebody new acted weird and pushed us around, we'd take care of it ourselves. We didn't worry about NASCAR slapping him on the wrist because *we'd* take him out."

In 1962, Panch struggled to balance his time between business and racing. Despite his limited participation, he finished among the top five in eight races entered. In 1963, he turned his full attention to racing, running in a Ford for the Wood brothers.

The Wood brothers, known for their meticulous preparation and synchronized pit work, had an ironclad rule. Fans could look at, but not touch, their cars. Once, when Marvin had driven for them at Riverside, they headed home in their truck, pulling their racecar, which was tied down on a trailer behind them. Hungry and tired, they parked at a truck stop in Greenville to rest and get something to eat. Afterwards, they climbed back into their truck and started up the road again. All of a sudden, they heard a horrific roar. It sounded like a 727 aircraft coming down on them, but instead of a crash, the noise kept on, no matter their speed. Finally, after looking out the windows and seeing no plane, they pulled to the side of the road and then walked to the back of the truck. To their surprise, they found a drunk in Marvin's helmet revving the racecar's engine. They jerked him out of the car and left him on the side of the road.

According to Panch, in those days, uninvited hitchhikers weren't unusual. "One night coming back from Memphis, Jim Pascal and Bill Blair pulled into a truck stop and while they were inside, a little kid climbed into the tow car. Since he hid in the back seat, they didn't hear him until they were well on their way down the road.

"Bill Blair is an imposing fellow. He told the kid, 'You're going to have to get out of there.' They pulled off the road but the child refused to leave. Figuring he'd scare him, Blair said, 'I hate little kids. I'm mean and I'm going to kill you.' The kid replied, 'You're not mean and you won't hurt me,' and wouldn't get out."

While they were stuck on the side of the road not knowing what to do, a trooper came by and asked "What's your problem?" When they explained, the trooper pulled out a flashlight and shined it in their backseat. He said, "This is the third time in a month I've had to take this kid out of a race driver's car."

Another Panch story relates to driving in Asheville. "The little track ran around the baseball field and the night was hot. After the race, I was very, very thirsty and couldn't wait to get something to drink. Since there was a big crowd, the concession stands were sold out so I went to a faucet. When I found the water turned off, I walked through the pits where I saw a crewman pull a fruit jar filled with a liquid and cherries out of an ice bucket. I remembered how my aunt who lived on a farm had canned cherries and how good they tasted. That fruit jar looked nice and frosty so I asked the guy if I could have a drink. He said 'Why, sure,' and handed the jar to me. I felt half dead from the heat so I took three or four good swallows. It wasn't my aunt's recipe and it almost killed me. The guys sat back and laughed at my unknowingly gulping their moonshine."

Motorsports historian Bill Chubbuck says that Panch was once on his way to a race when he lost control of his car. It went off the road and landed upside down in a river.

Determined not to miss the race, he climbed up the river bank and hitched a ride to the track. When he arrived, he found his driver had totaled his racecar in practice.

In 1963, Panch was preparing for the Daytona 500 when he had an opportunity to test Rick Cunningham's Maserati sports car. As he shot down the track like a bullet, the car went airborne. It flipped out of control, landed upside down, and caught fire with Panch trapped inside. Horrified onlookers scaled the fence and ran to his aid. Dewayne "Tiny" Lund jumped into a pace car and sped to its side.

"That's the only time I've been scared in a racecar," says Panch. "Because the doors opened into the top, I couldn't escape." His rescuers lifted the car high enough for him to kick a door partly open. He was able to wiggle halfway out, but before he was free, the fuel tank blew up, knocking his would-be lifesavers backwards. They were forced to drop the car on him as it burst into flames. Seeing his legs still kicking, the men went back into the inferno and lifted the car again while Tiny Lund pulled him out. It was one of the few times Panch had worn a fire suit. His clothes were burning, but he was able to roll on the ground and put out the flames.

"When they lifted the car, they all burned their hands. Steve Betrowski went temporarily blind from his burns, but regained his sight. If it wasn't for those guys I'd be dead."

While Panch was trapped in the car, everything good and bad about his life flashed before him. "It was as clear as watching TV and it caused me to stop and think. I changed my lifestyle, my whole way of living." Badly injured, but thankful to be alive, he decided that Tiny Lund, who had risked so much to rescue him, should drive in his place in the Daytona 500. Lund, who was without a ride, jumped at the chance and won.

In spite of his injuries, Panch ended the season thirteenth in Final Point Standings and the experience didn't hold him back. "I was very fortunate. I won seventeen major Winston Cup races and my best racing years, and my really good money, came after that." The next year, he ran in less than half of the Grand National races, but managed to rank tenth in Final Point Standings. In 1965, he moved up to fifth. He retired after the 1966 season.

Panch credits his health and being on his own when he was young for his success as a driver. "I couldn't bounce back on anybody because no one paid my bills and I had to look after myself. Racing meant a living and I enjoyed it but there's no comparison with today. I tell people if they paid money back then like they do now, I wouldn't have to be nice."

CHAPTER 24

Bettie Panch: Racing's Family Advocate

Mission Statement, Women's Auxiliary of Motorsports:

To enrich the sport of NASCAR with a commitment to its families through fundraising and wellness programs for those requiring medical or financial assistance.

In addition, the Women's Auxiliary of Motorsports, Inc. helps support organizations with likeminded missions and purposes.

One of the most important organizations in racing is behind the scenes. In its beginning, it was known as the Grand National Racing Wives Auxiliary. The name was later changed to the Winston Cup Racing Wives Auxiliary and is now the Women's Auxiliary of Motorsports. Originally founded to give financial assistance to families after driver injuries, it provides leadership and friendship opportunities, playing a supportive role for drivers' families.

Bettie Panch was one of the Auxiliary's original founders and its first president. The wife of racing pioneer Marvin Panch, she had a special insight into the group's beginnings and its evolution. Sadly, Bettie Panch died shortly after this interview.

The racing world has long been known for its sense of community. But in the early days, wives, unable to accompany their husbands into the pits, were left to fend for themselves. Those who were not tied down by the responsibilities of home traveled from track to track as they followed the racing circuit. Sometimes they struck up friendships in the stands or on the sidelines but, most often, they were alone.

In the early sixties, NASCAR was beset by fatalities and injuries. Lacking insurance, many faced financial ruin, drawing their families into bankruptcy with them.

In 1963, Marvin Panch was in a terrifying wreck at Daytona in which over sixty-seven percent of his body was burned. It was months before he recovered and his medical bills were astronomical. His mental and physical suffering was excruciating and his family suffered with him. Having endured these difficult times, his wife Bettie became aware of the hardships of other drivers' wives and their need for financial and emotional assistance.

"Marvin was in the hospital for three months and we were from out of state, had no

98

family, and had two little kids to support. There was nobody other than our friends, and I realized how lucky I was to have them. The experience made me think about those who weren't that fortunate.

"In 1964, a bunch of us got together. We wanted to join families and get to know each other so when someone had an injury or death we could help. We also wanted to make it a social group because back then, there wasn't anything for wives. We started out small, wrote up our bylaws and then got a charter. We had it inspected by an attorney so it would be right."

By 1965, the group was in full swing. The organization's first officers were president and founder Bettie Panch; vice-president Martha Jarrett, wife of driver Ned Jarrett; recording secretary Coleen Baker, wife of driver Buddy Baker; corresponding secretary Betty Smith, wife of driver Jack Smith; and treasurer Margaret Baker, mother of driver Buddy Baker. The board of directors included Betty Baker, wife of driver Buck Baker; Magadalene Clements, wife of mechanic Louis Clements; and Evelyn Hylton, wife of driver and mechanic James Hylton.

"There were only eleven of us when we started and we didn't have any outside support or sponsors. Our first great challenge was figuring out how to raise funds. Since our fees were only fifteen dollars a year, we passed the hat and begged when we needed money." Sometimes fans and manufacturers helped but hours were devoted to projects. The group put on fashion shows, baseball games, and auctions, and published and sold cookbooks. One year, they raffled a Volkswagen dune buggy.

"At that time, there wasn't the kind of money there is today. People couldn't just hand you a million dollars or even a thousand. When we started, we trudged along, coming up with money any way we could to keep the club going. We had dances in Daytona every February to start off the season and we held an auction. I think we were the first people in racing to have an auction of memorabilia. Once, when USAC driver Jim Hurnibese came into a dance, we took his tie and tie clip and auctioned it. He was very gracious about letting us have it."

Finally, after an enormous amount of energy and effort, the organization was able to establish a trust fund to aid families of series participants who were killed or injured. It also became a support group. "The club has enabled all of us to get to know and reach out to each other; otherwise we would only know what we read in the papers. Some wives couldn't go to the races because of small children and everybody did their own thing at the track. They were often feeding the pit crews or helping score.

"I went to every track where Marvin raced and did all of his scoring. When we started out, I couldn't afford to get on an airplane so I had to drive from track to track with two children." Determined to be sure her husband got credit for every lap, Bettie would take their children out of school on Friday morning and turn around after each race to get them back in their classes on Monday.

"I was proud of my kids, because they had perfect attendance and I have to say they were good. I had an arrangement with the school so I could check them out by 11 o'clock on a Friday morning. We came through racing hard and it was rough but I don't regret it."

When Grand National changed to Winston, the club's name changed too. Not wanting to continually go through more name changes, and wanting to include others, the group made a permanent name change several years ago. The Auxiliary also joined forces with the Busch Series Ladies Association and the Ladies of the Craftsman Truck Series to form one strong organization. It's now called the Women's Auxiliary of Motorsports.

"In the early days anyone could join, as long as they were a NASCAR member. Now, membership opportunities have expanded to include mothers, sisters, women working within the sport and NASCAR fans. There is a national director and an office in Charlotte."

According to Bettie, today's young women have many opportunities, but in the early days it was different. The sport was looked down on and wives suffered from its stigma. Since many of the wives had never held an outside job, the group afforded them professional opportunities. Holding office, being exposed to other achieving women and working in fundraising gave them leadership skills and helped them develop self-confidence. Times have changed with big sponsors and the media had a lot to do with it but some of their press conference savvy has come from the club.

Bettie's female friendships with racing wives lasted a lifetime and the organization has survived over forty years. The families who have benefited have been grateful. In 2004, the Women's Auxiliary of Motorsports, Inc. was honored with the designation of "Proud Charity of NASCAR." There are now almost five hundred members and its fundraising events continue. "Today, there are a lot of people around to help take care of racing families."

CHAPTER 25

Benny Parsons:
Stormtrooper from the North

Benny Parsons has been named by NASCAR as one of its Top Fifty Drivers. His record includes five hundred twenty-six starts, twenty poles and twenty NASCAR Winston Cup wins, including the 1975 Daytona 500 and 1980 Coca-Cola 600 at Charlotte. He was the first to qualify at over two hundred miles per hour at Talladega and was 1973 Winston Cup Champion. After retiring from racing, Parsons became a well-known motorsports radio and television broadcaster, a position he held until the day he died.

Parsons came from the "other side." In stock car racing, that didn't mean the other side of the tracks. It meant the Mason-Dixon Line. Although he was originally from the south, he first gained attention in Detroit with outstanding wins in ARCA. In 1964, hoping for a spot on the Ford factory team, he returned to his southern North Carolina roots to race Grand National. He performed well at Asheville-Weaverville until sidelined by a broken radiator. Discouraged, he went to the Midwestern short tracks where he earned two Automobile Racing Club of America championships. He ran four NASCAR races in 1969 and won the ARCA three hundred miler at Daytona. His big break came in 1970 when he was offered a ride by car owner L. G. DeWitt to replace his injured driver, Buddy Young. Parsons' performance was so outstanding, DeWitt decided to keep him. Within four years he was Winston Cup Champion.

"If you grew up in North Wilkesboro in the fifties," says Parsons, "you were around racing. I was born in Wilkes County, North Carolina, in the northwestern part of the state. When I was six years old, my parents left for Detroit looking for better jobs, more money, and a better life. They couldn't afford to take two children with them so they took my baby brother and left me behind. I lived with my grandmother until I was eighteen.

"After I graduated from high school, the first thing I did was head to Detroit. My father had a taxi company and a gas station. One Saturday morning, I was hanging around the station when two fellows, Wayne Bennett and Ben Gold, stopped by with a racecar on the back of their truck. I said 'Wow!' Being from North Carolina, I knew what it was and I was impressed. I asked them, 'Where are you going to race?' They answered, 'Anderson, Indiana.' Then, they said the magic words, 'Do you want to go?'

"My trip to Indiana was just the beginning. I'm sure they thought I was going to help, but what could I do? You have to have knowledge to be useful and at first I was just in the way. Three years later, in 1963, those same two guys bought an old Ford racecar, fixed it up, and sold it to me for fifty dollars, to start my racing career. The first year, I ran two races at Mount Clemons, Michigan, and Flat Rock Speedway outside of Detroit. I continued to work and race for the next twelve years."

Parsons says being based in Detroit around the automobile industry greatly influenced his performance. "Most guys were racing Fords and I got to know the Ford representatives. If I wanted to talk with them, all I had to do was make a phone call, and that had a big effect on my racing progress. One of the guys who helped me was Jack Bowsher, a driver and car builder who became my mentor, and helped me become more competitive. His emphasis on preparation was instrumental in my ARCA success.

"Living in Detroit helped me, but it also hurt me. Most of the people who became stars in racing were in North Carolina, South Carolina, and Virginia. I wasn't Richard Petty and I wasn't part of the racing community. The biggest obstacle I faced in NASCAR was breaking into the racing family. Rex White was in Maryland for awhile but when he came back down, he at least spoke the language.

"In the old days, people raced because they enjoyed it. Few made serious money, but they made a living at it because they worked at it. One thing I've learned from racing is, there is no substitute for hard work. In racing, I didn't quit at five, I worked up to fourteen hours a day seven days a week. Quitting time was just a number and a lot of times, I wondered why. In 1975, I won the Daytona 500 and those questions were answered. When I went into Victory Circle, it was all worthwhile."

According to Parsons, that lesson transfers into the non-racing world. "Most people who have left racing and gone into private industry are successful because they know the clock doesn't mean anything. Success includes preparation, focus, and dedication, all added together, not leaving any part out. Of course, you have to have a goal. You can work fifteen hours a day, but if you aren't focused on the job at hand, that work is for naught."

In looking back, Parsons says, "People ask me about my favorite car, my favorite track, and my favorite race. Some are Fords; some are Chevrolets; and some are Oldsmobiles. My favorite things are memories. The strange thing is, you can talk about terrible events that happened and in the retelling they come out as comedy. Twenty years ago, this was not funny, but today I can laugh. One June, I was racing at the Texas World Speedway in College Station. It would have been one hundred degrees in the shade, if there had been any, and I pulled into the pits and asked for the water hose to spray on my grill and myself. I wanted to wet my suit to shock my body and get going again.

"While I was spraying, the car behind me spilled gasoline and a spark caught it on fire. Everyone began screaming, 'Fire, fire, go, go,' so I took off. At the end of pit row, a man began frantically waving. Thinking my car was burning, I sped out in search of a fire truck. As I went around the track, I kept looking in my mirror for flames. When I came off turn two, I saw a fifty gallon water tank bouncing behind me. When I'd left the pits, its faucet had caught on my racecar's window, uncoiling the hose and jerking the tank out."

CHAPTER 26

Everett "Cotton" Owens: King of the Modifieds

Everett "Cotton" Owens is considered one of the best NASCAR Modified drivers to have ever lived. Always preferring dirt to asphalt, he won over 400 Modified and late sportsman races, fifty-four Modified during the 1950–51 season. Beginning with the inaugural Darlington 500, he ran sporadically, managing to win at least one race each year from 1957–62, and excelling as a driver, mechanic, and car owner.

Owens is a member of the Motorsports Press Association Hall of Fame, the Darlington Records Club, NASCAR Mechanics Hall of Fame, NASCAR Top Fifty Drivers, and NASCAR Legends. Owens was a constant speedway threat, particularly while running the "Hemi" in the late fifties. His drivers included David Pearson, Buddy Baker, Pete Hamilton, Ralph Earnhardt, Ray Hendrick, Bobby Isaac, Junior Johnson, Marvin Panch, Fireball Roberts, Mario Andretti, and Marty Robbins. (A special thanks to Ryan Owens for his contribution to this story through the Cotton Owens website, www.cottonowens. com.)

Born in 1924, Everett Owens was nicknamed "Cotton" because of his pale blonde hair. Raised during the Depression, he and his family moved wherever his father found employment. Since times were tough, that was often, but they finally settled in Spartanburg, South Carolina where his father set up a garage, deep in the heart of southern racing country.

Beginning work as a young boy, first at a grocery store, then at a cotton mill, Owens saved his money to buy a car, which he did when he was sixteen. "I've always loved speed. Before the war, I had a '34 Ford nobody could catch. After the war, races were held at the Piedmont Interstate Fairgrounds on Saturday afternoons. I threatened to quit my job if my boss didn't let me off."

After serving in the Navy, Owens worked as a mechanic in a wrecking yard for the D. N. Tinsley Company. One day, Atlanta driver Gober Sosebee, who had wrecked his '37 Ford at Richmond, came to the yard wanting a new body put on his car so he could run the next Saturday night. Cotton said, "I can do that," and he did. The car was ready on time and Sosebee ran it and won.

"After building Gober Sosebee's car, we felt like we could build a racecar also. We built a '37 Ford and Harold Ballard and Bud Moore carried it to Hendersonville to race on Saturday afternoon. I went to Hendersonville after closing the shop at noon... got to the racetrack and saw Bud and Harold walking up to the pits. I asked them where they were going and they said they were going to get a professional driver to drive the racecar. I said, 'Hold on 'til I get my chance to drive.' I won the first heat, started on the pole in the main event, led up to five laps to go and the switch cut off. I found the problem and got it going again, went back up to the door of the lead car as the checkered flag fell, and finished second in my first race.

"I started out racing in 1946 in a '37 Ford, because it was cheap and the fastest thing running. I raced because I loved it and the reason I loved it was because it was challenging. I wanted to see what I could do, how far I could go. If you do it all, build your own racecar and drive it, you feel a great sense of pride and you never get over it. I built the engines and then drove them myself and won races. That feeling of accomplishment is still with me and makes me feel good when I think about it.

"I started out racing in 1946 in a '37 Ford," says Cotton Owens, "because it was cheap and the fastest thing running." (Courtesy Cotton Owens.)

"In the beginning, I drove my own modified car, and later raced cars for other people. In the early fifties, I started building my own again. I worked on customers' cars in my shop during the day and my racecar at night. Racing was a way of life but what my family went through was unbelievable. At that time, I don't think anyone was making a living at it and there were horrible accidents."

Drivers tried to prevent accidents any way they could, sometimes through superstitions. "There were a lot of racing superstitions back then, like bad luck being associated with peanuts. I had been in a race in Charlotte where I was involved in a wreck and tore up my car. Since I couldn't find a coupe, I built a '37 Dodge Coach. That was the car I liked best and I have its 354 cubic engine in my office now. Once, I towed it to the track and somebody threw a bag of peanuts inside by the firewall.

I got in, ate the peanuts and threw the shells out the window. I didn't realize they were landing on the running board of the car next to me. Bill Snowden had towed that car all the way from St. Augustine, Florida. He saw the peanuts and said, 'I wouldn't do you that way,' then hooked up his car and left!

"I felt awfully bad about it. I hadn't paid attention to the superstition and I loved peanuts. I ate them in my car, sat on the pole, and won the race."

Owens says, despite superstitions, he doesn't believe anything bad will happen to a person "until their mark is on the "wall." "I've seen people killed on racetracks and people killed on highways. No matter what you do, when your mark is on the wall, you're gone."

During the time Owens raced, the "mark on the wall" was often related to fuel spills. "Fire was the most dangerous thing. In 1956, I went down the back straightaway on the Daytona Beach Road Course and ran up on a car swerving from one side of the road to the other. I backed off but that car hit another car in the rear. The car it hit exploded in a ball of fire. I locked my car down, turned to avoid the wreck and spun on the inside. Then, I went out into the palmettos on the left side of the road. When I looked up, I saw the car that was hit facing me. By the time I got my window down, the driver had jumped to the ground with his clothes in flames. Before I could get out, he ran in the road in front of the oncoming racecars. As soon as they passed, I chased after him through the palmettos on the opposite side. As he ran, he caught the palmetto bushes on fire. I got him down on the ground and tried to cover him, but the ground was so hard, I carried him back to the roadside. He was still conscious, although the fire had burned off his clothes. When I touched his hands, the skin came off, as if he were wearing gloves. I kept him there until help arrived and didn't think about how I looked. When I saw my car catch fire, I told others to keep him seated and ran to put it out.

"Some policemen came over and started pulling on me trying to get me to go to the hospital. When Bill France and Joe Littlejohn tried to get me to go, I told them to leave me alone. I hadn't been in the wreck, but in caring for the other driver, his skin had come off on me."

Owens was involved in an accident in 1951 in which he was badly hurt. Despite a severe eye injury, he continued to win races afterwards. "After my wreck, I had double vision but I did whatever it took. I quit looking at the track and just looked at where I was going. If there was a hole, I ran through it. The man who owned my racecar said, 'I'll give you that car if you'll just hang it up. Make it a museum piece and quit.'

"The next Sunday, we went to Columbia and I pretty near lapped the field. I got in a groove, kept my eyes on the other cars, didn't back off, and won. After that, I raced using only one eye."

The next year, Chrysler came out with the Hemi. "It was so easy to build that engine and make it outrun other cars. I elected to go with the Hemi in '52 and ran it as long as it was available."

Owens ran Modified and Grand National, but calls himself a Modified driver. "I wasn't really a Grand National driver, although I drove a lot of Grand National cars and won nine races. I only ran one whole year and was second in points to Lee Petty. I finished seventh in the first Darlington 500 and raced once or twice a year after that. The biggest races I won were U.S. Modified Championships. They were a hundred miles and paid lap money."

One of Owens' favorite tracks was the old Daytona Beach and Road Course. "It was four and two-tenths miles long and learning to broadside your car in the turns was hard." He won three beach races during his career, two in Modified and one in Grand National.

"In 1957, I went to Nashville in a 1957 Pontiac I'd won in at the 'Beach.' I used the same car and ran for a hundred miles before I crashed and tore it up so bad I couldn't tow it. The only man there from my part of the country was Neil Castle. Since he was carrying his car on a trailer, I asked him if he'd haul my car back to Spartanburg and let me tow his. He hauled my car and I towed his Ford and it was a whole lot easier. Racecars were trouble to tow when they wrecked."

In 1959, Owens went to the new Daytona International Speedway and was awestruck. "I remember looking at that monstrous track, thinking how big it was and realizing we would actually run there. I prepared mentally and physically for weeks before I went to that race. Because I was building the car, I was living off coffee and when I arrived I couldn't pass the physical. My urine was so full of sugar from the coffee, I had to go to the hospital to have my blood checked. It turned out all right, but the doctor told me I'd have to sleep before I could pass. That track was a challenge, but I set a record.

"I've had many memorable moments in racing, but the main one was when I took a '60 Pontiac to Daytona and won the first live televised race for pole position. In 1962, I participated in a spring race with two '62 Pontiacs. A. J. Foyt was to drive with me, but the race was rained out. Before I went back, Junior Johnson called and asked to drive my second car. I took the one Foyt was driving and set a new track record for qualifying.

Dragster Hubert Platt (left) and Top Fifty NASCAR driver Cotton Owens talk about racing's early days at J.B. Day's Raymond Parks Birthday Party in Easley, South Carolina, June 5, 2005.

"Junior said, 'You got the better engine.' I said, 'Junior, I don't. I built them both.' We traded motors and he ran the same speed he had been running. I took his motor and ran it, never missing a beat, but we both fell out of the race. Junior ran out of gas and my transmission broke.

"That year, I was encouraged to move to Dodge but they didn't have anything to out-run Pontiac. I told them if they'd go back to the Hemi engine I'd do it. The Hemi builds more horsepower than any other engine. It's used on dragstrips today and it's the hottest thing out there. Dodge promised if I'd sign, I'd get a Hemi, so I signed under those conditions."

There are always funny stories in racing and Owens has many. His most frustrating ones involve Charles "Slick" Owens, a Holman-Moody parts-man and friend. "Slick got caught for speeding in Virginia and signed his ticket *C. Owens*. I went to Martinsville to race Grand National in the latter part of that year. When I arrived, Martinsville Speedway president Clay Earles told me, 'Cotton, a gentleman has a warrant for your arrest.' I said, 'Clay, for what?' He said, 'For speeding in Virginia.' I said, 'Clay, I ain't never been caught for speeding in Virginia!' He said, 'Well, he's got a warrant. See the guy after the race.' After promising I would, I saw Slick. I told him about the warrant and asked, 'That isn't you, is it?' As it ended up, it was him, but after the race, instead of saving me, he jumped in the back of a van and headed back to Charlotte. When they finally caught him, they put him in jail, but Glen Wood got him out." Another time, Slick went on a date in Daytona, introducing himself as "Cotton."

In recalling the old days, Owens says, "Racing's had TV exposure, but it's not what we used to see. We had more competition and side-by-side racing but now it's follow the leader. Our cars were inspected to be sure they were stock, but today's cars are modified."

He also says cars weren't as hard to build. "We just put in roll bars, built safety hoods and safety wheels, and put on racing tires. We had AMA specs for wheel base, size of the motor, compression ratio and valve size and we could only use a 2½ inch exhaust pipe running stock headers. Today, they can build all the horsepower they want.

"The cars are crash-safe, but have nothing protecting the fuel cell. Bars protect the driver so cars don't crumble, but bodies can only stand so much impact, and they jerk drivers' bodies apart. That's what happened to Dale Earnhardt. When we drove, the cars folded and absorbed a lot of the crash. Today, drivers can hit a wall and die without a mark on them. Cars should be softer, with gas tank protection. Soft walls help but the cars don't give."

Owens still lives in Spartanburg with his wife Dot and still has his garage, where he displays his beloved old Hemi engine. He enjoys rehashing the old days with fellow drivers and competing against them in vintage races.

CHAPTER 27

Johnny Allen: Addicted to Speed

Johnny Allen raced from 1955 until 1983. He is considered one of the most capable drivers of the fifties and sixties, although he rarely had proper equipment. Allen began racing with a 1955 Plymouth, but raced midget, sprint, stock and open wheel in USAC, ARCA, Busch and Grand National. In 1957, he placed seventh in Final Point Standings and he won the 1972 Greenville-Pickens Championship. He drove performance trials and tested for Ford and Pontiac. Holly Farms and Braun Plywood were among his car owners.

"I've always been hooked on mechanics," says Allen. "I was raised in California, and in the old days, you could get a driver's license at age fourteen. As a teenager, I worked with a construction company during Christmas and summer vacations to get my first car. During the week, I was in a work program at school where I attended classes half a day and worked half a day to earn money to support it. On weekends, my Daddy took me to races. We went to midget, stock car and old jalopy races in the Los Angeles area."

Racing took hold of Allen like an addiction. "I wanted to get out there, to see what it was like, and the feeling never left me. After I got my driver's license, I took my friends to watch races all around the LA area. Famous drivers were there and that made it intriguing. They came to California in the winter because racing was held year round.

"In high school, the only course that interested me was math. I eventually dropped out to join the Navy and got my GED while in the service. I was stationed in Corpus Christi, Texas, where I was an aircraft mechanic and I hooked up with a guy who was interested in stock cars. We went to local tracks and became associated with a race shop where they worked on the local guys' engines. Since I worked midnight shift, I could go over during the day and work in the shop. One of the drivers was an older guy called Ankrum Crawford, whom we all called "Spook." In Texas, that's what they called a guy who drove wild and squirrelly. On the track, Spook was all over the place.

"Spook had an old Kaiser he ran on a little quarter-mile asphalt track. When he decided to build a new car, he asked me to help. I told him I wanted to drive and he gave me a chance to test the car. Since he liked what he saw, he let me race. The first time, we had engine problems, but I won my heat race during the second week and that set me off."

Because he was still in the Navy, Allen's racing time was limited and since he couldn't race, he would talk about it, or read *Speed Age* magazine. The publication featured track stars such as Fireball Roberts, Curtis Turner and Joe Weatherly and the money those hot doggers made seemed like a fortune.

"In 1955, I was still in the Navy but I ran one race on a mile-and-a-half track in Arkansas. I got out in September and, in 1956, Spook took a leave of absence from his job and sold his old Kaiser." Allen sold his car and used his Navy discharge money to buy a load of parts from a junkyard. The two then went in together on a '55 Plymouth and headed for NASCAR.

"There were four of us, Spook, his wife and dog, and me. We left Corpus Christi for Daytona and followed the circuit." Spook towed the Plymouth behind an old '48 Desoto he'd adapted to be their motel. He and his wife slept on a makeshift bed in the back seat while Allen slept in the front.

"We ran in the Daytona race but fell out early due to broken steering. The next race was down in Hollywood, Florida. We were fast and sure we'd do well, because we were accustomed to short track racing, but then the hot dogs showed up. We thought we were something until we saw the competition and realized how pitiful we were.

"We didn't run well, but we bought our first racing tire. We had been running street tires which ran hot and were fast to wear out. Since the racing tires held the track better and lasted longer, we bought a Firestone Super Stock in West Palm Beach, Florida. We couldn't afford four, so since the right front wheel took more beating, we put it there. The other drivers were running them too, but we thought we had something and we kept on following the circuit until we reached Fayetteville."

The two soon hooked up with a Chrysler dealership. Allen enrolled in the GI training program and he and Spook worked on commission. The business gave them a place to keep their car, a break on parts and enough money to keep them going.

"Spook was an excellent mechanic and super-fast. With my help we could make good money working on cars in just a few days. I also had money from my GI training bill but with racing expenses so high, we lived hand to mouth."

Despite the fact nobody else was running Plymouths and his car was sorely underpowered, Allen performed so well he attracted the attention of the car's automaker. "Ronnie Householder was head of Plymouth Performance and he saw how hard we were working. He said we needed a better car and offered us a new Plymouth for twenty-five hundred dollars. That was an awful lot of money to us, but the dealership let us buy it on installment. The car was from the new '56 Plymouth Fury series, a special sporty model that just came out that year. It was basically a stripped-down version run through the assembly line with no undercoating. They put a Chrysler suspension under it and added a high performance engine. Spook was listed as the car owner but he and I were partners."

Allen and Spook ran their first race with their new ride in July in Asheville-Weaverville. By the end of the season, Allen had thirty-two races, coming in twelfth in Final Point Standings.

As time passed and Allen got more involved, racing became more consuming. "I liked the adrenalin, the excitement, the competition and trying to master the automobile." His enthusiasm paid off. In 1957, he ran forty-two races and moved to number seven in Final Point Standings.

"In 1959, I went in with Don Bailey on a 1957 Chevrolet and Paul McDuffie built the engine. It was a great car and we took it to USAC. At that time, I'd run two or three midget events and decided I wanted to work my way to Indianapolis and get into open wheel racing. Don agreed and we planned to settle in the Indianapolis area and run our car on weekends and midget and sprint during the week."

Those hopes never materialized but their stock car racing continued. They finished second in a USAC race in Milwaukee and then won a 500-lap ARCA race in Dayton, Ohio. "That helped sustain us. We went to several other USAC races before heading to California where they raced in the winter." Another set of dreams bit the dust in the west when a crash in Las Vegas took out their car and they didn't have money to fix it.

In early 1960, Allen got an opportunity to drive NASCAR for Michigan's Braun Plywood Company and he and Bailey headed for Daytona. Their car was built by Roger McCluskey and Bill Cheesbourg, who were, ironically, both Indy drivers. The plan was for Allen to drive the car early in the year and return it to McClusky and Cheesburg when the USAC circuit began. Those plans changed when the car's owner saw Allen come in fifth in the Daytona 500. He decided to give him the car and have the other drivers build a new one.

"We went to Martinsville and then to Darlington where they were paying big money for a convertible race. We couldn't afford to run two cars and we couldn't run the car as it was so we cut off the roof and made it a convertible, making the top re-attachable. There were a lot of independents back then and the practice was common."

The car was running third when the right rear tire blew, suddenly sending it into a spin from which it went airborne. Allen shot over the fourth turn wall and into the scoring stand, taking all the supports out from under it. The car finally came to a stop upside down in the parking lot where Allen miraculously escaped with only a bruise to his foot.

"When it was all over, I crawled out of the car and looked up. I just knew I was going to see mutilated bodies." Fortunately, the day was hot and all the scorers had moved to the opposite side of the stand to see the clock and be in the shade. Since the accident took out the stairs, race officials had to get a ladder and a fire truck to get people down. No one was badly injured despite the drama, but the car was in pieces.

When the owner decided not to put up the money to build a new car, Allen feared his racing career was ended. But good luck came at just the right moment.

"We were befriended by an Atlanta nightclub owner named Tommy Starr. Chevrolet gave us a body; we salvaged a few parts from the old car and Starr put up the money for rebuilding the rest of it."

Don Bailey served as Allen's chief mechanic but their pit crew was all volunteer. Among them was a standout named Jimmy Summerour. "Jimmy was devoted, totally committed, and became our main man. He was a great motivator, friend and decision-maker. We couldn't have done as well as we did in the early sixties without him and we built that car in two weeks. No matter what we needed, he always came up with it."

One of the things Summerour devised was a race radio. Anxious to improve pit-to-driver communication and try new technology, he bought one as soon as they were available. The first time he used it, he was unable to contact Allen, but found himself talking to a lonely man in a California logging camp. He kept the man updated on the race during their conversation.

In spite of their efforts, hard times continued to follow the racing team. "We struggled along, tore up the car, lost an engine in Charlotte and went in the hole. We were behind on our rent and our furniture payments." With one race to go, Allen pinned his hopes on the racing community. "We were really scraping to get the car to Atlanta. We got a block from Tom Pistone, got enough parts to get our engine together and went to the track."

Unfortunately, due to a plug in the block, the engine lost oil pressure and locked down before they could qualify. The desperate Allen put out a call to his competitors.

His call was answered by Rex White, that year's soon-to-be champion. "I've got an engine and I'll let you use it," said White. "It was running good in Charlotte when we pulled it out, but it's got five hundred miles on it. I don't know if it'll run another five hundred but you're welcome to it." Allen thankfully accepted his offer.

"Rex sent his crew with me to get the engine and bring it back and I had it in the car the next morning. We qualified for the race and finished second, winning enough money to bail us out for the year. I told Rex he had saved our lives. When I tried to pay him, he said, 'No. I won't take any money but I do want my engine.' That was above and beyond what people do for each other and helped us get started."

According to Allen, one big problem was the lack of durable parts. "During the fifties and sixties, there was an awful lot of attrition. Racecars just didn't have the equipment they have now. Strong parts were available, but everything on the car had to be stock and we had to pass inspections to prove it. We were very limited as to what we could do and you could break parts easily, especially on dirt tracks. To compensate, I had a pattern I would always use. My style was to start out driving conservatively, trying to take care of the car, staying close in the competition and pacing myself. I tried to make sure I'd finish. Later, I didn't have as many people to beat because so many fell out. When it came close to the end, I would gain as many spots as I could to get my best finish.

"When I got an opportunity to drive a car for Holly Farms in 1962, I found that was the style they wanted. Junior Johnson had just left. His style had been 'Flat on the floor and wide open. Stop if it breaks.' Junior and his Holly Farms mechanic had been in controversy because Junior claimed the cars weren't well prepared. The mechanic argued Junior just broke them. I continued to drive conservatively, but the cars still broke.

"On June 16, 1962, I had my first Winston Cup win, driving for Holly Farms at Bowman Gray Stadium. Rex White sat on the pole and I sat outside the pole. That little quarter-mile was a really narrow track with the finish line near the first turn. When we came to the final lap, we were neck and neck and Rex was leaning on me from the inside. I had the choice of pulling back and letting him pass me or gunning it. I knew Rex would beat me if I backed off, so I stayed on it." Determined to win, he zoomed over the finish line ahead of White but plowed into the fence. "It tore up my front end, but the win was worth it." Allen had to walk back to the finish line to claim his trophy.

"At the time, there were a lot of factory-backed teams who were tough competition. Sometimes I outran them and sometimes they outran me. I believe if the cars had not broken we'd have had several wins. Holly Farms shut down their team at the end of the season. That put me out of a ride and I had to go hunting again."

It wasn't long before Allen found himself snared by racing politics. "If you weren't racing full time and going where the parties were... if you weren't in the right places, at the right times, you weren't considered. By then, I was married and had more overhead and I began thinking hard about my future. At that time, racing didn't hold a future. Constantly working my way up and into a good car and then having circumstances take me out was very discouraging.

"I looked back at the guys who were superstars when I came into racing: Curtis Turner, Fireball Roberts, Joe Weatherly and Buck Baker. Those guys were either dead or already looking for another profession.

"In '63, I drove a Ford that was halfway factory-backed and first built by Holman-

Moody. The car was being kept up by a guy named Rattus Walters who lived in Washington, D.C. We didn't get the good stuff and didn't have a crew chief, so we struggled again. In June, I went to Atlanta where I blew the front tire. The car went through the guard rail, bounded out of the track, and when it flipped the engine flew out." Allen broke his foot and nose and messed up his hand, temporarily halting his racing. "A car wrecked that badly is destroyed and if your owner has only one car, it puts him, and you, out of business. That's the way it was with independents.

"After the wreck, I continued to seek rides and drive through 1967. I'd been working for Ford and Pontiac doing performance trials and special tests on a contract basis. In between jobs, I went in with a business partner and started a tire and wheel store in Greenville. I finally began running on Saturday nights around South Carolina, North Carolina and Georgia in the late model Sportsman Division, now called the Busch Series. I competed with drivers such as Harry Gant, and Ralph and Dale Earnhardt, but I raced as a hobby, with no money in it. It proved to be a form of psychotherapy. I'd run my company during the week, then get rid of my frustrations on the track." Despite his semi-withdrawal from driving, Allen continued to make headlines, winning the 1972 Greenville-Pickens Championship. He finally fully retired in 1983.

"I would have liked to have had more success," he says today, "but it has a lot to do with timing and luck. As far as a driver getting a good ride, the whole thing was politics. You had to have a good car and everybody wanted the best, but if drivers didn't own their rides with sponsors tied in, they had to solicit them.

"In looking back, I have to say racing was very fulfilling. Most people start at the bottom and work their way up. I started at the top and worked my way down. I experienced everything, from dirt tracks to super speedways. That's what racing and life is about, making constant adjustments. The results weren't always what I wanted but I have no regrets. It was a lot of work, but a lot of fun. I lived my dream and I wouldn't trade that for anything."

CHAPTER 28

James Hylton: Standing on Principle Pursuing His Dream

If anyone ever deserved to be NASCAR champion, it was James Hylton. That elusive dream was never fulfilled as, year after year, the determined and hard-working Hylton came inches short.

Beginning as a mechanic, Hylton helped propel Rex White and Ned Jarrett, two of NASCAR's top drivers, to national championships. In his first two years as a driver (1966–67), Hylton competed in eighty-seven races with forty-four top fives and seventy-one top tens. During both years, he came teeth-gnashingly close to winning Final Point Standings. In 1966, he attained the record of highest finish in Final Point Standings by a Rookie of the Year, losing the position by less than 2000 points to David Pearson. In 1967, he held the points lead for six months before losing to stock car racing "King" Richard Petty. The third excruciatingly close second-place came in 1971, when he lost to Petty again by only 365 points. A master of consistency, he remained in the top five and top ten for twelve years.

Known for "telling it like it is," he was a rebel whose outspoken manner endeared him as much to drivers as it alienated him from NASCAR.

In uniform, Hylton became the sport's crusader, attempting to right wrongs committed against him and his competitors. He may never have been Points champion but he was the champion of the independents, the underdogs who lacked financial backing. Although NASCAR disparaged Hylton, the organization listened to him, and adopted many of his ideas. One of those ideas was the implementation of "plan money," funds guaranteed to drivers who follow the Cup circuit and qualify.

Despite innumerable obstacles, including lack of sponsorship, the tenacious Hylton never gave up and remains active in the sport today. Although he officially retired in 1982, he continues entering races and qualifying. Hylton Motorsports of Inman, South Carolina has been in existence and involved in racing since 1965.

"The bottom line is, I've done something all my life the people sitting in the grandstands pay hundreds of dollars to see and wish they could do. I learned how to drive a racecar driving a tractor. It had plows in the ground and I had to compensate for its front end push. It may have only gone three miles an hour, but I learned a lot from it. You can learn techniques driving any machine with a steering wheel on it and anything becomes high performance if you're in the right place.

"I've been involved in racing since day one. I was born in 1935 in Roanoke, Virginia and raised on a farm. There were thirteen children and no racers in my family. That's just something I wanted to do on my own. We were dirt poor but we had heavy equipment and did all kinds of construction work. At twelve, I was driving a bulldozer and after that I drove a tractor on a regular basis. I'd get on those Virginia hills and do a four-wheel drift. The whole machine would start sliding down the side of the hill. When that happens, you jump, correct it, or follow it. I always stayed with it, never jumped off, never did lose one.

"I was interested in speed even in the third grade. I distinctly remember our little school. It had windows but no air conditioning. When anything loud came by, I had to see it. Some guy came by on a motorcycle without a muffler and I jumped up. My teacher wore out my hands with a ruler."

When Hylton was fifteen, he began building a '37 Ford coupe with a friend whose parents had a farm. Both worked on a car in the barn while helping each other. "We got the things built and wanted to test them. His Dad had the prettiest alfalfa field. We got out in that field to do a lap or two just to see if everything was working. When we were done, his alfalfa field was gone. Needless to say, our cars were gone too. Both wound up on my father's farm.

"One day, we weren't satisfied with the way my car was running. We didn't have any seats so I used an old crate and sped down a dirt road. The road was full of ruts and gullies. As long as you stayed on the high side, you were fine, but when you got up to speed it slid down in the ruts. The car had a straight axle in its front and was solid from one side to the other. It dug in when the wheels went down and fishtailed. After that experience, I went to the dentist. That was my first stock car injury."

There was a Grand National racetrack in Roanoke that attracted Hylton like a magnet. The first time he went, unable to afford a ticket, he sneaked in with a friend, swimming across sewage in the Roanoke River and making a hundred yard dash to the bleachers. When the security guard saw them, he just shook his head. They watched Lee Petty and Curtis Turner battle it out and Hylton was hooked. On a Saturday when he was sixteen or seventeen, he went to the dirt track at Starky to race. "I knew a lot about tractors, but not racing. I asked around, looked at other drivers' cars and they helped me. I got in that race without a clue and ran as hard as I could.

"Billy and Bobby Myers were two of the best Grand National drivers and they were in the race. Dirt tracks get big ruts in them as the race goes on and back then, tracks weren't well maintained. There was a big hole in turn one and the Myers sandwiched me in. One was on the outside, one on the inside and they ran me right into the hole. When I hit, the car bounced out like a bowling ball. I hit one of them on the inside and one on the outside. They went off the track, one inside the infield and one outside the infield. It was all an accident, but I ended up in third place. I was lucky to come out of it. If I hadn't ricocheted off them I would have turned over. Since I was from Virginia and they were from North Carolina, I became a favorite. The fans and other drivers thought I was a wonder boy.

"The next race was the next day in Pulaski, Virginia at a desolate half-mile highbank up in the mountains. It's a nice little racetrack now, downsized a little. I learned a valuable lesson there and go back once in a while for old times' sake.

James Hylton on May 19, 1967, in Junie Donlavey's #48 Ford at Beltsville Speedway in Beltsville, Maryland. (Photograph by Bob Williams. Courtesy Larry Jendras, Jr.)

"I qualified well and wound up leading the race down the straightaway, with a white flag going into turn three. I'd worn out my right front tire but didn't know it. If I'd cooled it, I could have won the race, but I blew the tire and went over the embankment. There was no fence and on the other side were crossties and junk. The last thing I remember was landing on them upside down and totaling my brand new car. I'd only gotten two races out of it.

"I raced around Roanoke for several years, then married and moved to Tampa, Florida. We lived on Cherokee Avenue, and across the street, a race driver named Frankie Schneider worked on his car on a vacant lot with a little shed. I hung around him and eventually brought my car down from Virginia. I'd help Frankie and he'd help me. The guy was a master racer and he taught me how to make my car work. I had a 'nothing' car, but Frankie worked on it, showed me what to do, and I began winning. He took two old junk carburetors, cut them in half and put them together and made a four-barrel. We ran alcohol and the thing was leaking, but it would fly.

"I worked with Frankie a couple of seasons. He'd go back up to his home in New Jersey in the summer and return to Florida in winter. The one year I helped him, he won thirty-two races around the Tampa area. It was a toss-up who was the better driver on the short track, Frankie Schneider or Rex White. When we'd go to the short tracks, everybody bet on who would run second.

"One day in 1959, Rex called me wanting to know if I'd work on a Grand National car. I told him I'd have to think about it. One second later, I said, 'When do you want me there?' My wife Evelyn and I loaded up and moved to Spartanburg. I worked with Rex until about 1964, and that's when I learned about racing. Rex made a lot of adjustments to the cars which we still use today. One was raising and lowering the car with a bolt you put a wrench in, called a jackscrew. Holman-Moody got credit, but I was there when Rex came up with the jackscrews. Before then, we had to get close and cut a spring off to get the car fixed.

"We had rubber bushings for the sway bar. Rex came up with adjustable frame buckets and that was the beginning of the study of chassis, of working on frame and suspension. I learned about chassis from Rex."

White was also known for his pit crew and their eye-catching uniforms. "My most memorable moment in racing was when we thought Rex won at Darlington. We had our red Alpine hats on and we jumped up on that '60 Chevrolet and were on our way to the Winner's Circle. You couldn't see the car for the people on it.

"Once in Daytona, Rex wanted somebody to read the instruments while he checked out his car. At that time, top speed around the racetrack was 150 miles per hour. We got everything ready to go and I got in with Rex. He took us out of pit row and jumped up on the bank. Mind you, I'd only been around that track in a street car. The first time around, we went down the backstretch and I kept looking at Rex and looking at his feet to see if he was going to lift off the throttle. He was driving in that banking at 150 miles per hour and it was terrifying. I didn't read any instruments for a lap or two.

"Working with Rex, I drove the tow truck everywhere we went. I told him up front I didn't want to be a mechanic; I wanted to drive racecars. Rex went along with that, taught me, and let me drive his car around the track for practice.

"I worked for Ned Jarrett in 1964 and Dick Hutcherson in 1965. By '65, I was getting frustrated. I said if I couldn't figure out how to get a car, I was going to quit. That year, I met Bud Hardjay in Tampa and drove his car at local tracks. Since he wanted to go to Grand National races, he came up with the money and we became partners. We bought a '65 Dodge from Cotton Owens and a dirt car from David Pearson. We gave Cotton five thousand dollars for the turn key car, got us a truck and equipment and took off racing. It was an $18,500 investment and we started with the Riverside California Road Race.

"Back then, NASCAR wasn't strict like it is today and if you showed up with a car, they'd let you race. We'd practiced by speeding through the mountain roads of Virginia at night and people said we were crazy, going out there to start on a road course.

"I finished twelfth in the race, then went to Daytona with the same car and finished ninth, and we were on our way. We ran the same car with the same engine all year and never wrecked. Afterwards, we moved to Inman, South Carolina, started a little shop and overhauled the engine. With what I'd learned from Rex and his crew chief Louie Clements, we were able to do the setups, build the engines, and build gears and transmissions. With no money to speak of, we did it all. Back then, there was no body technology and with our mechanical know-how, we 'had' the other drivers on chassis. It gave me the advantage I needed because I knew how to handle a car and make it last longer. Now, you can pay $200,000 to hire a crew chief and go to parts suppliers and buy speed. In those days, you couldn't do that. What it boils down to is in 1966 I was runner-up to David Pearson, almost beating him for the championship. No driver has run second in their rookie year other than me. That record stands today and that's a fact.

"We've done all kinds of racing since, including ARCA and NASCAR, and now we're running Craftsman trucks and Busch. We've done it with hard work without a major sponsor so I don't know whether to be happy or mad with Rex for what he taught me.

"I'm a rebel and a hell-raiser. I was brought up by good, honest parents who believed in the American way, lived the good life and taught their kids the same. I've led a clean life and I wouldn't change it, but sometimes that's hurt me. I've tried to be honest with people but sometimes they've made me wonder if it was the right thing to do.

"If you see something you know is dead wrong with NASCAR, they will either accept it or fight you. It's NASCAR's ball game. Their attitude is, if you don't like it, go somewhere else. They don't like anybody interfering in their operation. When I was with Rex at Darlington, I was young and had a pretty wife. I came out of the garage area and saw a bunch of drunks around our car agitating her. That got my dander up. We needed a fenced area where our girlfriends and families could be safe without drunks pawing them and I was instrumental in getting it."

At that time, NASCAR only allowed a pit pass each for a driver and car owner. "I raised hell until they gave seven pit passes, so families could get in."

Hylton was also responsible for NASCAR's "Winner's Circle Plan." "In the old days, promoters across the country paid you a fee to show up. The deal was, we'd get about as much money to show up as the $700–800 the race paid to win. That kept independent drivers surviving. NASCAR made the promoters end the deal money and then we were starving. We wanted to get them to pay more money to the back of the field so we could keep operating, or, have a purse for the hot dogs and give us the rest. We tried to have a meeting with Bill France Jr., but he wouldn't talk. His theory was he'd talk one-on-one all you wanted, but three or four together... no way.

The independents appointed me to speak for the group and I took it seriously. It all came down at Martinsville. I asked France to have a meeting and told him if he didn't include the whole group, we were leaving the track. At 12 o'clock, there was still no sign he would talk to us. I said, 'Let's load up this junk and get out of here.' Everybody started loading their trailers, pickups and trucks. About a quarter to one, an official said, 'Junior wants to see you.' I went upstairs to Bill's office, where he was sitting behind his desk, pulled a chair beside it and sat there. We didn't say a word for fifteen minutes. Then, he said, 'Go get them and we'll talk.'

"He had a big motor home parked in back and we all got in. We gathered on the median in the middle of a dual lane highway outside of Martinsville. That's where Plan #1 was born. The way the plan worked, there would be $2500 for the first independent, then $2200 and so forth, broken down to twelve places. Last place paid $800. That gave us money other than purse for survival. I told France, 'It will be good for everybody, the drivers and the car owners. We'll have better-looking cars and we'll run better.' He agreed to the plan. We got enough money to sleep in motels, buy decent suppers, and update our cars.

"When the people who ran up front decided they weren't going to stand for it, NASCAR added the 'Winner's Circle Plan.' Under that plan, if a driver won a race, he got $10,000. The next race he showed up for after winning brought another $10,000, and then they'd break it down. NASCAR considered us money grabbers, but they use that idea today."

In the old days, there were more independents then factory drivers and they always pulled pranks on each other. They'd go to tracks three days ahead and have time to play. At North Wilkesboro, when Hylton and the other drivers found Elmo Langley under his

"The bottom line is I've done something all my life the people sitting in the grandstands pay hundreds of dollars to see and wish they could do," says James Hylton.

hauler taking a nap the dickens got into them. Hylton had a military smoke bomb and decided to give Langley a scare. He threw the bomb under the truck and yelled "Fire! Fire!" Elmo woke up, saw the smoke, and jumped up bumping his head, and then rushed to the cab of the hauler and threw up the hood.

Once when Richard Childress was racing, the dickens got Hylton again. "Back then, we carried a gallon jug for water during the race. I put ExLax in his jug and it worked. About halfway through the race, he had to get out. We were always cutting up. In the modern era, every time there's a little bump, it's 'See us in the oval office after the race.' NASCAR fines us, slaps our hands and tells us not to do it again.

"We had our own 'oval offices' and we were self-policing. If a guy turned us around intentionally, we'd take care of it. The guy who was doing the turning knew he'd get it and nine times out of ten, in the next race, he *got* it. If the guy was running for points, it could take him out of contention."

In 1968, Hylton was injured at Rockingham in a wreck that totaled his car. His concussion was so bad he lay unconscious for two days and remained in the hospital for weeks. "I was running against Bobby Isaac when he blew an engine and I hit the oil. Since I was going for the lead, just about every car on the racetrack gave me a whack. I was in an old van seat without a head rest and my head hit the roll bar. It was a setback. I had double vision from October until August of the following year. I passed the physicals because nobody knew and I overcame it by holding my head high. When I rode like I was looking at birds, I could have clear vision, but when I didn't, I saw two of everything.

"I'd missed the season's last race so I didn't race again until January when I went to Riverside. Ronnie Householder gave me a second-hand racecar and Chrysler helped me a little. I started out qualifying seeing double and by the time I got my head up, I was in the corner. I went down deep, scared Ronnie to death and was lucky to make it. I qualified in the top five and became his hero."

Hylton says the old days were challenging but he misses them. "Now, they're making movie stars out of participants and they've gone Hollywood. You can hardly turn on the television without seeing a race driver. It has a lot to do with the way people drive on the highways. They fantasize they're race drivers. You speed up, the other guy speeds up. You slow down, he slows down. People draft so close you can't see them and cut you off like I've never seen. I think racing's to blame for that and it comes directly from TV.

"When I started, racing was a matter of getting a car, getting people to help you, and figuring out the mechanical part. Now, technology doesn't linger long. Something new is always popping up and you have to be on top of things. Race shops have forty to sixty people working on one automobile, in plants that cost millions of dollars.

"The sport's become more military and money's taken over. You can't just put a decal on your racecar; you have to pay NASCAR. The cost of putting on an ad and running a race is staggering. Drivers have to 'salute' the chain of command, and if they don't have wealthy connections, they have a rough row to hoe."

Teams no longer fraternize and the camaraderie of brothers helping brothers is gone, yet the sport is still demanding and grueling for independents. "Racing is a very hard life and we're always on edge, trying to get to the next track; wondering whether it's worth it; resting up and deciding it is. We go to work at eight in the morning seven days a week and we usually stay past ten.

"When we're not in the shop, we're on the road. Tracks make you leave at five so that's our rest period. Sometimes, we drive all night without sleep and eat while we're driving. When it's raining, we're in the rain and when it's blistering hot, we're in the sun. Because our equipment is in the infield, we walk miles back and forth at the track. Most people putting those kinds of hours into a regular business would be multi-millionaires, but there's no pension and we're on our own."

Hylton says despite all the hardships, he still races because the sport is fun. "I don't know if you can call me successful, but I've had a good time. Racing is like a drug or an incurable disease. It's a drive that's uncontrollable, with no halfway house for it. Once you have it,... you have it for life."

Hylton recently attempted to qualify for the Daytona 500. He missed by one car position.

CHAPTER 29

W. C. "Junie" Donlavey:
Racing's Angel

Known for giving new drivers a break, Junie Donlavey was a standout car owner responsible for the entrance of some of motorsports' most famous names into big-time racing. This personable man with the big heart reached deep into his wallet to give new drivers a chance. Involved in Modified, Grand National, and Winston Cup, he sponsored many young soon-to-be stars. When he took new drivers under his wing, it was as if an angel had appeared. Ironically, Junie believes himself to have been a beneficiary of his own guardian angel.

In 1997, along with fellow car owner Bud Moore, Junie was presented with the coveted Bill France Award of Excellence. The award is considered to be one of Motorsports' highest honors.

Born in 1924, Donlavey was raised in Richmond, Virginia, where he's lived all of his life. He got his racing start under the influence of his uncle who operated a radiator shop. "I went to my first race at age fourteen at the Richmond Fairgrounds," says Donlavey. "My uncle had sprint cars, and I enjoyed watching and helping him work on them before each race. He could take a car that was really torn up and put it back together like new. The cars had to be perfect so he worked his brains out, not leaving anything undone, even small details."

As a teenager, Donlavey saved money from working after school in his uncle's shop to buy his first car and at fifteen he paid fifty dollars for a Ford Model A. "It ran like a champ. I always had a favorite car, and my favorite was always Ford. The best engine I had was Ford and I've run Fords all my life.

"I thought I wanted to be a pilot, but when I was eighteen I married and joined the Navy and was in for three years as a metalsmith. When I came out I worked for a year for my father. He taught me more about working on automobiles and I took over his business."

Soon, Donlavey, who spent his free time going to races, expanded his work on cars from the garage to the track. At the end of 1949, he heard that a driver from New Jersey, who'd raced in Florida, had headed back home through Richmond and left his car to be sold. In early 1950, he and a friend pooled their money and bought it. Donlavey began running it on a newly opened short track nearby.

"We began running Modified within a 300 mile radius but after going to races in the Carolinas, we got into stocks. I drove a couple of races but found I liked working on their engines more than driving them."

For Donlavey, racing opened up a new world. "I met so many nice people and I looked forward to that at each track. I could meet more people in a season than most people meet in two lifetimes. Normally, people don't travel much, just on vacation, maybe two weeks a year. Racing gave me an opportunity for a lot more. Back then, there were no interstates and the main highways didn't have much traffic. I was able to see the country and it was fun. I learned how to get along with different people and not be one way in my thinking. If I was in a group of six people, we'd have six different opinions about everything, but it taught me to see their side and reason out what I believed in. I could have lived a hundred lives and not learned what I've learned in racing."

Donlavey says people who have jobs nine to five often miss those experiences and racing made him feel part of a group. "In racing we were involved in each other's lives and the people made up for everything we went through. We knew what each of us did and who did what well. We could see every need and share how to do things differently. Years ago, people would say, 'I found if you do this or that your car will run better.' Today, drivers don't communicate with competitors and give any secrets away. Racing's a lot safer, but money's taken the place of community. There isn't a close relationship like we had."

Donlavey says getting to know Rex White was one example. "We couldn't have met a nicer young man. He was a good driver and a good mechanic. He worked on cars like

Sonny Hutchins wins at Beltsville Speedway in Beltsville, Maryland, in Junie Donlavey's #90 Ford on September 1, 1967. (Photograph by Bob Williams. Courtesy Larry Jendras Jr.)

the rest of us and we watched him succeed. Since he ran mostly GMs, we had fun running a Ford against his Chevrolet. Winning a race was nice, but it was the people who made the moment."

That also included the fans. "People think they just bought a ticket, sat in the grandstands and watched something happen, but after the races, they were with the drivers. Most tracks didn't have garages and when the race was over [the fans] piled into the pits where they had access to everyone. We used them on our pit crews and to score, and they pitched in to help load equipment. I have close personal friends I met as fans who were part of our racing community."

No track had a stronger feeling of community than the old Daytona Beach and Road Course. "Running through the sand on the beach was fun and it was like a big gathering of friends when we went. We didn't have modern equipment back then so we just took what they ran on the streets and beefed up the parts. I liked to bring out a street car and expose it to the public as a good racecar, but since we didn't have engine shops, we had to learn from experience."

Among his fondest memories are engines' sounds. He listened for a loud sharp crack when they started and had trained his ears to hear horsepower. "I'd listen to tell how weak or strong they were and if a guy had an additive, I'd smell the difference. Our biggest obstacle was the competition. There were so many competitors, we kept our eyes open, looking to see how they did their work, how good it was and how sharp. If something they had looked good, we added it to our own. Rules didn't cover everything but, back in the old days, some of those guys really knew how to work around them. It wasn't called cheating, it was ingenuity. We'd make engines go from two to three hundred horsepower up to seven hundred. What we came up with was amazing and we all worked closely together."

For Donlavey, close relationships extended beyond the track into the spiritual realm. He believes he's been protected by a guardian angel, the first time at ten.

"I remember it was in the middle of winter. We had about three feet of snow on the roads, so nothing was moving. My father cleaned out our kerosene stove and put the ashes on the back porch. They were cool but the wind was blowing. At about 2:30 in the morning, the wind ignited the ashes and set the house on fire. We were ten minutes from being burned up when a gentleman walking down the street saw the fire and beat on our door. He got us out but the house burned to its foundation. When I hear people talk about a guardian angel, I think of that. Why was a man walking down the road through three feet of snow at 2:30 a.m.? Why was he right there at the right moment when our house was burning? God had that man walking down that road.

"I've been close to death many times but always come out of it. Once, when I was returning from Columbia, a car sped toward me down the highway in my lane. When he came close to me, I pulled over as far as I could and closed my eyes. I felt the crash of the car, but opened my eyes and was still going straight. It was like I was gone, but came back."

Others have had close calls too. The most unusual Donlavey remembers involved his driver Ken Schrader. In 1987 at Daytona, Schrader was leading the race into the last lap when he came off the number four turn and spun. The car flipped into the air and landed on Harry Gant's car's hood. Gant's car carried Ken's car across the finish line. When the car finally slid off, it was torn to pieces.

Alarmed, rescue workers rushed over to cut out the window mesh. The shocked but unharmed Schrader was unaware of the damage. He said, "Don't cut that window. If you do, my car owner will kill me."

"Daytona was one of the funniest places I've ever been around," says Donlavey. "One day Joe Weatherly's crew cleared out the center of the beach and Joe got into his modified. The road going down to the beach dropped off with a pretty good slope. Joe came up from the beach on that hill, hit the top of it on the street, and the car flew into the air like he was a Hell Driver. Seeing a policeman standing near where he landed, Joe took off. The policeman chased him all over Daytona. It was dangerous but it was funny. Guys used to do a lot of that, having a lot of fun, sometimes running their cars into swimming pools."

Donlavey gave Weatherly his first Grand National start, running a Hudson in the 1952 Southern 500. Weatherly went on to win twenty-five Grand National races. An "angel" to those with talent but no money, Donlavey led many, who otherwise had no chance, to racing greatness. His other drivers included Jody Ridley, Mike Wallace, Ricky Rudd, Ernie Irvin, Chad Little and Harry Gant. He was also responsible for giving NASCAR legend Buck Baker the opportunity for a racing comeback.

CHAPTER 30

Dewayne "Tiny" Lund: From the Cornfields to Talladega

A man who loved pulling pranks, Tiny Lund was a generous, fun-loving driver addicted to racing. Described as a two hundred seventy pound kid, his childlike antics garnered attention on and off the track. Despite his unusual approach to the world, Lund was a serious racing competitor who was willing to do anything, even risk his life, to help others. Named as one of the Top Fifty Drivers in NASCAR history, the enormous Lund was a short track master. In his 21-year career, he won five Winston Cup races and five Grand American titles. Lund was awarded the Most Popular Driver title in the Grand American Series for four consecutive years and also raced in Japan as NASCAR ambassador. The following is based on a 2005 interview with his widow Wanda Early and former driver Rex White.

Rex White recalls the first time he met Lund. "I was going to a race in Council Bluff, Iowa and had a mechanic install a new transmission in my Chevrolet. When he did, he didn't put in any grease. This wouldn't have been a problem had I been aware of it as I was towing it on the ground without a drive shaft, but when I got to the track, I put in the driveshaft, took the car out to warm it up and tore out second gear. Since I didn't have an extra transmission, I took the one out of my tow truck and put it in so I'd be able to race. Despite my efforts, since it was the wrong ratio, I didn't run well. Afterwards, I had the chore of changing it back.

"I was about to put it back in the truck when two guys stopped by to help. One was named Kenny Miler and the other was a giant of a man called Tiny Lund. When we finished, Tiny invited me to his house to shower and eat. He told me he was also a driver but had torn up his car and was out of funds.

"Tiny had played basketball and football in high school and been offered numerous scholarships but he turned them all down to race. I encouraged him to come south when he got his finances together and he did, bringing Kenny with him. They stayed at Billy Myers' shop for awhile and I helped him set up his car.

"Tiny was a good driver, especially on dirt, because he was raised in the Iowa cornfields. He loved to get his car sideways and throw dust on spectators. When he wasn't racing, he liked to fish and we spent many an hour on the Catawba. Back then, we'd tie

124

Tiny Lund in the #55 wins at Beltsville Speedway in Beltsville, Maryland, on April 26, 1970. (Courtesy Larry Jendras Jr.)

a line to a milk jug and let it float, then return and check to see if a catfish was on it. We'd sometimes put jugs out at night and then hunt for them with flashlights. When the fish took the bait, those jugs would go flying.

"When he could finally afford it, Tiny bought land at Moncks Corner, South Carolina and opened a fish camp. For years he held the world record for his fifty-five pound fresh water striped bass." According to his widow, Wanda Early, fifty-five had already become a meaningful number to Lund. He wore it in high school athletics and painted it on his racecar.

The fish camp soon became a gathering place for drivers and there were many pranks. "One time," says Early, "Buddy Baker came to the camp and went out on the water with Tiny. It was extremely hot and the fish weren't biting so he told Tiny he was burning up and couldn't take the heat any more. Tiny said, 'Why don't you just jump in the water and cool off?' When Buddy got into the water, Tiny sneaked over to the other side of the boat, got into the water and swam beneath it. He then grabbed Buddy by the leg and pulled him under. Horrified, Buddy thought he'd been caught by an alligator."

"Tiny was a good-natured kid," says White, "but he was constantly playing pranks on people and animals. In a garage, he was like a bull in a china shop and I believe he could have broken an anvil. When he was around, we couldn't work. Tom Pistone and I were the smallest Grand National drivers and Tiny would pick us up and throw us over his shoulder like sacks of flour. When I'd had all I could take, I'd lose my patience and chase him out.

"One year at Darlington, Tiny hurled water from the roof of our hotel onto people below and then went down to the pool and threw people in. The Charlotte track had a cheetah that was always kept in a cage. As rough as that big cat was, Tiny would take him out and wrestle with him. They would get down on the ground and roll and play. Tiny was a con artist and the funniest human being I've ever met. Everyone I knew had a Tiny Lund story. He was every driver's friend and every driver's nightmare. We didn't have a clue what he might do to us.

"I remember when we were in Columbia and Tom Pistone was there. Tiny and Tom were close friends and both of them were going to race. They were about to get into their cars when Tiny picked up Tom and handcuffed him to the fence. The announcer said, 'Gentlemen, start your engines,' and there was Tom dangling.

"Drivers always put their helmets upside down in the back of their seats. While Tom was struggling to get down off the fence, Tiny filled Tom's helmet full of ice water. When Tom finally got loose, he rushed to his car, grabbed his helmet, and popped it onto his head. The water was so cold, it took his breath.

"Another time, Tiny put a snake in a driver's car during a pit stop on a caution lap. The driver was terrified of snakes and when he saw it, he slammed on his brakes and jumped out, and then ran across the track with the cars coming.

"Once David Pearson spun Tiny and after the race Tiny went after him. David tried not to show he was afraid while Tiny pawed the ground like a bull. 'David, I'd like to know why you spun me,' Tiny demanded. Pearson told him he was trying to pass him and if he hadn't done it to Tiny, Tiny would have done it to him. Suddenly, fire flashed from Tiny's eyes. He put his huge arm around Pearson's neck and put him in a headlock, but instead of killing him, he rubbed cherry pie in his face.

"Tiny was funny but he was also likable," says White, "and he'd give anyone the shirt off his back. That's not to say, people didn't get irritated. When he played tricks he could be obnoxious. He enjoyed aggravating people and liked a good fight."

"Tiny could win a fight with one hand," says Early. "He didn't get into many, because nobody wanted to risk being hit by a man of his size. Tiny was so large, if racecars hadn't been as big as they were in the old days, he couldn't have raced. Sometimes others would start a fight and Tiny would finish it."

Lund used his size to his advantage, but also to the advantage of others. In 1963, Marvin Panch was testing Rick Cunningham's Maserati sports car at Daytona when it went airborne, flipped out of control and landed upside down. Because the doors opened into the top, Panch was trapped inside.

Lund and other onlookers rushed to the scene, lifting the car while Panch tried to kick a door open. Before he was free, the fuel tank blew up, knocking his rescuers backwards. Seeing Panch was still alive, they went back into the inferno, lifted the car again and Lund pulled him out. Panch was badly burned, but survived.

Panch and his sponsors, the Wood brothers, were so thankful they asked Lund to drive Panch's Ford in the Daytona 500. Thrilled, he avoided pit stops, pushed the car to its limit, and sped ahead of his competitors to victory. It was a fabulous win and the only NASCAR win on one set of tires.

Thereafter, Daytona was Lund's favorite speedway. "Daytona is the Super Bowl of

NASCAR," says Early. "Winning the 1963 Daytona 500 was Tiny's most important accomplishment and how he did it was a Cinderella story."

Lund proved he could be a super speedway winner, but his real love was the dirt track. He preferred Fords and Camaros, but was happy to race in anything. Although he never got a long-term sponsor, he drove whenever he could, sometimes picking up rides when he arrived at a track. "He didn't really prepare for a race," says Early. "He went to the track and stayed on 'ready.' If a car was 'ready,' too, he'd jump in it and drive."

On August 17, 1975, Tiny Lund was killed in a violent accident at Talladega in which he suffered severe chest injuries.

CHAPTER 31

Charlie Glotzbach: "Chargin' Charlie"

"Chargin'" Charlie Glotzbach spent four decades in Grand National and Winston Cup racing. Known for his aggressive hotdoggin' style, he helped bring Chrysler products to the forefront of public attention.

During his career, he hard-charged through one hundred twenty-four NASCAR races, finishing in the top ten in 50 of them. Of those, he placed five times in the top five in twelve super speedway races. For a time, he was Cotton Owens' number one driver.

Glotzbach also played an instrumental part in the creation of the aerodynamic Dodge Charger Daytona through his work as a test driver.

(A special thank you to Ryan Owens for his contributions to this interview.)

Bob Myers of the *Charlotte News* once said, "If all Rebels and Yankees got along as well as Cotton Owens and Charlie Glotzbach, there would never have been a Civil War, unless it was run with stock cars." Known for "telling it like it is," Glotzback's opinions may have held him back at times, but many appreciated the honest, hard-driving young man.

At five years old, Glotzbach was already seeking out rides. Born in rural Indiana, he lived near a guy named Maynard Beard, who had peach and apple orchards. "As a kid, I would sneak off and go to Maynard's and he'd let me drive his tractor. Since I wasn't big enough to sit down on the seat, I had to sit on the transmission housing. That allowed me to push the clutch in and I'd pull a wagon through the orchards so the workers could load baskets on it. When I went home, I'd get my tail kicked, but that was where I learned how to drive.

"When I was older, I rode a bicycle twenty miles delivering papers. I made eight dollars a week, and when I was ten, I decided to buy a Whizzer motorbike. It had a rod thrown out of the motor, but I bought it for seven dollars and fixed it. I was too young to have a license, but I rode it around on dirt roads. Later, I sold the Whizzer and bought a Cushman motor scooter. I was always interested in cars so when I was about twelve, I took the scooter, sold it, and bought an old '34 Ford for fifty dollars. The engine was stuck and wouldn't turn over so I took the sparkplugs out, put fuel down in it and every day I'd go out and rock it. Finally, it broke loose. I still didn't have a driver's license, so I drove it up and down our long driveway. When my parents were gone, I'd take it out on the road.

There was a state cop who lived near us and someone always told him I had the car out. He'd tell my parents and I'd get grounded. I was always mechanically inclined and that's where the racing started. I'd drag race on River Road almost every night."

Glotzbach soon fell under the influence of NASCAR driver Art Binkley, who lived nearby. "I liked fast cars and I went with Art to some races. I went to Martinsville with him, and Asheville-Weaverville. During a race at Asheville-Weaverville, the track became so dusty on the backstretch, drivers couldn't see. A bunch of cars piled up and Art was in the middle of it. He stayed in the hospital three or four days and Larry Frank and I helped get his car fixed and tow it home. Later, he helped me get into racing. When I was sixteen, I had a '50 Plymouth and began running sportsman. My first race was in 1956 at the Jeffersonville, Indiana Sportsdome."

Glotzbach acquired a reputation for hot-footing the throttle, but also for his skill and by 1960, he was ready to try the southern stock car circuit. Persuading friends and relatives to help him, he spent 1960 and 1961 running NASCAR. After a lackluster attempt with a shortage of funds, he returned to the Indiana local tracks and ran an earth-moving business. Glotzbach spent the next five years honing his skills, then in 1967 shot into NASCAR like a bullet. Preferring super speedways to short tracks, he earned his nickname, "Chargin' Charlie," in 1967 while working for the K&K Insurance Dodge, racing a two-year-old backup car. Glotzbach shocked everyone by qualifying the car at 175 miles per hour. Shortly afterwards, he drove the same car in the Atlanta 500 and came in fourth. That year, he placed in the top five three times in nine races.

In 1968, Glotzbach's most memorable race occurred at the Charlotte National 500, which also included such greats as Bobbie and Donnie Allison, Paul Goldsmith, Pete Hamilton, Cale Yarborough, Buddy Baker, Bobby Isaac and David Pearson. Pearson and Issac were fierce rivals in Final Point Standings and the race was a major fight in their war for the championship. Glotzbach, who at that time had never won a major NASCAR event, qualified on the pole. The race was postponed for a week due to rain, but when it was finally run, it was a nail-biting thriller.

At the drop of the starter flag, Glotzbach sped down the straightaway wide open. Within seconds, the track was a battlefield. Never wavering, Glotzbach stayed in the top ten, lap after lap, finally cutting off frontrunner Pearson. The two dueled to the end, swapping positions, until Glotzbach gunned his car beneath the checkered flag and won. The other drivers and the fans were stunned. He continued to astound the racing community for a span of five years.

According to Cotton Owens, "Glotzbach became a legend oldtimers still remember with reverence and he deserves a place on the list of drivers who made stock car history. His record includes twelve pole positions and four victories. He placed second eight times, and also had five thirds, eighteen fourths and three fifths. That's thirty-eight finishes in the top five."

After 1972, Glotzbach backed off from NASCAR, working with Hoss Ellington from 1973 through 1976 and driving occasionally for Dick Bahre in 1981. He drove some for Junie Donlavey in 1992.

"I raced forty years," he says today, "from '56 into the early nineties. I liked the bigger tracks better than the small tracks and I ran as hard as I could." Glotzbach claims he may be out of NASCAR, but he's never really quit driving. He collects classic cars and runs in vintage and celebrity races. Glotzbach lives in Sellersburg, Indiana and is a member of the Old Timers' Club and Over the Hill Gang.

CHAPTER 32

Jim Bray:
Determined Canadian

Jim Bray was one of the first Canadian drivers to run Grand National and the second Canadian driver to run the Daytona 500. Drivers' most exciting moments are usually when they win, but Bray's joy was in the process. "I liked Grand National on the big tracks better than anything and was thrilled to just start, especially the Daytona 500."

According to Rex White, "Jim Bray's desire to race was humongous. His ability to get off from work in Canada on Friday, tow his car to South Carolina or Virginia, get in late with no one to help him, race, and then turn around in his still dirty clothes in time to return to work on Monday was phenomenal. It was nothing for Jim to travel two thousand miles and he did it for pure enjoyment. He loved racing and his willpower was strong. It had to be. He did all of his work himself without the equipment to win. Once his car was so beat up after a race, he couldn't tow it. My crew and I repaired it so he could pull it back home."

In looking back, Bray says traveling was hard, but not his biggest obstacle. His most difficult ongoing challenge was his frame of mind. "My Dad used to tell me I'd spin out, blow an engine, pop my tires, wreck and have nothing. My worst problem was thinking I couldn't succeed combined with my typical Canadian reserve. I was afraid to put everything I had into racing for fear of financial failure and jeopardizing my family."

Bray was born and raised in the suburbs of Toronto where his dad, a trucking company owner, took him to races on weekends. "In the forties, he and I went to sprint and midget races, and later we went to see stock cars. When people asked me what I wanted to be when I grew up, I told them a trucker or racecar driver, although there weren't many racers around. Drivers who were professional had to go to Indianapolis, but since half of them were dead in three years, stock cars made more sense to me.

"After going into the trucking business, I bought a racecar and began running races at Pinecrest Speedway. In 1952, I saw my first NASCAR Grand National short track event, held at the Canadian National Exhibition in Toronto. Jim Reed led most of the race, but his spindle broke and Lee Petty won."

Fueled by the excitement, Bray raced NASCAR that year. "I continued into 1953, but when I started a family, I stopped. I didn't run often in '54, and not at all in '55, but in 1956, I won my first two races, running in the rain, at Pinecrest." Located north of Toronto, the track was considered upscale because spectators could watch the cars from a covered grandstand.

By the late fifties, Bray had three children, and a consistent racing schedule was impossible. "In 1957, I went to the Grand National in Toronto again and helped Reds Cagle and his brother Hoss as a volunteer in the pits. Rex White was leading the race but, in the last lap, Jim Reed spun him and crossed the finish line first. Hearing the angry fans, Reed ran into the press box and grabbed the microphone. He said he didn't mean to spin White and didn't want a riot and insisted White take the win.

"Afterwards, Hoss Cagle said he wanted to introduce me to a real race driver and took me to meet White. He said, 'Here's a guy who weighs 132 pounds with 125 of it in his right foot.'"

In 1958, Bray quit the trucking business and became a car salesman, and his interest in racing intensified. When he learned there would be another Grand National race at Toronto, he decided to look up Cotton Owens. He also thought about White and wanted to see him. During the race, Owens drove a Pontiac and White drove a Chevrolet. Lee and Richard Petty were also in the race, which was Richard's inaugural Grand National.

According to Bray, "It was raining when the race started and Rex was leading but spun. Lee won by forcing Richard into the fence, to keep Cotton, who came in second, from passing him." The incident left Bray dumbfounded.

"After the race, I said to Lee, 'You were a little rough on your kid, weren't you?' He replied, 'If he's going to be a racecar driver, he's going to have to learn to stay out of the way.' I said, 'A win at any cost, spinning your own son in his first race.' Lee gave me a funny look and then turned away. That night, I got a chance to be with Rex and we talked for hours.

"In 1959, I heard Rex was racing in Trenton, New Jersey and went there to find him. Cotton said, 'Rex isn't here. He cut the top off his '59 Chevy and is running convertible.' Since Cotton only had one guy helping him, I served as his jackman. He placed second, due to a broken return spring in his throttle, and Tom Pistone won."

That fall, Bray took his family to Darlington for the Southern 500. "We arrived several days early and watched a driver practicing. Surprisingly, that driver was Rex. His was the first Grand National car I saw on the track. A driver named Len Page needed help so I worked in the pits while he raced.

"In 1960, I spent a lot of time with Rex in Daytona and, in 1962 I tried to buy one of his cars. Instead, he guided me to a 1960 Ford. In March, I took the Ford to Atlanta, but the race was rained out. Because a Canadian couldn't import a used car and I had to go back to work, I towed the Ford up to Richmond and left it at Emanuel Zervakis' shop.

"The next Atlanta race was also rained out. I finally ran the car in the Eastern Late Model Division and everything played out in sixes. I drove a '60 Ford, ran three of the six races, came in sixth in each of them and was sixth in points.

"The first of April, NASCAR ran a race on a half-mile dirt track in Richmond and since my car was already there, I decided to drive. This time when it rained, track officials wouldn't give up, finally beginning the race at 6:00 p.m. I'd never had a lap of Grand National practice and was running on a track I'd never seen that was covered in water. Worried I'd be in the way, I ran too low and the car bogged down in the mud between the third and fourth turns. I couldn't go forward and couldn't get out and Larry Frank

(Left to right) **Rex White, Bobby Johns and Jim Bray at the Living Legends of Auto Racing Annual Banquet. Jim Bray was one of the first Canadian drivers to run Grand National and the second Canadian driver to run the Daytona 500. Drivers' most exciting moments are usually when they win, but Bray's joy was in the process. "I liked Grand National on the big tracks better than anything and was thrilled to just start, especially the Daytona 500."**

sideswiped me. Scared I'd be killed, a bunch of fans jumped over the fence and pushed me out. I placed 13th and received a hundred dollars. Rex White won the race.

"Since I'd needed tires before the race, Rex had sold me a hundred dollar set of recaps on credit. After the race, when I tried to pay him, he refused the money. He said, 'You didn't make any money. You only took in a hundred and you want to give that to me?' I finally insisted he take it, but I'll never forget the experience. Rex White is that kind of guy."

In those days, drivers sometimes drove all night to get to a race. In September, Bray ran at New Oxford, Pennsylvania on a Saturday night and then drove to Richmond to race the next day. After qualifying, he was so exhausted he fell asleep in the line-up, where he was awakened by the start of the engines.

In late 1962, Bray took his car to Buffalo, New York where he left it until he hauled it to Daytona to run Sportsman-Modified. "I qualified second in Sportsman and thirtieth overall, at 144.3 mph with three-year-old tires. But, I had a problem. I'd taken my fan off when I qualified and forgotten to put it back on. The car got so hot in the line-up, it never cooled. After that discouraging experience, I sold it."

In spite of the tremendous effort required, Bray's attraction to racing continued. "My dream was to run a Rex White and Louie Clements racecar. In 1963, I bought Rex's gold and white Chevrolet from his 1962 super speedway win. I ran it in NASCAR, in USAC at the Indianapolis Fairgrounds, at Langhorne, Pennsylvania, and in a couple of MARC [now ARCA] races. In January of 1964, I towed it to Riverside, but the scorers lost track of my laps and, twice, I ran out of gas. I had a MOOG chassis parts sign on my car and was their first Grand National sponsorship.

"After the race, NASCAR called and asked if I'd race in Daytona. I said that the car was worn out and I was broke, but they guaranteed seven hundred and twenty-five dollars to start and I took the car.

"In Daytona, I discovered the car's front spindles and hubs were both cracked. Bill France told Ray Fox I needed two front corners from his last year's Chevrolet and sent me down to his shop. None of the parts fit properly but they got me through inspection and qualifying, and I ran a few laps. After the race, I towed the car to Rex's garage in Spartanburg and sold it. J.T. Putney won 'Rookie of the Year' in it several months later.

"In 1965, I drove from Canada to Daytona where I met Shorty Johns. Since his son Bobby had a Ford ride, he'd brought their Pontiac from Miami without a driver. I helped him get it through inspection and agreed to drive for him. Before qualifying, someone left the radiator cap loose and the engine got hot. I qualified and ran in the 500, but because of engine problems, again, only made a few laps. I didn't race again until 1973 when I ran Winston Cup. My last Cup race was at Dover in '74."

In 1990, Bray saw the man who'd bought his old Ford and purchased its remains. "Eventually, I'll restore it as an original 1960 Grand National. Its first race was the first World 600, so it has history." In 1999, Bray bought a CASCAR car to tour tracks in Canada. "I still have it, and I'm still racing it."

Bray and Rex White were destined by fate to be friends, despite the distance between them. The proof is as follows:

In the early days of racing, few drivers had gold cars. "When I started racing," says Bray, "my car was black, but I painted it gold. A while after I met Rex, both of our cars were gold." Their friendship just passed its golden anniversary.

In 1979, White was in the trucking business and Bray drove to California on a business trip. "I was following behind a car transporter along a road in New Mexico when I thought back twenty years past to when Rex won the championship. I looked across the interstate and there he was. We were both thousands of miles from home and passed each other."

At the time when White's daughter Brenda died, Bray coincidentally came down from Canada. When he arrived at the funeral, Rex looked at him and said, 'I didn't know how but I knew you would be here. I told myself, Jim will show up.'

"During a business trip in 1990," says Bray, "I was traveling an interstate in West Virginia, when the driver of a truck I passed blew his horn. When the driver kept blowing and blowing, I thought I had a problem. I slowed down so he could get beside me and it was Rex."

Bray still drives thousands of miles to see races and to see Rex. They talk about old tracks, old cars, and old times, into the night.

CHAPTER 33

David Pearson:
The Cunning Silver Fox

Considered by many to be the greatest driver who ever lived, David Pearson was known for his driving skills, ability to "read his competitors," his focus, and his racing strategy. As cunning as a fox, Pearson has won the highest percentage of races started in history, usually through careful pacing followed by hard charging at the end. With 105 NASCAR wins and three championship titles, he has been named one of the Top Fifty Drivers in NASCAR history. Pearson has 113 career poles and 64 wins on super speedways, and was Rookie of the Year. He still holds the record for the most wins and poles at Darlington. In 1969, he was the first to break the Daytona 190 mph speed barrier. He was Winston Cup Champion in 1966, 1968, and 1969.

Pearson and Richard Petty "owned" the super speedways in the seventies, and their battles were the fiercest in NASCAR. Fans knew the two would take first and second place and often bet on who would place third. They were thrilled by Pearson's mastery of the "slingshot pass" and the Petty-Pearson rivalry.

Pearson eventually drove for Ray Fox, Cotton Owens, Dodge, Holman-Moody, and the Wood brothers. Because he is a private person who avoids the media and self-promotion, little has been written about his life. The following is from a rare 2006 interview.

It's been said, "David Pearson didn't drive a car, he wore it. He knew its capabilities and its limitations, when to pace and when to charge." Pearson could be a poster child for NASCAR and in many ways his experiences represent those of the sport itself, paralleling its humble beginnings and its burgeoning popularity. Born in Whitney, South Carolina, in 1934, Pearson was destined to be a great driver. He grew up in the heart of racing country near Spartanburg, an area deeply entrenched in its moonshining roots.

Pearson became hooked on racing as a youngster when, attracted by the noise at the track at Spartanburg Fairgrounds, he climbed a tree to see what was happening. "I'd always been interested in cars, and I decided right then, that was what I wanted to do with my life.

"As a teenager, I worked with my brother in a body shop. I didn't make but forty or fifty dollars a week and the first car I bought was a wrecked Ford coach. I gave thirty dol-

(Left to right) David Pearson, Rex White and Charles "Slick" Owens at J.B. Day's Raymond Parks Birthday Party in Easley, South Carolina, June 5, 2005. Pearson could be a poster child for NASCAR and in many ways his experiences represent those of the sport itself, paralleling its humble beginnings and its burgeoning popularity.

lars for it, chopped the fenders off and made a little ol' street rod out of it. There was a pasture down below our house where I jumped gullies and turned it over. My Mom told me if I'd get rid of it she'd give me fifty dollars. When she gave me the money, I took the car to the junkyard and sold it for twenty-two dollars. I made a profit right then and there, turned around and got something else. I'd do anything to make a dollar to get an old car to work on. At one time, there were eight or nine racing teams out of Spartanburg and I used to hang around all of them to see what mechanics and drivers were doing."

One of Pearson's favorite spots was Crawford Clements' shop. "Crawford and his brother Louie were good to me. I asked questions about what made a car push and what made it loose and they explained how to do different things to make a car faster."

In 1952, Pearson ran dirt tracks in a '40 Ford, starting in an outlaw race and winning thirteen dollars. As his winning streak continued, he attracted the attention of the racing community, including Spartanburg promoter Joe Littlejohn.

Pearson wanted to run late models, but a good running car was expensive. In 1960, he bought a '59 Chevrolet from Jack Smith and began running Grand National, but the car had been run on dirt and needed constant repair.

In 1961, Littlejohn was at the Charlotte World 600 when he learned that Ray Fox had come without a driver. He instantly thought of Pearson and recommended he drive Fox's car. As Pearson tells it, he went to Charlotte, tested the car and ran well. "Ray Fox asked me how it felt. I told him I didn't know how it was supposed to feel. I'd never run that fast in my life!"

Pearson and the car were a perfect match but the race was filled with famous competitors. "All the hot dogs were running, so during the race I told myself, 'If they can do it, I can do it. This car doesn't know who's driving it... me or the other guys.'"

Pearson ran well until almost the end. "I was about seven laps ahead when I had a flat and thought surely I'd lost, but, after turn four, I saw the flagman. I said, 'I ain't going to stop now,' ran the last lap on three wheels and won. It was my time and the good Lord was with me. That was my most memorable moment in racing and I'm proud of it. This little hillbilly boy had never accomplished anything, except on the dirt tracks. Winning the Charlotte World 600... was something else.

"After the race, Fox asked if I would run the Daytona Firecracker 250. I said 'Yeah' and went on to win that. Then, I ran the Atlanta Dixie 400 for him and won that. No one had won three super speedway races in a year, so I was set. I ran a few more times with Ray before he quit racing and then drove for Cotton Owens. In 1966, we won the Championship.

"In 1967 I went with Ford's Holman-Moody and won championships in '68 and '69. In 1969, we were testing in California, when Ford pulled out of racing. We went out to eat and when we came back, we were told to load up. I started driving for the Wood brothers and stayed with them almost until I retired."

According to Rex White, Pearson patterned his style after Fireball Roberts and Joe Weatherly. "He's still eager to win and a force to be reckoned with. A few years ago, I saw David at the Piedmont Fairgrounds in Spartanburg, where fans had a race and reunion. Forced into the wall the previous year, he was itching to get even and had spent months preparing his car. He tore out in front of everyone and zoomed into first."

Although he says he doesn't have a favorite, Pearson is fond of the track at the Fairgrounds. "The hardest track for me to get around was probably Martinsville. At the time, I didn't have a short track car and the harder I tried, the worse I got. When I'd relax, I'd start passing but if I ran well, I'd push faster and slow down again. I was lucky to win one race there. I won at Darlington and I won often at Charlotte and Michigan. It didn't really matter where I went. All of the tracks were good when I won."

Smart as the fox for which he's nicknamed, Pearson's strategy was using his head. "It was a faking thing. I had to outsmart other guys and show them what I could do. If I could beat a guy coming through the corner, I didn't let him know it and I'd figure out where he could beat me and adjust my car. I'd let him run faster and then at the end, I'd run wide open. Since I was quicker, I ran ahead of him.

"Racing's something I always wanted to do and if you want to do something bad enough, you can do it. When I ran, we didn't have power steering and we had little spoilers. Leonard Wood says I ought to try one of the new cars. He says they don't bounce or wiggle like they did at Daytona in the old days where even going through the dog legs, cars became loose. Today's cars have so much down pressure you can hold them wide open and sit on them.

"In the old days, we had to figure things out, work on our cars and do everything. Now that it's easier, lots of guys don't know what to say to their pit crew. They complain their car's pushing or loose and let the mechanic figure it out. Some drivers can *only* tell if it's pushing or loose. One day when a driver said his car was pushing, I asked if he could spin it out. When he said yes, I told him if he could spin it out, it wasn't too tight and to drive it to the point he couldn't. They don't do things like we used to and they know a lot less.

"Racing was real good to me," adds Pearson. "I didn't make the money they're making now, but a dollar was worth more than today and I made a good living. If I had it to do over again, I wouldn't change a thing and I can't grumble one bit."

Pearson was known as "The Silver Fox" because of his cunning and premature gray hair. He was also known as "Little David, the Giant Killer," because he defeated big-name Goliaths.

CHAPTER 34

Ronnie "Papa" Sanders: Master of Short Tracks

Ronnie Sanders' racing history is impressive. He has won more than 500 races, ten track championships and the 1982 Winston Racing Series, Southeast Region. In 2005, Sanders won the Thomas Concrete World Crown 200 at the Peach State Speedway. He is still running as this is written and still winning races.

Sanders began racing in 1967. In the four decades since, he has seen firsthand how the sport has changed.

"I'm happy with what I've done, but I would have liked to have been in a really competitive Winston Cup car, at least one time, well funded, with a good professional crew."

Sanders first became interested in racing as a young boy. "My uncle, J. R. Stinchcomb, used to get me from school to take me to the Peach Bowl and Lakewood. Atlanta Raceway opened when I was about sixteen years old. David Pearson was my hero, because he wasn't out for show, he was a racer.

"I decided to race in 1959, while helping a neighbor with his '37 Plymouth, but I didn't have an opportunity until I could build my own car. When I finally bought my first one, I ended up taking it to the racetrack and selling it."

Starting on a small track in Senoia, Georgia, Sanders began with a "run 'til I spun" racing strategy and it usually occurred on the track's third turn. "My wife Bobbie fussed every time I spun out, so I told her if she thought she could do any better, to try it!"

Her husband's biggest fan and greatest supporter, Bobbie Sanders is known to be a woman of strength. She's *had* to be in order to survive in a field as demanding as racing. "It's been rough," says Bobbie, "and wives can get burned out. It was really hard when the kids were little, but it's not as bad now they're grown. Ronnie's mother always told me, 'I'll keep the kids, you go with Ronnie.' I've had a lot of long nights but I learned to take it one day at a time and say, 'This, too, shall pass.' We have met a lot of great people and have become friends with many of them. All in all it has been a great life and a lot of fun.

"Ronnie, and racing, have come a long way from racing on dirt. I remember one track we went to in his early days was in a cow pasture. Another track would not let him run because his car had a quick change rear end and they were not allowed in the highest class at that track. We stayed and watched the race and, halfway through, Ronnie leaned over

Southeastern Winston Racing Series Champion Ronnie Sanders began racing in 1967. One of the most fierce and respected personalities in the southeast, he has raced over 30 years and seen firsthand how the sport has changed. (Courtesy Ronnie Sanders Photo Collection.)

and said to me, 'Sure glad they did not let me run.' The drivers were a little wild, to say the least. When he raced for the first time at Middle Georgia Raceway in Byron, Georgia, on asphalt, he fell in love with that track and that was the end of his dirt career. I much prefer his racing on asphalt."

According to Ronnie, strength is important for wives and a necessity for drivers. It's the most important physical trait a race driver can have. Another important trait is focus; before a race, a driver must be mentally prepared. For him, that includes having a close relationship with God. He believes God can perform miracles, both on and off the track. Once during a race at Daytona, Sanders was going down the straightaway wide open when the car in front of him spun. Just as he was about to barrel into the driver's side, the wind caught the car and lifted it upwards in time for him to pass beneath it before it came down.

Another night, after winning a race at Huntsville Motor Speedway, he prayed with Raceway Ministries Chaplain Eddie Barton and was saved. It was a major event, changing him forever and affecting every part of his life. He now attends Raceway Ministry Bible Study on Wednesday mornings at Atlanta Motor Speedway and is a member of Fellowship Baptist Church. Since his involvement, he's been more at peace and more focused, because the two go hand in hand.

"When I arrive at a track I try to stay calm and concentrate on the car, getting everything like it should be and setting the tires. Once the race starts, I concentrate on what the car is doing. If I need to change something, I can do that when I pull in. A part of

Ronnie Sanders with his wife Bobbie. Having raced for more than four decades, Sanders is one of the most well thought of drivers on the circuit.

staying calm is remembering how to breathe. You have to breathe to have stamina and you can't do that if you're tense. You'll be mentally and physically whipped.

"A driver also has to learn his car's limit and drive it just at the edge. Of course, when I started, I didn't do that. I just drove it wide open until I hit something."

In addition, drivers must be on constant safety alert. Two of the biggest problems he's seen on the tracks are lack of respect for other drivers and unsafe tires. Sometimes, drivers who are several laps down won't move so others can pass, and some track rules permit racing on tires that are unsafe.

"Some of the tracks require drivers to buy the track's tires and sometimes the tires are no good. I've run on junk tires when they charged us $120 apiece. For $120, we ought to have a premium tire. I have blistered a tire because they were no good, and the hotter it got, the worse they were. Those tires were usually bought at a low price and sometimes three years old."

Strategy is also important; planning, or the lack of it, can win or lose a race. "One year, when I was running at Mobile, I let a guy go ahead of me because he was running harder than I wanted to run. I could run him down, but I couldn't pass him. I began to think I'd made a mistake, but it worked out in the end when his tire went out and he spun."

Winning marks the end of a race, but not the work. "When a race is over, I think about what I could have done to make it better, mentally making notes for the next time, when I come back. If the car ran well, I try to remember exactly how it was set up. Every time we leave a race, we know how we left it. We put the car on four scales and weigh each wheel. I make a lot of notes, including what shocks and springs we used in it."

Looking back on how racing has changed, Sanders points out three ways: one, it's a big bucks affair; two, drivers race, but know little about their cars; and three, children are being groomed for the sport as early as two. Sanders says young drivers need to learn the mechanics of the car and why it works, not just get in and drive. He also firmly believes children shouldn't be pushed. "There are a lot of kids out there whose mamas and daddies want them to race, want them to be racing stars. Parents need to let kids be kids, not have them racing at five. Let them be kids first. If they want to race when they become teenagers, let them decide."

Having raced for more than four decades, Sanders is one of the most well thought of drivers on the circuit. "Ronnie approaches everything well," says 1960 Winston Cup Champion Rex White. "He rationalizes things before he does them and he's a totally good person. Ronnie Sanders doesn't have a drop of bad blood in him. He came into racing when you had to have money. If he'd had the right equipment and crew, he would have been a Winston Cup Champion."

"My most difficult obstacle has been financial," says Sanders, "but I've never jeopardized my family for racing."

Bobbie agrees. "It's been important for him to make a living for us first and foremost. His family's been his biggest priority, but racing's something he's wanted to do and has enjoyed. We spend money, but don't borrow it. He's never borrowed money to buy a motor or car."

At the beginning of his career, Sanders received most of his financial help from his uncle. Now, in a weird turn of events at age sixty, he has a sponsor. "In the early nineties," says Ronnie, "I sold a car to driver Ronnie Kittle so he could run asphalt, and drove for him some. He went into racing with a guy from South Carolina for a couple of years and when he came back, he offered me a working sponsorship. I maintain his two cars and can drive either one of them. We don't drive alike, but I've learned what he wants and that's helped me. Racing is a very expensive game. He's made us competitive enough to win a little money and that keeps us going."

As well as maintaining a successful professional relationship, the two have become close friends, helping and competing with each other. Sometimes racing the same tracks, they're frequently seen at Peach State (Jefferson, Georgia), Cordele and Pensacola.

The Sanders live in Fayetteville, Georgia, and have two children, Pam and Ricky. Ricky has competed in the NASCAR truck division and currently competes in the ARCA series. Ricky owns a race shop in Stockbridge, Georgia, where he builds pit boxes for race teams and sells race haulers.

CHAPTER 35

Morris Stephenson: Pioneer Racing Reporter-Promoter

Born in Marian, Virginia, Morris Stephenson's racetrack career began with basketball and a set of irresistible influences. His grandfather was editor of the *Marion Democrat* and his best friend was a sportswriter's son.

While still in high school, Stephenson became friends with Dick Thompson, an Emory Henry College journalism student who loved the challenge of facing off on the basketball court. Thompson's father was a sports editor with the *Bristol Herald Courier* and Dick soon became a sports writer for the *Roanoke Times* and covered Martinsville Speedway. Shortly afterward, he was hired as the speedway's full-time publicity director, one of the first in the business. With writing already in his genes, the young Stephenson quickly fell under his friend's influence and followed in his footsteps. He took a job as sports editor in Marion and later in Salem, where he was introduced to the old Starky Speedway. After brief stays in Harrisburg and Danville, he moved to Rocky Mountain, Virginia where he covered racing and general sports, while working part-time in publicity for the Franklin County Speedway and Natural Bridge Speedway, both owned by Whitey Taylor. Together, Thompson and Stephenson were among racing's first pioneers in public relations. In 1992, they combined their talents for *From Dust to Glory*, a highly acclaimed book on Clay Earles' impact on the Martinsville Speedway and southern stock car racing's pioneers.

"Starky was a little community in Roanoke County with a top-notch dirt track. I was covering sports for the *Salem Times Register* in Starky when a man named Tim Sullivan asked if I'd run races in the sports pages. I said yes and began spending time talking with drivers. I didn't worry about keeping up with stats because Tim stayed after the races on Saturday nights, waited for the inspectors to tear down the engines, and brought in the official results on Monday mornings. I worked with him for two years, then went to the *Virginia Leader* newspaper in Harrisburg.

"While I was in Harrisburg, I wrote an article about a driver who was preparing a '63 fastback for Grand National. He convinced me to write about Grand National races because they were getting so popular. I didn't know much and wanted to know more, so I hung out with him." Stephenson's new interest, combined with an endless source of drivers, made for good stories. The next time he changed jobs, he accepted a position covering races in Danville.

Danville was the home of NASCAR's most famous black driver and a hotbed of racial conflict. "One of the first things I did," says Stephenson, "was look for Wendell Scott. When I finally found his shop, it was like nothing I'd seen. Next door to his mom he had a tiny work area where he and his friends worked on his racecar in a one-car garage. There was hardly room to walk and it was hard to find anything.

"When I told Wendell I wanted to do a story about him, he appreciated the offer but warned, 'You may not want to do it now because of racial tension.' I said, 'Wendell, you're racing now. I'm going to report on what happens to you in each race and start with a feature that runs in two parts.'

"The paper had an artist who was really good. I told him to go see Wendell and draw a picture of him to use with the photos I had from the track and his shop. He returned with a great portrait in which Wendell stood in his racing uniform, holding his #34 car, with an air-brushed cloud of dust behind him." The story was well received. "I never heard any complaints and my boss was proud our town had a Grand National driver." Realizing that Scott had insight into the racing community, and wanting to produce more stories, Stephenson came up with a plan.

"I told my boss that Wendell told great stories but couldn't write newspaper articles. I suggested Wendell come in on Mondays after the race and sit down and tell what he'd experienced. He could talk about drivers such as Johnson and Petty and reveal what went on in the infield. My boss thought it was a good idea and said to try it.

"Wendell's articles ran as a weekly column named 'Off Track.' Every Monday Wendell came in and I got everything down verbatim, so it would sound like him. We included the tricks drivers played on each other, freaky things that occurred, disagreements and gossip. While other columnists wrote about Sunday races and big names, we focused on the little guy. The crowning touch was our artist's picture of Wendell.

"Later, I wrote the first national story on Wendell for a stock car racing magazine. A two-parter called 'The Shoestring Stormer,' it was appropriately titled and I wished I'd thought of it.

Over time, Stephenson and the Scott family became close friends and Scott's story of the little guy's struggle caught on, giving fans a view of racing they couldn't get elsewhere.

"In 1967, I left Danville to work for

According to Morris Stephenson, "Racing against each other, drivers were bitter enemies, but the night before the race, they'd be at a bar in a beer joint." (Courtesy Morris Stephenson Photo Collection.)

a weekly called *The Franklin News* in Rocky Mountain. I handled sports and general photography, covering everything from murders to wrecks. I lived in a mobile home park until
I found a house and Wendell and his family often came to visit. Because segregation was
still a big issue and there were no blacks in the trailer park, he'd haul his racecar to the
front of my trailer, but wouldn't get out.

"Wendell had little money and there were few places blacks could stay so he and his
family slept in their tow vehicle. One night when he stopped by on his way to Bristol, I
told him I'd make sandwiches before he left and to come inside. Afterwards, I had a big
upset with the landlord over it.

"Wendell put in a good word for me with the other drivers, and helped me work myself
into their circle. By that time, Dick Thompson was directing public relations for Martinsville Speedway and he helped me too. Back then, racetrack promoters were begging
for fans. I'd tell them I was from the newspaper and needed credentials and a couple of
passes. If I asked for four extra tickets, they'd send ten or fifteen, suggesting I bring my
whole family. They told me to give some to friends and tell them to 'come on down.'

"When I took my father to Bristol to see his first Grand National race, I introduced
him to Fireball Roberts and Joe Weatherly, and he thought that was something. From
that day until he died, he was a big race fan.

"There's always excitement in racing, but it meant more to me than that. I saw the
same people week after week and we formed a strong bond. I loved the drivers, the wives,
the volunteer pit crews, the fans and the whole racing community. They were a tightly
knit bunch and great individuals. In those days, racing was a family-type thing and we
were a family ourselves. Racing against each other, drivers were bitter enemies, but the
night before the race, they'd be at a bar in a beer joint. After practice on Saturdays, most
of the drivers stayed in motels and parties were everywhere. Before we met, my wife went
with a friend to a dance near a track and Cale Yarborough showed up. He turned a lot of
ladies into race fans.

"Since I'm a small guy, two drivers who endeared themselves to me were Rex White
and Tom Pistone. I'm a little taller than Rex and a few inches taller than Tom. Most drivers were either good-sized or powerfully strong. They had to be to control their cars. Many
of them had run liquor and they were tough. There were fights in the pits, the infields
and stands, among fans, between drivers, and between the drivers and fans.

"When I moved to Rocky Mountain there was a fast little three-eighths mile asphalt
track named Callaway Speedway, but called the Franklin County Speedway by locals. A
guy named Squeak McGuire owned it but Whitey Taylor later bought it. He renamed it
Callaway USA but nothing changed. Everybody still calls it Franklin.

"When I first began working at the *Franklin News*, there was no racing coverage. I
asked my editor, 'Do you know how many people go to Franklin County Speedway on a
Saturday night? There are five thousand people up there. We're missing people who would
buy our paper if we carried racing.'" Stephenson talked the editor into it and was soon writing his column again. Combining news from local tracks and drivers with what was going
on with the big boys, he soon turned his attention solely to racing and explored its legacy.

"Aside from the daily newspaper in Roanoke, we were probably the only one in our
end of the state that wrote about racing. People looked down their noses and called it a
redneck sport.

"While I was writing for the paper, I worked in publicity at the Franklin County
Speedway and at a three-eighths mile dirt track called Natural Bridge Speedway, also pur-

chased by Whitey Taylor. My job included writing racing programs, stories and press releases, and taking action shots." Before long, Stephenson was distributing press releases, pictures and articles throughout the state.

"I was having a blast and bringing in extra income. I knew guys such as Harry Gant and Wendell Scott, Richard Petty and Marvin Panch, but I was more attracted to the underdogs because they never had any money. If it hadn't been for the help of the Petty family and some of the factory drivers, people like Wendell would never have raced."

In the sixties and seventies, promoters featured big-name drivers because they brought in hundreds of fans. "Part of my job was persuading drivers to come. Since I knew them, I could talk with them and promoters found we could lure them with 'show money.' The extra dollars guaranteed they would show and the track could advertise them. The ante got bigger and bigger as drivers outdid each other and promoters paid more to get drivers to come than they paid for purse money.

"Once, Wendell and his family drove from Danville, Virginia to Riverside, California to race but his old tow truck broke down and he got there late. The drivers had already qualified and the field had been set. The other drivers went to the track owner and told him they wanted Wendell in the field so he would have money to get back home. They refused to run without Wendell.

"Today, I'm constantly reading about one driver not being able to stand another driver and calling him a name or taking a swipe at him. They truly don't like each other." Years ago, when drivers wrecked, it usually wasn't intentional. "Harry Gant was racing at Franklin County Speedway when his car and another driver's car locked on the fourth turn. They slid down the outside wall and Harry's car burst into flames. He finally escaped without being hurt but it scared the heck out of me."

Stephenson watches young drivers develop and sometimes predicts their success. "The first time I saw Jeff Gordon was in his rookie year. He was probably eighteen or nineteen but looked fourteen to me. My sister was a fan and told me to watch him. I told her Jeff Gordon would never make it as a race driver." Known for his good looks and media savvy, Gordon is now one of the winningest drivers on the NASCAR circuit.

In the old days, drivers weren't as publicity-oriented but most made public appearances and one who loved the attention was Curtis Turner. "During the late sixties, a Ford dealership had a grand opening and Turner was to appear. My friend Harmon was going and said he'd call me when Turner showed up so I could write a story. At ten-thirty, Harmon called and said, 'You're not going to believe this. Curtis Turner has President Lyndon B. Johnson's old limousine and it has bulletproof glass and a whole lot of stuff in it.' When I arrived, I saw the biggest black limousine I'd ever seen. The bumpers had holders for flags, and inside was a fold-out bar and a mobile phone."

Fascinated with the phone, Stephenson pressed Turner to explain how to use it. The proud race driver admitted he didn't really know how it worked, but one should be careful talking to girlfriends. He said the technology wasn't advanced and wives with home phones could eavesdrop. Turner admitted he'd learned that the hard way.

"Turner said he wanted a drink and we agreed, so he opened the bar and filled three glasses half full of whiskey. We drank as he told stories and I took notes. When I got out of the car, I realized I'd had too many. I called my buddy at the newspaper, told him to cover the story and went home and slept. When I returned, they'd brought in a band and Turner was dancing, still going wide open. I found out I couldn't party with Curtis Turner."

CHAPTER 36

Linda Vaughn:
Elegant Entrepreneur

Linda Vaughn made a life-changing decision as a '60s teenager when she entered a beauty contest. When she became Miss Atlanta International Raceway, a new world opened. Seizing the opportunities the position offered, she became a successful business-woman. A natural politician and publicist, she charged upward and through the glass ceiling of a male-dominated sport while most women were wrestling with issues of liberation. For years the only female allowed in the pits, she became one of the most active, well-traveled, and recognizable figures in motorsports.

According to Atlanta Motor Speedway president Ed Clark, "Linda Vaughn can work a room better than any United States president. I've seen her go into a room of three hundred people and leave in thirty minutes, having spent time with each of them and having made every one of them feel special."

As 1961 Miss Atlanta International Raceway, Vaughn made a flamboyant entrance onto the speedway and into fans' hearts. A gorgeous blue-eyed blonde who was a dental hygienist by trade, her first title was Miss Georgia Poultry. Later, she entered Miss Atlanta International Raceway and took the contest by storm, becoming a familiar figure at race-tracks all over the country. Dressed in custom-made costumes, lovingly sewn by her mother, she dazzled everyone she met with her vibrant good looks and warm personality.

Raised in Dalton, Georgia, Vaughn is the daughter of Mae, an accomplished seam-stress, and Seabe, a former sheet-metal worker (famous for his liquor stills), who was the son of a sheriff. Her track queen title took her far from her roots and put her on a path-way to fame.

"I thought I was hot stuff," says Vaughn today. "I became addicted to racing and it's in my blood. When my year's reign was ending, Fireball Roberts suggested I enter the Miss Firebird contest. I was Miss Firebird for three years. The pay was twenty-five dol-lars a day and back then that was good. I traveled and signed autographs along with Richard Petty."

Spectators went wild each time she appeared. Dressed in a costume with sparkling red sequins, she balanced atop a huge red phoenix with its wings spread open and back, waving to fans as she circled the speedway on a trailer pulled by a convertible.

According to Atlanta Motor Speedway President Ed Clark, "Linda Vaughn can work a room better than any United States president. I've seen her go into a room of three hundred people and leave in thirty minutes, having spent time with each of them and having made every one of them feel special." (Courtesy Linda Vaughn.)

"I love people and the fans were great. The most fun I had was the reception I received as I came down the straightaway. It was thrilling to hear people yell out my name and sometimes they ran beside me."

Drivers also sought her attention and often pulled pranks to get it. While staying at a motel, she left her room to find her sports car propped on its end against the wall. Later, she learned it had been pulled to the second floor but taken down at Fireball's insistence.

Funny things were always happening to Vaughn. Once, when she was riding on the Firebird around the Darlington track, one of its wings collapsed. Managing to hold on and keep her balance, she just kept waving.

When the time came to replace Miss Firebird, Vaughn quickly sought another contest. In 1966, *Hot Rod Magazine* coordinated a national search for a spokesperson for the Hurst Company's floor-mounted gear-shifting products. A perfect candidate, Vaughn was chosen Miss Hurst Golden Shifter over two hundred other contestants. This time she wowed fans by wearing a clinging gold jumpsuit while on a standing perch on the back of a gold Oldsmobile or Pontiac convertible fitted with a replica of an eight-foot Hurst shifter.

While she was being pulled around the Darlington track in the Oldsmobile, the system holding the shifter broke. Terrified, she held on for dear life, but waved as it fell, going down with it into the back of the car. "It was like the time at Daytona when my bra strap broke. I kept waving and went on with the show. My mother was driving the pace-car that day, and luckily had a safety pin."

Showmanship came naturally to Vaughn, but behind the scenes her glamorous role was demanding. Known for her hard work and energy, she made over one hundred annual appearances.

The "Sweetheart of NASCAR," Vaughn was also a member of the Hurst Armed Forces Exhibition Team, appearing at military installations and hospitals and touring Vietnam. She received the highest award of her career from Bob Hope at a SEMA show for her contribution to the armed services.

"I have a Ph.D. in racing," says Vaughn. "I got my own education, inquiring about everything from media coverage to auto parts. I surprised people in the industry because I turned it into a business and my desire to work showed. It was a long process with a lot of hard work, but racing's my love and my passion. Racing opened up travel opportunities for me and I was able to see the world. Sometimes I was the only female passenger on the plane. I've had fans come to see me in Australia."

Vaughn, who never forgets a name, enthralls crowds with show-stopping good looks and a natural charm. Graciously pausing when asked to sign autographs, she networks easily with fans and motorsports executives, proving beauty can come with brains.

In the sixties, Vaughn was an irresistible and refreshing sight on the racing scene. Unlike most beauty queens, she approached each new opportunity as an adventure and a stepping stone. When the media began highlighting motorsports, she hosted ESPN's *World of Speed* and made movie appearances in *The Gumball Rally* and *Stoker Ace*. She taught herself public relations and marketing skills. By 1983, Hurst had promoted Vaughn to vice president of public relations and she credits George Hurst and Jack Duffy for her success. "I'm thankful to them for believing in me."

A high achiever by nature, she admires others who attain their goals. "I admire Richard Petty, Bill France, Jr., Wally Parks, George Hurst, and all of the people who made racing history." She also admires the cars. One of her favorites is the popular 1957 Chevrolet. "I received my first real kiss in a '57 Chevrolet. I look at that Chevy today after all those years, and there's still a price for that car." It has looks and still holds its value.

"It's a classic," says Vaughn, "and that's how I would like to be remembered."

CHAPTER 37

Harry Gant: "Mr. September"

Harry Gant was the oldest racecar driver to win a NASCAR Winston Cup race, having started the circuit at age thirty-nine. He won 19 races in 475 starts and finished second in the series in 1984. He was in the top ten eight times, and in 1985 he won the International Race of Champions title. His astounding success earned him a place as one of NASCAR's Top Fifty Drivers. He was the National Motorsports Press Association Driver of the Year in 1991 and was inducted into the Charlotte Motor Speedway Court of Legends in 1995. Gant was modest and hard- working, and popular with drivers and fans. He was nicknamed "Handsome Harry" for his movie star good looks, and "Mr. September" after winning four successive September 1991 NASCAR races at Darlington, Richmond, Dover Downs and Martinsville. Gant retired from Winston Cup in 1994, then briefly competed in NASCAR's truck series and substituted for the injured Bill Elliott. His enduring popularity and media appeal have enabled him to continue to be involved in racing as a Skoal Tobacco spokesperson.

Gant was born in Taylorsville, North Carolina, where his Dad, JC, challenged locals to back road races. By the time he was in his early teens, Gant owned a hot rod and a Model A and was following in his Dad's tire tracks.

"None of us were mechanics. All we did was build houses and farm. The main thing my parents taught me was work, work and work. They said, 'If you build something, don't throw it together. If you do something, do it right.' One day when I was twelve, my Dad and I were hauling lumber and I got aggravated because the work was so hard. He said, 'You've got people with easy jobs and people with hard jobs. If everybody's job was easy, we wouldn't have one.' Our motto was 'Do what you have to do and enjoy it, whether it's shoveling a ditch, digging a hole or cutting down trees.'

"When I was a child, the thing to do was to gang up and go to Grandma's for Sunday dinner. I had a bunch of uncles who had old Plymouths, Dodges, Fords and Chevrolets and they'd drag them up and down the dirt roads to see who was fastest. Everybody raced around Taylorsville and I grew up around it.

"Our neighbor, Lawrence Poole, had a li'l ol' '40 Ford coupe, painted red-orange and numbered seventy-seven. He'd go to the crossroads in front of my house and work on it at the filling station, and then try it out on the highway and circle back to his house. I numbered my car seventy-seven, when I started racing.

"My Dad was a Lee Petty fan and always bought Oldsmobiles. He hung out with the younger guys who drove Fords and Chevrolets and when they'd argue about which one was quickest, he'd challenge them. He bought a Super 88 in 1955 when they first came out. Every morning, when he drove his carpenter crew to work in Statesville, he tried to find a Ford or Chevrolet to race. Those Oldsmobiles were fast but I stayed with Chevrolets. I liked their simple engine and they were winning races. When I raced Sportsman I could buy a short block assembly for only three or four hundred dollars. I'd put in Corvette rods, cut the clearance, put a cam in it and race."

Taylorsville was surrounded by short tracks, but Gant didn't see a big race until he was fifteen. "When a group of guys from town bought a twenty-seat booth on the Darlington backstretch, my Dad decided to go. The race was on Labor Day, which was a school day, but since he had an extra ticket, he asked if I'd ride along. Fireball Roberts sat on the pole and won in a 1957 Chevrolet. After the race, he signed autographs and we went down to look at his car. I kept going to Darlington every year afterwards until I started racing.

"When I was older, I bought a 1957 Chevrolet. My Dad had a '57 Oldsmobile with three carburetors and we'd wash our cars together. After he finished washing his, he'd take off the breather and challenge me to a race. There were churches below our house and we'd drag between them.

"I started racing professionally when I was twenty-four; ran two races in 1964 and won the 1965 Hickory Championship. Because I won the championship, I was promoted to Sportsman and, in 1966, I began running late models. I ran Hickory, Kingsport, Nashville and Maryville and, a lot of times, went to Savannah. I'd race on Wednesday night, Thursday night, Friday night, Saturday night, and Sunday and then come home at daylight on Monday morning to work on houses. Everybody who helped me had a full time job but we could pop our car out in forty hours, go to the track and race it. One year we ran ninety-two races with only one racecar.

"After I started racing, people asked if I'd drive their cars. I'd get out the record book and see how much money they'd won. Since I'd only get ten percent, I decided I could make more money in Sportsman than in Winston Cup. I averaged more races a year, but I could make a hundred fifty thousand dollars.

"In 1969, I received a paper saying I was running second to Red Farmer in Final Point Standings. I thought if I traveled more I could catch him, but I didn't. We were running Firestone tires for the Gene White Company and, in those days, drivers who were top finishers on Firestone tires got a bonus of ten thousand dollars. It was three times what NASCAR paid for second place so that's what we did. I expected a check from Firestone at the end of the year, but I waited and waited and never received it. Finally, Firestone sent out a book on their payouts and I saw where the guys who'd run third and fourth had already received theirs. I called the Gene White Company in Atlanta and they told me to call Humpy Wheeler. I was then told to go to his office in Charlotte. When I arrived, Little Bud Moore was talking to Humpy so I waited on them for an hour. Finally, Humpy came out and said 'Come on, let's go eat.' I sat at the table eating, scared to say anything. When we were finished, I pulled out a paper showing my races with my Firestone finishes. They'd mixed up my name, but I got the check and that kept me racing.

"After twelve years, I began driving for other car owners. Driving for a team meant listening to what other people said and I found that hard. I had an engineer before I quit racing but I didn't like to talk to him. I'd come in mad because the car wasn't handling right and he'd have a hundred questions. When I wanted to jump out and change some-

Harry Gant is among the most famous race drivers, but his real love is the land. Bonded to the soil, he finds peace away from the crowds at his farm in Taylorsville, North Carolina.

thing, I couldn't, and it took me a long time to get over it. I think a reason why the young guys do well now is because they listen. Old guys have trouble listening but the new guys don't.

"Today racing blows my mind. For example, the Busch cars. Drivers only run twenty or thirty races yet they have thirty or forty people working on four or five racecars. After I retired from Winston Cup, I ran Sportsman again. I'd pull the car into the garage, pop the sheet metal up, bolt it and keep on truckin.' Now, it takes them forever. They put the body on in one place and paint it another place. It doesn't make any difference because they're just going to tear it to pieces.

"When I raced, drivers could get extra bounty money. Fans got bored when a driver beat everybody on the same track too many times so promoters offered a bounty to winners from other tracks to come and beat him. The promoter at Hickory sometimes offered five hundred dollars to beat a driver who was on a winning streak. But Hickory had a steadfast rule. A driver couldn't win the bounty if he took another guy out."

Once when Gant won six races at Hickory, a guy in Tennessee called and told him Jack Ingram had won six at Coburn. He offered Gant bounty money to come up and beat him because Ingram was hurting attendance.

"I accepted his offer and won the race. That made seven in a row. It was easy running so I went back the next week. We won, but we backed into it as something happened to the guy in the lead. The next week, we went back again. A South Carolina driver, Butch Lindsey, was leading the race when Jimmy Hensley decided to lap him and accidentally caught the back of his car. Butch shot across the track and came down on my hood. I sped into the third turn with his car still there. The motor was boogying down so I slammed on the brakes. The car slid off and I went on around. My air cleaner was mashed down flat on the carburetor but somehow I won. After the race, since luck was going our way, we went back again. We were running third in the last lap when Jack and Butch went into a turn and got together and their wheels went up in the air. Butch's springs flew out from under his car and Jack's car busted a tire. Ten races in a row were the best we'd done, but the guy was so tired of us, we made it our last."

Another of Gant's wreck-wrenching wins occurred at Martinsville. "I won my second Winston Cup race at Martinsville with the car torn all to pieces. I was leading the race when Rusty Wallace went up in a corner and got down on the inside, spun out and turned me around. As I was sliding, a car came by and clipped my front end, knocking me back around. Then, somebody came right into my nose. I ended up with a half-round play in the steering wheel and the grill knocked out. I don't remember if I lost a lap, but I backed up and took off down the track and into pit row. The pit crew jerked out the sheet metal and since I couldn't see over the hood they stomped it down. I was so mad I couldn't stand it and kept going out and coming back in. I told the crew a ball joint was bent but they said there wasn't time to fix it and to go on. The car had awfully good brakes and a really low gear. Down the straightaway, I could run behind somebody and when they'd go to the left, I'd put my brake on, drop down and take off. When I'd hug the curve and keep going, I passed everybody. At Martinsville, if you back off a little bit, you can go faster, so when I got to fifth place, I took it easy and won."

According to Gant, his most difficult, and most memorable, race was in a Busch car at Darlington. "The throttle stuck wide open going into the third turn and I almost couldn't switch it off. You can't lift your arm up easily when you go around curves. I flipped the switch off and cut down to the inside, then switched it back on to get out of the way. When I did, the second car went by me, so I left it on to go down the straightaway. I switched it off at the pits but was going too fast to turn in, so I switched it back on. Then I saw the leader and I thought if I switched the throttle on and off, I could catch up to him. I switched that throttle off and on and caught up, and switched it off and on until I won. When I drove to the Winner's Circle, the throttle stuck fast to the floor. Darlington was my favorite track because power wasn't the object and I always knew I'd do well, if I didn't hit the wall or wreck."

Gant's family was supportive, but dubious, of their son's racing career. "My Mom says the reason I didn't get hurt bad in racing was because she was praying for me all the time. She went to three races in her life. I was running a Hobby car at Hickory when my uncle and his wife came down and they all decided to watch me. At first my mother refused to go but they kept at her until she agreed. I was driving a '53 Plymouth and, going into the first turn, the wheel came off. The car flipped seven or eight times and my helmet flew out the window and my arm flopped outside. I just ended up with a sprain, but she said she was never going back to a race again, and she didn't, until 1981 in Martinsville. I drove the Skoal car and won in the first Winston Cup race there. She went to Charlotte in October and I won again, but that was her last.

"My Dad didn't act like he cared about my racing professionally but from the day I started until the day he died, I think he liked it. I'd build houses all day and spend time in the garage all night. He'd come in, see the car wrecked, watch us fix it, and say, 'Well, you got it torn up over the weekend, didn't you? If you'd work this much building houses, you'd make twice as much money.' He gradually got adjusted to it and, when we started winning races, he came every night."

CHAPTER 38

Robert Arthur "Bobby" Allison: Leader of the "Alabama Gang"

Bobby Allison was voted NASCAR's Most Popular Driver six times and named by NASCAR as one of their Top Fifty Drivers. He was NASCAR Modified Special Champion in 1962 and 1963 and NASCAR Modified Champion in 1964 and 1965, and in 1983 he won the Winston Cup Championship. He ranks fourth in the number of Winston Cup poles. Of his eighty-five Winston Cup wins, fifty were on super speedways and one was in a Mustang. He was a five-time runner-up in Final Point Standings. Allison was known as the leader of the "Alabama Gang," a group which included his brother Donnie, his son Davey, Red Farmer and Neil Bonnett, who became one of his best friends.

Allison has been inducted into the North Carolina Auto Racing Hall of Fame; Alabama Racing Hall of Fame; Living Legends of Auto Racing; Alabama Sports Hall of Fame; International Motorsports Hall of Fame; the Motorsports Hall of Fame; the Florida Sports Hall of Fame, and the U.S. Racing Hall of Fame.

"Racing has taught me there is opportunity for all people," says Allison, "regardless of their personality, their class or their shape. Anybody who wants to work hard can find their niche somewhere, as a mechanic, a crewman or driver."

Born in Miami, Florida, in 1937, Bobby was one of ten children. "My Dad was a service station and garage equipment installer, and, with ten kids, my Mom worked full time at home, twenty-three and a half hours a day. We are Catholic and I had a good Christian background and teaching. My Dad's motto was 'Always do the best you can, regardless of what happened yesterday,' and he insisted on an honest day's work for an honest day's pay.

"I was a little kid, around nine, when my grandfather, Arthur Patton, took me to the Opa Locka Speedway. At that time, the track had paved straightaways and dirt corners and I was impressed. I really got into stock cars and by the time I was fourteen, I'd made up my mind I wanted to race."

Bobby was seventeen and a senior in high school when Hialeah Speedway was built. The track was 1/3 mile and paved and he spent weekends there watching the races. Not long after the track was completed, race officials decided to form an amateur division. The only rules:

1. Drivers had to have a complete stock car automobile.
2. The car had to be equipped with a seat belt.
3. There had to be straps around the doors
4. Competitors must wear helmets.

Almost anyone could enter and no roll bars were required. Anxious to race, Bobby used shoe polish to paint a number on his '38 Chevy school car and drove to the track. "The first week, there were about thirty cars and I finished seventh. The second week, there were forty cars and I finished seventh again. The third week, there must have been fifty cars and I won the race." Convinced he was on the right track, literally, he decided he'd found his career. "Racing got my attention because it involved mechanical engineering, technology and preparation. It was a great big interesting picture from what I could see."

Born with natural driving ability, one of the things Bobby quickly developed was a feel for his car. "The first person who helped me was a guy named Roy Armstrong. He was an older racer from back in the thirties. He taught me how to handle and adjust my racecar, and how to set it up for different tracks. Each racetrack had a different personality and I got a big thrill from figuring out the best groove. I zeroed in on it and, if it moved, I could find it."

After Bobby got out of high school, a relative helped him get a job in Wisconsin, working for Mercury outboard motor magnate Karl Kiekhaefer. As a part of his job, Bobby tested speedboats and worked on cars for the Kiekhaefer racing team, including those of Buck Baker, Speedy Thompson, and Herb Thomas. After a year, he returned to Miami where he took a job sweeping floors in Bobby and Shorty Johns' garage. "In the beginning, Bobby Johns was the driver I admired the most. He and his Dad ran a little sportsman car, and although they had no big financial sponsorship, they raced against teams who had more money to win. Bobby taught me not to worry about someone else having a car that was bigger or fancier and I learned to take what I had, get the most out of it, and do the best I could."

In the late fifties, Bobby decided to expand his racing territory. He began by exploring the speedways of Alabama. He instantly fell in love with the state and he and his brother Donnie decided to move there. Bobby soon became known as the leader of the "Alabama Gang." The "Gang" took racing by storm and was perceived as a speedway threat throughout the country. "In south Florida," says Bobby, "the purses were so poor it was pitiful. I still had to keep my job as a mechanic, even when I raced well. When I went to Alabama, I found the purses were big."

Unlike some drivers, Bobby seemed to exist on adrenaline, functioning well without sleep in spite of his grueling schedule. "My racing strategy was working hard and getting my car in shape. I kept myself in good physical condition but I didn't worry about getting rest. Sometimes, I'd race on a Saturday night and go straight to a win on Sunday."

Unfazed by the demands of the racing circuit, his biggest obstacle was keeping a sponsor. "I drove for lots of different race teams, but I never had total support. I think it may have had something to do with my personality."

Bobby was a fierce competitor who was involved in many driver feuds. One of the most famous racetrack fights in history occurred during the 1979 Daytona 500, which was the first complete televised race. On the last lap, Bobby's brother Donnie was battling with Cale Yarborough when each bumped the other and Cale's car pushed Donnie's into the

"Racing has taught me there is opportunity for all people," says Bobby Allison, "regardless of their personality, their class or their shape. Anybody who wants to work hard can find their niche somewhere, as a mechanic, a crewman or driver." Allison is shown here with Appalachian State University racing historian Suzanne Wise. (Courtesy Suzanne Wise Photo Collection.)

wall. Both drifted down into the infield and when Bobby got the checkered flag, he stopped to examine the damage. Cale saw Bobby stop, went up to his car, saw his window netting was down and hit him with his helmet. Within seconds, both drivers were in a brawl. Fans were thrilled by the sight of a fight and a race on the same program, and NASCAR interest soared.

Always retaining his sense of humor, Bobby later said that Cale used his nose to hit his (Bobby's) fist. "One thing racing has taught me," he says today, "is to control my emotions."

Bobby won his first Grand National race in 1966 in a Chevelle he built. In 1967, he drove a Holman-Moody '67 Ford Fairlane to a 500-mile Grand National win at Rockingham and from then on the rest is history. "When I won at Rockingham, Fred Lorenzen was crew chief but Ralph Moody was in the pits and ran the operation. He became my biggest hero because he was the brains behind Holman-Moody."

The win was as a turning point in Bobby's career. "All of a sudden, I could win and make more money than I could in my job."

In looking back, Bobby says two of his most formidable rivals were his brother Donnie and Richard Petty. "Richard was my fiercest competitor, week in and week out. I struggled on dirt but he was one of the few drivers who was good on dirt and pavement. He was good on road courses, too."

Bobby's most thrilling moments were his first 500-mile win at Rockingham and his wins during the 1988 Daytona Speedweek. In a spectacular series of events, he won the Daytona 500 qualifying race on Thursday and the Goody's 300 NASCAR Busch Series Grand National Division on Saturday before zooming to a Daytona 500 victory on Sunday. Davey came in right after him, marking the only father-son first and second finish in Daytona 500 history. Sadly, it was to be Bobby's last Winston Cup win. Later that year he suffered massive head trauma in a wreck at Pocono, ending his racing career.

In the early nineties, unable to drive due to neurological problems, Bobby became a car owner. From 1990–1996 he sponsored numerous drivers, including Hut Stricklin and Jimmy Spencer. In 1992, his son Clifford died in a racecar crash and Davey was later killed in a helicopter accident. The Allison family's recovery from these devastating events was a horrific struggle.

Today, Bobby credits his wife Judy, his strong Catholic faith, and his father's words as having given him strength. With Judy by his side, he continues to work hard and do his best as his father taught him. "I've had some really good days and I've had some tragic days. I'm thankful I've made it and for the people who've helped me. Judy and I have battled with so many tragedies, but she has done a great job in helping me get through them. I've had a great career and the Lord has been good to me."

CHAPTER 39

Dave Marcis:
The Wingtip Wizard

Dave Marcis' racing career has encompassed five decades during which he amassed five Winston Cup victories, ninety-three top five finishes, two hundred twenty-one top ten finishes, and fourteen pole positions. He placed second in Winston Cup Final Point Standings in 1975, finished two seasons in top five in Final Point Standings and finished six seasons in the top ten Final Point Standings. He started in 881 Winston Cup events and holds the record for the most consecutive starts, at 32, and most total starts at 33, in the Daytona 500.

Marcis, who was easily identified by his trademark Goodyear caps and wingtip shoes, serves as primary test driver for the IROC (International Raceway of Champions) series, and has taken in over seven million dollars in career earnings. He has raced more miles than any other driver in Winston Cup events at Talladega, Daytona, and Michigan, and is a member of the Darlington Record Club: 1972 AMC Matador/1976 Dodge. He is the 2001 winner of the Buddy Shuman Award.

"We have done so much with so little for so long that we can now do anything with nothing." The words on this sign, which hung in Dave Marcis' shop during his racing years, symbolize the extent to which Marcis' dedication, determination and hard work have made him successful.

"My love for racing began when I was a child," says Marcis, "hanging around my father's garage and wrecking yard. I've been monkeying with cars since I was six years old." Raised on a farm in Wisconsin, Marcis was always tinkering with cars and machinery. When his parents weren't home, the farm and his father's business became his playground. "I have a sister, Toni, and a brother, Donnie. When my father was gone from his wrecking yard, my brother and I would hotwire old cars and tear around the fields. We tore the heck out of those cars, rolling them over. It probably should have killed us, but we got a big bang out of it. Later, when a friend did grading work at a racetrack, I'd go with him and we'd tear around the track in his street car.

"When I was fifteen, I was cutting up cars, taking the gas tanks off, and dumping the gas left in them into a can to use for my road car. I spilled a lot of gas on my pants and my boots. I waited an hour until they felt dry, then, thinking there wasn't a problem,

In the past, drivers frequently gave advice and assistance to one another, and Marcis says that is a way in which racing has changed. (Courtesy Dave Marcis Photo Collection.)

continued my work. When I cut a bolt, it popped loose and fell down in my shoe. I was wearing engineering boots and the leather was thick and still wet with gas. They went up in flames and caught my socks and pants on fire. I jerked my pants down but couldn't get them off because of the boots."

All of the skin on his legs was burned and Marcis spent a year out of school getting skin grafts. "When I turned sixteen, I'd missed so much and was so far behind, I quit. That didn't go well with my mom, but by then I had my own wrecking yard where I cut up junk cars and sold them for scrap."

Marcis had become a young businessman, but his life hadn't settled down. "One day I went with friends to another wrecking yard to pick up a car. The guy who ran it had a log-jammer truck with a boom on it. The car didn't have a rear end in it and the idea was for the truck driver to pick up the car and set it down on the truck's platform, while my friend Herbie Kurth sat in it and steered. As the car was being lifted, the cable on the truck slipped and the clutch got hot. The car flew up and hit the boom and the truck's driver released it. When he did, the car went hurtling down to the ground with Herbie jumping out as the dust was flying.

"When I was seventeen, I went to my first race at State Park Speedway in Rib Mountain, Wisconsin. I'd heard there'd been racing before World War II, but when the war broke out, racing ended. In the fifties, some of the fellows who'd raced wanted to start again, so they put an ad in the newspaper saying they were starting a racing club. Anyone who was interested was to meet at the bowling alley.

"The membership fee was a hundred bucks. That was quite a bit in those days, but I didn't have to pay all at once and those who joined that night could pick their car number. The club used the money to rent a racetrack from Otto Holtz."

As soon as the club took over the track, Marcis pulled an old '49 Ford from the wrecking yard. "My Mom didn't want me racing so she wouldn't let my Dad help. Since I was forbidden to work on my car in his garage and there were no race shops in the area, I relied on my farm repair and welding experience. I took the front fenders off, but was afraid to cut a wire for fear the car wouldn't run so I finally loosened them, rolled them into a ball, tied them and hung them on the firewall; then, I took out the headlights." Marcis welded old pieces of black pipe to the frame to make roll bars, used an old lap belt to make a seat belt and took off for the dirt track.

"My only link to racing was *Hot Rod Magazine*, so I read articles about Richard Petty, David Pearson, Rex White, and Ned Jarrett. I got to know some of the older guys at the track, but there was a whole crop of us young guys coming along, full of piss and vinegar. We began with one race a week; then another place opened a dirt track and we had two. Another guy opened a blacktop track and our racing started to grow." Within a short time, Marcis was running seven times a week.

"The older guys knew more, had money to get better parts and were buying trick stuff out of California, but my car cornered better. When I didn't have chores to do, I was always working on my car, getting parts from the wrecking yard, and I could beat them because it handled well.

"In those days, we just had one shock and racing was all about chassis. I monkeyed with the springs and made sway bars out of drive shafts from old Fords and Nashes. The Nash had smaller drive shaft tubes and solid shafts and I could heat them and bend them to put on the front of my car. The first ones I made bent when I went into corners, but then my Dad took an interest and gave me a hand. He knew about heat-treating so he taught me how to dip them in oil, how hot to make them, how long to dip them, and how to make them turn colors. Finally, I was able to make a sway bar that stayed put and I taught myself to build wheels from trial and error. I continued to run locally in Wisconsin, learning lessons about roll bars and the importance of having a harness, after several wrecks.

"As time went on, I got rid of the Ford, built a '52 Studebaker, and moved up to a '57 Chevy. I won twelve thousand dollars in three months, running the Chevy with one set of tires. Those tires were so hard they almost threw sparks. It had a 327 cubic inch engine and, during the season, all I had to do was take it apart, clean it, fit the bearings, do a valve job and put rings in it. Once I started racing, I didn't have a regular job and a friend named Geno Hartjes helped me. After a race, we'd go home and tear the engine apart and put a new set of rings in it, and then be ready to race the next day."

Marcis was a wizard at car building and everything about racing appealed to him. "I liked the noise, the people I met in the grandstands, the smell of Castrol, the taste of Martinsville hot dogs and really good barbecue. In the old days, we'd all have a few beers after the race and the fans were there too. I met my wife Helen, who was a school teacher, at a racetrack in Tomahawk, Wisconsin. She had a cousin who raced and her mother was a big fan. At the end of the race, we'd all go up to the beer stand to wait to get paid. Helen always brought her mother, who was in a wheelchair, to see the drivers."

In 1965, Marcis competed in ninety-two events in three months and won fifty-two first places. "Up north, the fastest cars started in the back, but we got paid to race and for time trials. We made ten or fifteen dollars for that. The promoters usually gave a trophy for the 'Fast Dash,' but when we won the heat and the feature, we made a hundred twenty-five bucks a night, and that was a hundred twenty-five dollars seven times a week."

"When I went to NASCAR, I bought a car from a fellow after seeing his ad in *National Speed Sport News*. Elvin Perry, who lived in Louisville, Kentucky, had a '64 Ford being driven by Charlie Glotzbach. He told me it was originally a Holman-Moody car, used by Fred Lorenzen. I bought the car, rebuilt it, and took it to the IMCA race at the Minnesota State Fair on Labor Day weekend." Despite a lack of money and old recapped tires, Marcis ran well. "I placed second in the 300 lapper and, the next day, when they held the 500, I pulled in third."

There were good times, but there were also disappointments. "For instance, when my car was running well and I thought I could win, something would happen or break. During a race at Hickory, there was a rule drivers could only make one pit stop and had to do it before the 150th lap. In those days, guys were playing tricks with their tires and taping over the numbers. We could run Goodyear T-16 or T-70 and the T-16 was a little softer. That night, I had T-70s, which were the hard tires and I won the pole. When the qualifying ended, the cars lined up to start and Dale Inman came over to me. He asked how long I thought I could run on my 'gum balls.' I told him I didn't have 'gum balls,' but he didn't believe me so I pulled off the tape. That night, I lapped the field and on the 149th lap, I stopped to pit. When I drove back on the track, a breather line on the rear housing broke and all of the grease ran out."

In 1967, deciding he wanted to continue to race for a living, Marcis headed south. "The southern people were as helpful as the people in the north. If someone had a car and I needed a part, they'd loan it to me and there were always people to help in the pits who didn't get paid. My strategy was to stay out of trouble and to keep up with Richard Petty and David Pearson, because they were always up front. When I went to my first race in Charlotte, I didn't get through inspection so I went back home, fixed everything on the car and went to the Cracker 250 in Atlanta, Georgia that fall. It was the first NASCAR race I ran and James Hylton won. In 1968, I went to Daytona to run ARCA with my '66 Chevelle. On my way, I broke the connecting rod in my truck in Bowling Green, Kentucky. All I had were racing tools and I had to fix it in a rest area parking lot. I took the oil pan off, unbolted the rod from the crank and used a torch to unstick the piston. I couldn't pull the rod out, so I cut it off, hoping the piston would stay. I then took the torch and cut off the other end of the rod. Using the part of the rod that clamped around the crank-shaft, I taped it all with duct tape, bolted the rod back on, added STP and dumped the used oil back into it.

"I drove from Bowling Green to Daytona at twenty-five miles per hour. The truck was vibrating so hard I could barely hold onto the steering wheel and by the time I got there, the tape was gummy and the oil pressure almost to zero. Smokey Yunick let me repair my truck at night in the parking lot by his garage, running a drop cord out of his building so I had light. I worked at the racetrack by day and the parking lot at night."

Although he performed well, the next years were a struggle as Marcis established himself as an independent. Then, midway through the 1974 season, NASCAR pulled away from big block engines. Nord Krauskopf of K&K insurance was sponsoring a Dodge with a Chrysler Hemi driven by Bobby Isaac with Harry Hyde as his crew chief. When the Hemi cylinder head was banned, Krauskopf became miffed with NASCAR and parked his cars for the rest of the year. Later, as the '75 season approached, he decided to send

Hyde to talk with Marcis about testing the small block. He asked if Marcis would drive it at Charlotte and Rockingham so they could decide whether to race the following year. He said if they did, they wanted Marcis as their driver. Marcis quickly hired Dick Trickle to drive his car in Charlotte and Rockingham so as not to lose his points and accepted Hyde's offer.

At Charlotte, Marcis didn't finish due to a blown engine, but Trickle came in eighth. At Rockingham, Marcis' small block blew again and Trickle finished in Marcis's car. Two depressing months followed before Krauskopf hired Marcis, but in 1975, he won his first Winston Cup race in a K&K car. At the end of the 1976 season, Krauskopf decided to get out of racing, but Marcis was well on his way to an outstanding career.

In recent years, Marcis has credited racing with having given him a good life and a good education. "I quit school, but racing taught me lessons the hard way. I had to learn self-discipline and I learned a lot about business. I began managing my money and didn't buy things I couldn't afford. I had a lot of respect for what I bought because I worked hard." In the early days, drivers either learned those lessons, or they went broke. They also relied on, and learned from, each other.

When Marcis first started racing, there were no racing shoes and one of his biggest problems was burning his heels on the floor of his car. When David Pearson suggested he buy a pair with leather soles, he bought wingtips and his problem was solved. In the past, drivers frequently gave advice and assistance to each other and Marcis says that is a way in which racing has changed. "Back then, drivers went up and down the roads and shared more accomplishments together. We helped each other when our cars broke down, borrowed parts back and forth, and have stories that go on and on. What's so sad is today's drivers don't have any stories. They take an airplane to get to their racecar and get back into their airplane and leave. How many stories can you make out of that?"

CHAPTER 40

Bob Glidden:
Dragstrip Champion

Bob Glidden is said to have a doctoral degree in determination. Considered a dragstrip icon, Gliddon won ten world championships in sixteen years, including five consecutive titles. He scored eighty-five national event victories. At the time he retired in 1997, Glidden was the winningest driver in National Hot Rod Association history. A dominant competitor, he was aided in his achievements by his wife Etta and sons Billy and Rusty, who served as part of his team. In 2001, Glidden was named as number four on the NHRA All-Time Greatest Drivers List and in 2005, he was inducted into the International Motorsports Hall of Fame in Talladega, Alabama.

One of eight children, Glidden was born in Indiana to a family of sharecroppers. He credits his unrelenting work ethic to his early days of laboring from daylight to dark on the farm. "When I was young, we had to work long, hard hours. We learned to work for what we wanted and, since we didn't have farm equipment, we did almost everything by hand. From the time I was five years old, I was up at four a.m. to help with the dairy cattle. We didn't have much back in those days and I did whatever was needed, which was a little of everything. That was how I became involved in working on engines. One summer, one of our tractors broke down. We couldn't get it into a shop to be worked on so I repaired it myself."

By the time Glidden was a teenager, the family had acquired a television and one of its advertisements caught his eye. "I still remember seeing TV commercials put out for Ed Martin Ford, claiming they had the fastest Fords, because they were involved in drag racing."

A National Honor student in high school, Glidden became fascinated with the mechanics of engine building. "I became so interested, I'd go to the dealership when I had time and hang around the racecars." After high school, Glidden accepted a job with Ed Martin Ford and bought a Ford which he drove during the week and raced on weekends. He worked for the dealership for eleven years and they helped sponsor his first racecars.

"People have raced on the streets forever," says Glidden, "but when I was growing up, drag racing had just become an organized sport. At first it was something I did to have fun and something I enjoyed, but as time passed, it became an opportunity. I realized if

Bob Glidden on the night of his induction into the International Motorsports Hall of Fame at Talladega Super Speedway in 2005.

I was well prepared and good enough, I could make money. Like everything else in life, it's not as simple as it looks, but I found if I practiced every day, it became routine."

When he was nineteen, Glidden met someone as interested in drag racing as he was, and married her. "Etta became very involved. She looked after the financial end and, when she wasn't working in the office, she helped mechanically. For years, she worked as my crew chief and won many awards. Our biggest obstacle was financial, trying to put together enough money to race, but we funded nearly everything ourselves, putting in long hours to have the money."

In the old days, as today, the public associated drag racing with danger, but according to Glidden, when he began racing, it was the tracks, not the cars, that posed the biggest threat. "The condition of the tracks we raced on was the most dangerous aspect. When I started, tracks were very narrow. They weren't nearly as smooth as they are today and guard rails were close. Today, the sanctioning body oversees the tracks and they have concrete walls instead of guard rails and are twice as wide. Updating the tracks was the biggest factor in safety. The cars are also built for safety and there's been improvement in chassis and parts. Accidents occur and people lose their lives, but that happens every day on the streets."

Glidden is a spiritual person who is both religious and superstitious. He always said a prayer before he raced, avoided the color green, stayed away from peanuts at the track and tried to repeat everything as he'd done it before. He says the most crucial lesson he's learned involves commitment. "I've learned the value of dedication in being successful, not just in racing, but in all aspects of my life." This includes his wife and children and he admires and appreciates Etta more than anyone else in the world.

A modest man, Glidden is grateful for his achievements and for his fans. "I've won ten world championships and each one of them was the greatest thing that ever happened to me. Racing has controlled my life and it has been my life but I've been a lucky person. I've come in contact with hundreds of thousands of people and had so many good experiences. I always greet the fans first, because in the end, they are the reason we accomplished what we did and made a living at it. I'm a hillbilly who loves to be around people and I hope they will remember me just as I am."

CHAPTER 41

Bill Chubbuck: Collector, Wrestler, Racer and Fan

If you've never been behind the wheel of a pounding jalopy or a thundering modified, you've missed something important in life. It's a feeling you have to experience and no one can adequately describe. Once experienced, it is never forgotten. I've seen tough, hardened men literally cry with joy at winning a heat race at a local track. They'll relive that moment a thousand times. When they see the big boys take the flag, they say, "I know how he feels," and they do. —Bill Chubbuck

Bill Chubbuck has one of the most extensive NASCAR memorabilia collections in the Carolinas. His collecting fervor is matched by his respect, not only for the sport, but for its pioneers. The sheer amount of Chubbuck's collectables, going back to the forties, requires he maintain two buildings to house them. It's been said, "If it were not for Bill Chubbuck, much of racing's history would be in landfills."

In 1990, Chubbuck formed Racing Relics, Incorporated for the restoration and preservation of racecars and memorabilia. In 1991, he was elected president of the Florida Wrestling Federation, and in 1996 and 1997, he was a Living Legends of Auto Racing honoree. He is also the author of *Coupes and Coaches,* a book that tells of racing's early days.

Chubbuck goes to extremes and it started in his youth. He spent most of his childhood in Massachusetts before moving to Miami as a young adult and he now lives in Waynesville, North Carolina, surrounded by thousands of racing artifacts.

"I can still remember my first trip to the speedway," he says. "In the early fifties, a neighbor named Mr. Moran took several of us tough inner city kids. We lived in a ghetto, but back then, we didn't know it. We just knew our neighborhood was poor and sprinkled with Polish, Irish and Italian immigrants, and oddly, some Egyptians. In that environment, owning a car was something special and using it for anything beyond basic transportation was unheard of. When I asked my parents if I could go to Saturday's race, I knew by the length of time it took for them to talk it over, it was something big. They didn't approve of auto racing and Mr. Moran was known as a brawler. I was told I couldn't

Bill Chubbuck (left) and Marvin Panch. (Courtesy Bill Chubbuck's Racing Relics, Inc.)

go because they didn't have the seventy-five cents I'd need for admission. I proudly showed them a dollar I'd earned and it, coupled with my temper tantrum, had the desired effect.

"Friday night, I lay in bed visualizing the few pictures of racecars I'd seen. The next morning, I ran my paper route and it seemed to take forever. I was slowed by Saturday collections and because I had to find my way back to the newspaper office without getting beaten and robbed by older boys.

"On Saturdays, Mr. Moran worked a half-day and I died a thousand deaths waiting for him to come home." Another long wait ensued as Chubbuck and two other boys waited outside of Mr. Moran's house, ready to go. Finally, they all piled into his car and headed for the track. "When Mr. Moran pointed out a racecar being towed in traffic, I knew we were approaching the promised land. As we got closer, we heard a dull droning. The good Lord and his band of angels couldn't have made sweeter noise.

"As we got out of the car, dust blew up from the parking lot and pits and we could hear a high-pitched roar as engines were revved. We finally got our tickets and walked onto the sacred grounds of the Norwood Arena. The place throbbed with excitement. There were smells of oil, exotic fuel, and burning rubber, and the sounds of straining engines, squealing tires, and screaming fans. It feels like it was only yesterday and I can still picture it.

"The first race was a novice qualifier. During the race, a huge LaSalle slowly rolled over and landed upright. The driver scrambled out and threw his helmet at the driver of a vintage Chevrolet. When the Chevrolet driver jumped out, the fight was on. People from the infield quickly broke it up, but it started again when a group of men rushed out of the pits. The infield crew eventually managed to get it under control.

"The event was a 'move 'em out to pass 'em' kind of race, finally won by a big old Hudson. When it ended, I prepared myself for the heat and then cheered myself hoarse. Eddie Hoyle took an easy win and I rooted for him when I watched the sportsman feature.

"That night, I didn't know I was watching men who'd become some of the biggest drivers in short track racing. When I look at that old program, I see the names of Ralph Moody, Garvin Cooper, Ed Flemke and Fats Caruso. By the end of the race, I was hooked and began planning to build my own racer."

It would be years before Chubbuck's racecar-building dreams would come true. Meanwhile, he hung out at a biker garage and hitchhiked rides to Saturday night shows at the Norwood Arena. Influenced by the roughness of inner city life, he became a member of a street gang. "I had a wild streak influenced by my environment. I was too young to get into serious trouble, but I served as lookout while other boys broke into buildings."

After several arrests, Chubbuck was sent to a boys' correctional school, but his big change came during high school. "By that time, our family had moved out of the inner city and I was involved in basketball, football and track. The football coach took me under his wing, became a part of my life, and straightened me out."

In spite of his many other interests, visions of checkered flags continued to haunt him. "My high school buddy was Don McTavish, 'The Flying Scot.' He became National Sportsman Champion, but later was killed in one of Daytona's worst accidents. In 1955, I built a jalopy at the gas station where I worked after school, forged my parents' name at the track, and was allowed to race as a minor."

Chubbuck still found time for school sports. He became captain of the basketball team and played so well he was offered a scholarship. He accepted and played for Boston University, where he majored in education, although he admits to trying out for the AFL Boston Patriots. Meanwhile, he found a sponsor who bought him a racecar. "'Coffee Shop Al' Russian probably spent seventy-five dollars on it, but for a seventeen-year-old kid in school in 1955, it was a bunch. My friend Bob Staples and I were given a 1947 Plymouth four-door. It was stripped and had a surplus aircraft seat, seatbelts and straps, with a roll bar crudely installed. A five-gallon surplus jerry can was bolted into the front of the trunk.

"We modified the suspension rods (rules required it to be stock, but nobody checked). We also lowered the car by heating the springs, chained the right front down as tight as we could and put a tiny little 15" tire on the left front, with a big 820 × 15 on the right. (We didn't know why we did this. It just seemed like a good idea.) Next, we brushed on a coat of Mobil Red paint and lettered 'Bill' over the doors and 'Mech-stapes' on the rear quarters. We numbered it 10 JR for no apparent reason, then borrowed a station wagon and trailer to tow it and headed for the Westboro Speedway.

"Westboro was a typical New England paved quarter-mile track. As we prepared for warm-ups, I strapped myself in and put on my helmet. I knew immediately I'd bitten off more than I could chew. At the gate, the pit steward held us back while the guy next to me got out of his 1939 Hudson coupe, took off his belt, got back in, and used his belt to tie his door shut. The steward motioned us out and I gave it the gas. The Hudson next to me fell back and as I approached the first turn, I eased up and steered to left, but the Plymouth had a mind of its own and continued straight. I let off the gas and yanked harder. The car lurched left as the old Hudson slid by and cars kept hitting my bumper. Shortly after, I was slammed in the rear. That was the fastest I experienced old 10 JR move.

I got it under control, strictly by luck, and headed into the pits." Despite his lackluster debut, Chubbuck continued to race for the next several years.

While in college, Chubbuck and his brother discovered wrestling. When they found they could earn extra money, they decided to form a tag team. "We were so big, we called ourselves 'The Larde Brothers.'

After graduating from college, Chubbuck temporarily gave up wrestling, accepting a teaching job in Miami. "I taught a variety of subjects, including science and a work program. I also became a dean. Later, I took up wrestling again, as 'The Mountain Man.' It was supposed to be a money maker, but it never turned out to be."

While in Florida, Chubbuck discovered the thrill of collecting racing memorabilia. His collection grew through the following years as he quit teaching and left Miami and moved to St. Petersburg where he started an auto salvage company and to Daytona where he had an auto rental and auto carpet business. "I started saving programs, souvenirs and anything else on racing. I also started racing again in a Mini Stock. In 1981, I suddenly realized I had a tremendous amount of 'junk' people wanted to buy. I didn't want to get involved in selling off individual pieces so during Speedweek in Daytona, I auctioned everything I owned in one day at a Howard Johnson's. At the time, I made pretty good money, but it didn't end my collecting; I felt such a sense of loss, I started again right away."

Motivated by a compulsion he couldn't explain, Chubbuck began buying up others' collections as well. "I bought out Dell Printing, the company that made all the programs for NASCAR from 1948–1962 in Greensboro, and now I probably have the most extensive collection of programs in the world. I once sold a house in Florida for a NASCAR collection, and I have Tim Flock's jacket, a stop watch given from Bill France to Tim Flock, and Marvin Panch's Daytona 500 trophy. I have one of Richard Petty's trophies and a huge aerial view of Daytona from Bill France's office." A lifelong lover of automobiles, Chubbuck has also added them to his collection, "I like unusual cars and have a half dozen, including several Australian UTEs."

In 1990, Chubbuck formed Racing Relics, a corporation for the restoration and preservation of racecars and memorabilia. "During my Daytona auction, I realized I was letting go of a significant amount of racing history and had made a mistake. Since then, I've accumulated a massive amount of memorabilia. The oldtimers are a quickly vanishing breed and I want to do what I can to perpetuate their accomplishments."

CHAPTER 42

The Rev. Frank Stark:
"Will You Win the Real Race?"

I would encourage people to find out where God is at work and join Him there. Much of Jesus' teaching was outside church—on the side of the mountain, at the well, from a boat, in a graveyard, in the dark of the night, under a sycamore tree—even on the cross. Jesus met the needs of people outside the four walls....—Frank Stark

The Rev. Frank Stark is founder of Frank Stark Raceway Ministries, Inc., a non-profit organization whose purpose is to provide an opportunity to worship for race fans at tracks on the NASCAR Nextel and ASA circuits. Its philosophy includes the following: "When we talk of the Great Commission, we usually think of going into all parts of the world. It is just as important to take the gospel of Christ into your world: where you work, where you play, where you take a vacation, etc. Raceway Ministries is another way to share the gospel of Christ with a lost world. Since unsaved people normally do not attend churches in large numbers, we must take the gospel to them where they are. We need to find methods of sharing the Good News that touch them in a secular society and communicate with them in terms they can understand and will listen to."

Stark was chaplain for the Automobile Racing Club of America (ARCA) from 1986 to 1996 and has helped other individuals, churches and associations organize ministries at various events. He also served as a consultant with the Home Mission Board and North American Mission Boards Special Ministries Unit in the area of Raceway, Truck Stop, and Gaming ministries. From 1997 to 2000, he served as a contract worker with the Missouri Baptist Convention as Resort/Special Ministries Consultant. Prior to that, he was a pastor for thirty-three years.

Frank and Betty Stark have devoted their lives to Christian ministry. Their most outstanding contribution has been in their founding and support of Raceway Ministries, Inc. He and Betty are recipients of the Southern Baptist Convention 1988 "Ken Prickett Award for Creative and Innovative Ministries." In 1997, they were honored with a United States House of Representatives tribute by the Honorable Roy Blunt, Congressman from Missouri. Frank has also been honored with the 1981 Life Service Award from Southwest

Baptist University in Bolivar (he is a graduate) and the Interfaith Witness Associate of the Year, from the Missouri Baptist Convention. Stark received the ARCA Spirit Award in 1996. On January 14, 2006, he was inducted into the Ozark Racers Association Pioneer Hall of Fame. He was pastor of the First Baptist Church of Strafford, Missouri for nineteen years and was also involved in truck stop ministry.

Because of the difficulty of drivers, racing officials and fans going to church services on race weekends, Stark brought services to them. He has brought many of them to Christ, changing their lives. Also conducting weddings, he has had a profound influence on those he has met. The Starks began their racetrack ministry in 1982 and retired in 2005.

The Atlanta Motor Speedway gave Stark an award for the 20th anniversary of Raceway Ministries at the Atlanta track and he was guest speaker at the Raceway Ministry tent on Sunday morning. After the service, a man told him he had attended services under the speedway's big oak tree twenty years before, but he was "just an old drunk at that time." Today, he is a Christian and a church member in Florida.

"Frank Stark reminds me of our Lord in Mark 6:34, King James version,"* says Atlanta Motor Speedway chaplain Bill Brannon. "When Frank saw the multitudes at the racetrack and there was no place to worship, he was moved with compassion and provided them with a worship service as he served our shepherd."

Stark was born in Billings, Missouri. When he was fourteen years old, his father took him to the old jalopy dirt races near Rogersville, where cars ran over a hill, down through a hollow and through a ditch filled with water. They also went to the fairgrounds to watch races during the fairs. "Drivers brought in Indy-type cars and ran sprint races. Later, we moved to a town called Greensfield and, in 1960, my brother Charles started racing. After that, we moved to Macks Creek."

Stark's interest in stock car racing was renewed in the mid-sixties when he was pastor at First Baptist Church in Strafford, near Springfield, Missouri. Louis Miller, who was a deacon, managed the Fairgrounds Speedway at the Ozark Empire Fairgrounds. The venue was the site of weekly races, and since his church member was so heavily involved, Stark decided to attend.

In the old days, when races were held, towns teemed with excitement and Springfield was no exception. "You could get in for a dollar," says Stark. "I'm not sure how many people the fairgrounds held, but it was jam-packed every Friday night. At first, drivers raced on either a quarter-mile dirt track or asphalt, but then they moved up to a half-mile.

"Rusty Wallace and Mark Martin have both raced there. Every Friday night, Louis would allow our family to go down to his box and watch the races at the start-finish line. Whenever there was an injury to drivers or crew members and they were hospitalized, I went to visit them."

In 1975, the Starks attended the Daytona 500 race where they thought there was a Sunday service for race fans and planned to participate. "We arrived early that morning and asked where the services were. The security guards looked at us like 'This is a racetrack, not a camp meeting.' They said nothing like that was held for the fans. There was a service inside the NASCAR garage for drivers and crew members, but we couldn't get to it without a pass."

Seeing thousands of people, an overwhelming need, and an opportunity, the Starks

*"And Jesus saw much people, and was moved with compassion toward them, because they were as sheep not having a shepherd: and he began to teach them many things."

Betty and Frank Stark

decided, "Somebody ought to do something," not realizing that the "somebody" would soon be them. "We began seeing the people, not the races," says Stark. "Seeing people is one thing; having compassion for them is something else. We need to see people and what they can become through the grace of God. When we began thinking of a NASCAR event, we began thinking of a city with 80,000–150,000 people. All of the services such as fire and police, ambulances, and hospitals were available. Churches were needed, too. If a city of 80,000–150,000 people had no church, every denomination would send church planters, but because a racetrack is a 'portable city' made up of race fans, the evangelistic opportunity was overlooked.

"Wherever you go, you are in the midst of a mission field and the racetrack is certainly a mission field. Fans may come looking for a drink of water and something to eat, but they can go away having tasted the living water and the bread of life, Jesus Christ.

"In 1981, our youngest daughter, Sandra, attended a Baptist Student Union where a speaker, Ken Prickett, mentioned several potential Southern Baptist projects, including holding worship services at Grand National [now Nextel] races. About two weeks later,

I asked Betty if she was interested in helping. Thinking we would be support people, I got in touch with the Home Mission and they, in turn, put me in touch with someone else, who put me in touch with David Bunch, who put me in touch with other people, who ... finally put me in touch with Ken Prickett. I didn't know Ken Prickett was going to hand us the ball and expect us to run with it. He was a man with visions and dreams and I believe they came from the Lord."

By the early eighties the Starks were using their vacation time to take the "Word of God" to the speedway, particularly at Talladega and Atlanta. They quickly realized the importance of the service they were giving as they suffered with the injured, comforted families with fatalities, witnessed, and drew people to Christ.

Prickett helped the Starks get started in their new endeavor by giving them names of contact people, one of whom was Don Namon, president of Talladega Speedway. "We went down to meet with Don in the spring of 1982," says Stark. "He was enthusiastic and helpful. He said he'd been waiting five years for something like our ministry to come along and told us to return to his office with concrete plans and we'd discuss them. That's how we got started in Talladega.

"We went to 1982's first race and had our first service. We didn't have a tent and had nothing to identify where we were going to meet so when people came by I'd say, 'We are going to have a service over here in a little bit,' and they would ask 'Where?' I said, 'Well, right over there,' and they looked and saw nothing. I told Betty to go 'over there' and stand and hold up her hand so they would know. I told her the next time someone came by and said, 'Where is the service?' I would say, 'See that good-looking young lady right over there? Just go over there. That's where we are going to have our service.' She was the first location for our services. We were near the front stretch, which was a very rough area, so much so that before it was over, they moved everyone out and we moved to turn three." Two years later, the Starks began working with the American Speed Association and in 1985, Stark gave up his position at Strafford and, beginning at Talladega, started Raceway Ministries as a Mission Service Corps volunteer for the ARCA and Grand National circuits.

Stark decided to move from part-time to full-time racing ministry partly because of a commitment he made at an evangelical meeting in Kansas City. The evangelist challenged the audience to break out of their ministry comfort zones and take the gospel to where people are. "This convinced me I should be doing more than I was to serve the Lord and I thought of the things I could do to break out of the comfort zone. I realized I would have to give up my church or the racing end of my ministry. I was in a very comfortable position as pastor of First Baptist Church, Strafford. I had a guaranteed income, health insurance, an annuity and a warm loving church. Walking away from that was quite a challenge." It was especially challenging because as parents of daughters Stephanie, Sara, and Sandra, Frank and Betty were concerned about the needs of their family.

A later evangelistic conference emphasized the unknowns the Starks would face. "The speaker challenged us to commit ourselves to a special service we felt the Lord wanted us to do whether or not we had financial resources or the personnel to do so. To the best of my ability I did this."

Betty recalls it as a scary time because, at an age when many people start to think about retirement, they instead embarked on something new. Frank's commitment meant moving from the security of life as a pastor to freelance missionary work, with racetracks as his mission fields. Fortunately, Betty was able to continue her job as nurse with the

Rex White (left) and Frank Stark

Visiting Nurses Association, and the Greene County Baptist Association employed Frank part-time for special ministries and multi-housing ministry and provided health insurance.

Their ministry soon expanded to include twelve states, and took on many different aspects. In 1986, when severe drought threatened the farmers in the southeastern United States, Frank and his family helped organize a haylift from the Midwestern region of the country, using trucks from race teams to transport the hay.

As he grew older, Stark began putting branch racing ministries in place to carry on after his retirement. "We are grateful now to have tents and buildings where people can worship. We put up a big tent and held services at Talladega for several years. I stayed with them until 1993, when I turned it over to them to do full-time. They have a great ministry there now with four or five locations."

According to Stark, stock car racing is a family sport and, along with rodeos, it is one of the only sports where you can count on having the national anthem and an invocation. It is also a place where the ministry of Christ can reap greater rewards than Point Standings. He loves to tell about a girl who found Christ at the track on her seventeenth birthday, a fan who turned his life around, and a reporter who made a profession of faith after writing an article about Raceway Ministries.

"You never know what God is going to use to reach someone. We have held services in buildings, out in the open and at a bar. At Darlington several years ago, a fellow from Canada attended the services. Sometime during that weekend, someone sang the song 'Where Could I Go But to the Lord.' He went back to Canada and then came back the next year and told people, 'That song haunted me so much all the way home and after I got home, I finally realized the only place I *could* go was to the Lord.' He said he had been saved and had won his entire family to the Lord."

There are many more heart-rending stories, such as one involving a service at Talladega. While in the Raceway Ministries' tent, J.B. Burt of Prattville, Alabama gave an invitation for people to accept Christ as their personal Savior. That morning, although he had "religion," Mark from Arkansas accepted Jesus Christ as *his* personal savior. He had joined three different denominations but had never heard of having a personal relationship with Jesus Christ.

"I think there was more joy in Heaven that morning than from all the race fans," says Stark. "In years to come, Jeff Gordon's trophy will tarnish and people will have to look in the record book to see who the winner was. When Mark accepted Jesus Christ as his Savior, he was given eternal life, and his name was recorded in the Lamb's Book of Life."

Some of his stories concern people you might not want to meet on the street. But, as Stark emphasizes, "God so loved the world that he gave his only begotten son that whosoever believeth in him should not perish. *Whosoever* is a small word, but it's a great word, because it includes everyone who lives and will ever live. *Whosoever* may include some people whom you don't want to include on your prayer list. Today, public enemy number one of the cross of Christ may be the champion of all if we win that individual to the Lord.

"At races, we have Legends cars, Bandoleros, trucks, and the big boys out there in late models. The drivers in those cars haven't worked on them. They haven't touched them. They believe in their crew chiefs and their pit crews, and that those Goodyear tires will hold up. A driver goes into turn number one, trusting his car. People need to come to a point where they can turn loose of everything in this world and put their personal faith and trust in Jesus. I pray people have already settled that, but if not, we'll be glad to help them."

Stark credits the phenomenal growth of Raceway Ministries to the support of local churches. "I tried to involve area pastors and churches in the ministry, which I believe leads to better understanding and communication between the racetrack and the community. Different ministries began to spring up at different tracks so we joined forces. In 1991, we formed the National Fellowship of Raceway Ministries and it has grown over the years. It's all interdenominational and we have services at all of the NASCAR tracks. What makes the organization unique is, each branch is a local group, with several locations for services and different family activities. We usually have forty or fifty people, but the numbers can jump to three hundred. Often, popular drivers attend and there are things for the kids. We may have face painting, pine wood and hot-wheel races, and concerts by singing groups, such as The King Echoes. We give out tracts encouraging people to come into the 'Winner's Circle,' because 'With Christ, You Are a Winner.'

"The most important part of Raceway Ministries is someone simply being there. I believe Christ would have us go outside the church walls and take His message to people who do not come inside the church house. People know we are there whether they come to our services or not. Signs advertise worship services and give testimony that Christian people care. We had almost a thousand conversions through our fellowship of Raceway Ministries last year, and we are grateful. God is alive and well and working at the races, and many other places. I encourage you to discover where God is working... and join him there."

CHAPTER 43

Mike Bell: Living and Breathing Racing History

As official historian and founder of the Georgia Automobile Racing Hall of Fame Association, Mike Bell contributes stories to many online and hard copy publications, including *Pioneer Pages*. Beginning as a freelance journalist, he has researched and written articles for over twenty years. Described as "living and breathing racing history," he fell in love with racing at an early age. Bell spends almost every free waking hour in archives and museums across the southeast, recording interviews with old racing legends and hunting down old tracks and pictures. His primary goal is documenting that which would otherwise be lost.

Unknown to most people, Bell suffers from congenital muscular dystrophy. He struggles to walk with a cane, but has never let his handicap get in his way.

Bell caught racing fever as a teenager going to races in Jacksonville, Florida where he was born. When he was fourteen years old his family moved into a new house and the boy who lived next door became his best friend. All was well except for one puzzling problem. On Saturdays, the boy and his father disappeared. When Mike finally got the courage to ask why, the answer surprised him and changed his life.

"The boy's father was a notorious street rod racer. Every Saturday, they'd go to the track at Speedway Park. I talked my Dad into going and the four us went the next Saturday. I climbed up in the grandstands, fell in love with the hot rods and knew I'd found home.

"The track was later known as Jacksonville Speedway, but at that time M.L. Vaughn was promoter and Pat Patrick leased it from a guy named Bob Matthews. Matthews had bought it in 1954 from Eddie Bland, who originally built it in 1946 from land belonging to the family farm. Matthews owned a lot of racecars and kept the track until 1962 or 1963 when Julian Klien bought it. Klien owned the Model A coupe with a 409 Chevrolet engine that made Leroy Yarbrough famous."

A highlight of Bell's life was watching Yarbrough race. "In 1961, he won thirteen races in a row in Jacksonville. They found a way to bar him for two weeks just to get a new winner, but when he came back, he won again.

"In 1962, my Dad and I were at Daytona when we ran into two gentlemen who were

When he was fourteen years old Mike Bell's family moved into a new house and the boy who lived next door became his best friend. All was well except for one puzzling problem: On Saturdays the boy and his father disappeared. When Mike finally got the courage to ask why, the answer surprised him and changed his life. (Courtesy Eddie Samples Photo Collection.)

building a new racetrack off I-75 in Valdosta, Georgia. They named it the Valdosta "75" Speedway and when it opened, we decided to go. It was like being at a street rod show and I loved those old cars."

The outing whetted Bell's appetite for hands-on experience. "I read *Hot Rod Magazine* and the modifieds, with their mix-matched nose-to-tail homemade parts, really intrigued me. When I was older, I began helping a guy named Wally Dutton with his car. During the day he was a mechanic for the Marietta Bread Company and at night he built racecars. Despite racing superstitions, his car was green with the number thirteen and his Flathead engine was the last Flathead to win a race at Jacksonville Speedway. Jimmy Capps drove it and the only reason he won was because the other cars dropped out. When the checkered flag went down, Capps' car was the only one running.

"Later, I helped Eddie MacDonald in the pits when he ran nearby, at Jacksonville,

Lake City and Valdosta. Nobody got paid back then because drivers couldn't afford it, but I was able to see everything first-hand and I loved listening to Eddie talk about driving and handling a car.

"I did whatever needed to be done and could get you dirty, changing the gears, putting in oil and gas, or wiping the car down. Since Jacksonville was an old dirt track, working there was a mess. The dirt had a lot of sand and wouldn't hold together, so they kept the dust down with motor oil and whatever it stuck to stayed. A lot of guys hated to run there, because they'd have to use gas for clean-up and it would take days.

"At Valdosta, drivers needed brakes but Jacksonville was the type of track that required nerves rather than brakes. Drivers could back off the throttle going into the turn, slow up a bit and keep going. Built like the speedways of long ago, it had two tight straightaways. The back straightaway wall was built with big old timbers in the ground with two-by-tens bolting them together, because on the other side was a street.

"Eventually, the Jacksonville Speedway ran NASCAR and I was there the day Wendell Scott won. Scott was the first African-American driver to win a Grand National. Many great drivers were there, David Pearson, Joe Weatherly, and the Petty team. It was the end of the season and the drivers hadn't rebuilt their cars so they were all old. When we got to the Speedway, Daddy got mad because he heard Maurice Petty had already wrecked one of the Petty Plymouths before qualifying, during the hot laps, crashing into the back straightaway wall. Many of the cars took the lead, then fell out, breaking down before the end of the race.

"The race was two hundred laps and by the time it was over, the track was in really bad shape with rut holes big enough to put a car in. I didn't have any idea who won because the dust and confusion were bad and I'd become bored. The announcer at first said Buck Baker, then two hours later, said the winner was Wendell Scott."

"The funny part was Joe Weatherly had dropped out of the race early and he and Curtis Turner were drinking in the pits. People said there was no alcohol in the pits at NASCAR events, but those guys were drunk. Joe Weatherly wanted the Firestone guy to pay a hundred dollar contingency for Wendell because he'd won while running Firestone tires. The Firestone guy told Joe, 'Yeah, I recapped Wendell's tires, but they had Goodyear carcasses.' He said he wasn't going to give Wendell the hundred dollars because he could see Goodyear on their sidewalls. Joe insisted the Goodyear guy had already given Wendell one hundred dollars even though he had Firestone treads. Finally, Joe, Curtis, David Pearson, and two or three other drivers ganged up on the tire man. By the time it was over, Wendell got contingencies for running Firestone and Goodyear tires, a hundred dollars from both.

"In the mid-seventies, the old Jacksonville Speedway was torn down for a housing project which never materialized. Developers discovered its former owners had used PCB fluids to hold down the dust, the same fluids used as oil baths for electrical transformers. They had, unknowingly, soaked the ground with super-toxins and the land remains uninhabitable today."

Bell's family was originally from Hochston, Georgia. In the early sixties, they traveled back and forth seeing relatives and visiting the speedways. Bell particularly enjoyed the tracks in Winder and Athens where he watched Charlie Burkhalter and Charlie Padgett. The Athens track was a small clay quarter-mile where the action was tight and winning depended on driver skill.

Bell graduated from Auburn University where he received a degree in mechanical engineering. In 1968, he was called to take an army physical, but was quickly turned down. His muscular dystrophy was already taking its toll. "I was told I wouldn't make a day of boot camp, much less the battlefield."

After attempts to find post-graduate courses in the automotive field, Bell settled into a job in Atlanta, Georgia, designing conveyer belts during the week and watching races on weekends. In the early eighties, he became devoted to watching sprint car racing and began driving to tracks in central Pennsylvania. He was at Williams Grove Speedway when he learned they were having an oldtimers' car show and reunion. He met a bunch of old racers, listened to their tales and became fascinated by racing history.

Soon, he was networking with other historians, comparing notes and writing articles. He helped Jerry Massey and other former drivers form the "Alabama Auto Racing Pioneers" in Birmingham in 1994 and, after becoming involved with the Atlanta Peach Bowl Reunion, he and its founder Jack Jackson decided to form a racing club in Georgia.

In March of 1997, a group of enthusiasts met at Gordon Pirkle's Dawsonville Pool Room in Dawsonville, Georgia. In that meeting, the Georgia Automobile Racing Hall of Fame Association was formed and Bell was named president. The organization now has over eight hundred members and continues to grow. Focusing on the preservation of Georgia racing history, GARHOFA has been instrumental in recording interviews related to drivers, tracks, and races in articles and film. Its quarterly *Pioneer Pages* magazine is a prominent periodical of motorsports history.

According to *Pioneer Pages* publication chairman Eddie Samples, "Because of his health problems, Mike Bell lives life on two flat tires, but he never complains. That should shed light on those who spend theirs idling in the pits. The growth of the Georgia Automobile Racing Hall of Fame Association is a testament to his devotion. The spell he has put on the organization will last for years to come."

CHAPTER 44

Mike Sykes: Old Timers' Racing Club Founder

At the mention of Mike Sykes' name, I immediately think of caring and compassion for vintage drivers. Mike has stepped up to help the oldtimers when nobody else has. He is sincere and dedicated to the endeavor. He is a true friend of the vintage racer. —Bill Chubbuck, Racing Relics, Inc

Mike Sykes was born in High Point, North Carolina, where his dad was a carpenter by trade. His dad's nickname was "Peanut," but the family knew him more as a "race nut" because, although he was never a real mechanic, he was constantly at the track. When he arrived at a race he'd earn his way into the pits as a go-fer, going to get parts or jacking up cars as a volunteer. He was willing to help anybody. Bob Welborn and Fireball Roberts were his heroes. Fireball, famous for his all out pedal-to the-metal style was his number one man.

Every time he went to the track, "Peanut" would take his young son Mike along. Since he was too small to be allowed into the pits, Mike, like many other "track kids," would pair up with other young children and sneak in. "I was only about six years old, but I met Fireball Roberts, Herb Thomas, Bill Myers, Jimmy Lee Ryles, Frank Mundy and Buck Baker. That entire bunch was there. Frank Mundy was a high roller in those days. We saw a lot of local guys too and those memories stand out in my mind. If the pit steward caught us, he'd run us off and we'd play in the infield. By the time I was ten, I went to all the races, Charlotte, Bowman Gray, Richmond, Martinsville, all kinds of dirt tracks and asphalt tracks, too."

In 1964, when he was at Charlotte, there was a big mud hole by turn three and Sykes and his friends played in it. They timed the starts and stops of the race by the sounds they heard and when the race started, they climbed on a rock from which they could watch. The cars raced around the track as fast as bullets, the noise so loud the children could hardly think.

All of a sudden the engines wound down and came to a stop and a dead silence fell on the speedway. The children couldn't see what had happened because they were short but the crowd was on its feet at the fence. "We could still hear cars, but we knew something was wrong. When we looked down the backstretch we saw smoke and we took off running. We were headed toward the medical center when I saw my Dad coming through the gate. He looked at me and said, 'Come on boy, we've got to go.' Later, I learned Fireball's car had caught fire and he was burned. My Dad never again went to a race."

Since his father would no longer go, Sykes had no way of attending races, except with his brothers. He found watching from the stands a poor substitute for firsthand experience. After he graduated from high school, he went into the army and served in Vietnam as an infantry soldier; when he was discharged, he had to make a career decision. Since he was still interested in racing, he called Bill Gazaway. "Gazaway had taken a job in NASCAR as competition director. I was working Modified and Late Model Sportsman events and he hired me to work as a Grand National safety inspector in Charlotte."

It was an interesting time for safety development. "A lot of ideas came up. The drivers hadn't started using window nets yet, but the fuel cell had come into play. I worked off and on with NASCAR for seven years."

Although there'd been technical changes, the sport remained largely the same as when he was young. "In those days there wasn't a lot of money, so racing wasn't all business and politics. We saw it as a sport and it was fun. There were practical jokes going on all the time.

"The funniest thing I remember is seeing Tiny Lund, who was huge, pick up Tom Pistone, who was small. He would catch Tom, turn him upside down, hold him by his feet and shake the change out of his pockets. Tom would cuss and Tiny would laugh. Tiny would turn Tom back over, hold him by his side and put the change back in his pocket." The comedy routine was repeated time and time again at the good-hearted Pistone's expense.

Sykes says his spookiest memories are from Talladega. "I always felt strange, when I went there. Some say the track is built on Indian burial grounds. Larry Smith, Tiny Lund and Randy Owens were some of the men who died there. One crewman had his legs cut off and another suffered a heart attack. Bad things were always happening and I was uneasy."

One night in the early seventies, Sykes and other race officials were camped by the garage gate at Talladega when a dozen racecars were sabotaged. "We didn't know whether it was by rice, oatmeal or sugar, but it was a foreign substance. How it was done was a mystery. At that time Johnny Bruner Jr. was a flagman, Johnny Bruner Sr. was chief steward and Mary Bruner signed in the drivers. Johnny Jr. had a motor coach parked right beside the gate. I was camped in a little van and another inspector, Pete Dunbar, was in his Winnebago. We sat outside drinking coffee and beer and watching television until ten or eleven o'clock that night and we could see the garage area from where we sat." Bobby Allison was among the first to find the mess in his car.

The incident led to the use of an electronic track surveillance system. "That was a problem because of the eye beams. Every time a bird flew by, the thing would wake us up. The siren would go off in the middle of the night, but we'd usually find nothing there. Later, they placed deputies in the garage area."

When Sykes divorced and was awarded custody of his children, his track career came to a halt. Although he could take his children to watch, he longed for the excitement of being involved and waited until the children grew older to attend races again.

For years, he was only seen at local tracks, but Marvin Panch, one of the Top Fifty Drivers in NASCAR, invited him to a Daytona race as his guest and he couldn't refuse.

(Left to right) Rex White, Mike Sykes and Marvin Panch enjoy old-time race driver reunions. (Courtesy Mike Sykes Photo Collection.)

Comfortably settled in Panch's motor coach, the two reminisced about the old days for hours, talking about people and races gone by. When Panch told about the Indy oldtimers and their reunions, Sykes started thinking.

"Why doesn't somebody do something for NASCAR drivers?" he asked. When Panch explained that nobody had taken the time, Sykes started thinking again.

"That night, I got to work on it. I got in touch with some local drivers from my area who had run Grand National and called guys from the fifties and sixties. We started hashing things over and decided to form an organization to bring us all together again." Calling the group the Old Timers Racing Club, they invited as many drivers, mechanics, officials and car owners as they could find—anyone who'd been involved and wanted to come. Two-hundred thirty people attended the first banquet and Sykes was stunned. It was as if a family whose members were lost, were united again.

It's now one of the largest groups of its kind in the nation, anyone interested can join and there's no need for qualifications. It doesn't matter how many races, if any, a member has won and there are no status boundaries. Those who only ran locally blend with Final Point Champions and help each other when needs arise.

"Some of the older guys were having a pretty hard time," says Sykes. "They couldn't buy insurance while they were racing and now they have medical hardships. At first, when we heard about problems, we'd just pass the hat."

It wasn't long before Sykes and other members realized there are hundreds of people suffering and expenses are huge. Assisting those who need help became a priority. "Our club is non-profit, and we have established a non-profit hardship fund. When we learn someone is in need, we give them help." The club charges a small membership fee and raises money through the selling of card sets and other endeavors. "We're not in the club to make money but I'm a firm believer we should help those old guys who started NASCAR, risked life and limb and laid its foundation. Their families did without and *they* did without. NASCAR should have set up and maintained a medical hardship fund."

If you would like to join or donate, contact:

> The Old Timers' Racing Club/Racing Legends Foundation
> c/o Mike Sykes
> 119 Northeast Drive
> Archdale, North Carolina 27263

A few of Sykes' Old Timers' Racing Tales

"Jimmie Lewallen once told us he was on his way to a race in Lynchburg, Virginia when they passed a train that had derailed, causing him to detour. When he finally arrived at the track, one of the first people he saw was Bobby Myers. Bobby looked at Jimmie and asked, 'Jimmie, did you see that train down the road?' Jimmie answered 'Yeah, why?' Bobby said 'If you get in my way, I'll spin you out like I did that train!'"

"Fred Harb was running hard at the old Hillsborough Speedway dirt track when he saw where someone had dropped a gas tank in the middle of the track. He grinned and thought 'Oh boy!' as he hit the tank. After another lap, his car quit running and he wondered why. He coasted into the pits and told his crewman he'd just run over a gas tank and put some poor sucker out. By that time, his crew chief Frank Hayworth came over and told him, 'Yeah, that's right.' He'd found Fred's mechanical problem. He was missing his gas tank."

"Wendell Scott was one of racing's first black drivers. Although some saw skin color, most of the other drivers came to like him as he was a friendly, enjoyable man who was, like them, determined to race. Although he had little new equipment and his family usually served as his pit crew, Wendell followed the circuit as best he could. Drivers who had spare parts often shared them with Wendell, who appreciated all he was given. Although he realized his chances of winning were slim, he pursued his dream anyway, never taking his car's position too seriously. A favorite story about him relates to his eating habits. Frequently, when Wendell was racing, he'd take a supper break. He'd stop his car, send his sons for hot dogs, eat them while sitting on the pit wall, and then get back in the race."

Some old-timer tales are true. Others may be racing legends. You have to judge for yourself. In the old days, fans were often too poor to afford a ticket, so they watched racing events from wherever they could. During a highly competitive race, things were down to the wire when the lead cars tangled. One car was hit with so much force; it flew out of the track and hit a tree so hard a fan fell out and onto the ground. According to former driver Johnny Allen, such occurrences were not rare. "A lot of wild stuff went on in the old days. I've known cars to go out of control, over an embankment and into a creek. One landed in a nest of bees."

Drivers were known to risk life and limb to race, but what is less known is how many times they risked their lives for each other. During a race in 1958, driver Bill Morton of Bluff City, Tennessee was seriously injured, pinned under his car, and rendered unconscious when his convertible flipped over several times on the 119th lap at Lakewood Speedway in Atlanta. Fred Harb of High Point, North Carolina, zoomed past in his Mercury, saw the seriousness of the wreck and immediately braked and backed up, positioning his car between Morton's and the oncoming racecars. Another driver, Jim Massey, crashed into the guard rail to avoid plowing into Morton's car.

CHAPTER 45

Betty Carlan:
First Lady of Talladega

Deep in the recesses of the International Motorsports Hall of Fame museum, away from the hustle and bustle of visitors, is a small office manned by a staff of one. Called the McCaig-Welborn International Motorsports Research Library, it contains a treasure trove of racing history from throughout the world. Betty Carlan, popularly known as "Betty at Talladega," is the collection's librarian and historian. An undisputed source of racing knowledge, she has turned her office into a sanctuary for those involved in research—or wanting good conversation.

Surrounded by racing memorabilia, at a desk full of "things to do," Carlan greets those who enter with, "The coffee pot's in the kitchen, make yourself at home." If there's a question, she either knows the answer or how to find it and, like many former teachers, she sets the rules. "It's Talladeeeeeega," she explains, "not Talla-day-gah. You have to pronounce it right when you're in here. It's my pet peeve and I correct everybody."

When asked what brought her to a job in the Hall of Fame library, she says, "Honey... how much time do you have?" A no-holds-barred, get-to-the-point go-getter, Carlan is nobody's fool, nor will she stand for anyone's foolery. There was enough of that going on when she was born.

Carlan was born in Talladega in 1928 to Reba and Gene Landreth. Gene, who had been blind since he was a baby, was teaching at the School for the Blind where he struggled to make ends meet as a band director. Thinking his wife might be having twins, he expressed his concerns about the cost of raising two children to their family doctor. When Betty's mother gave birth, Dr. Washam placed Betty in her father's arms, then took her back and handed her to him again as a second child. Gene was so overwhelmed, he nearly fainted.

Both of Carlan's parents taught Special Education and she followed in their footsteps. She graduated from the University of Alabama, where she played the trumpet in Colonel Carlton K. Butler's famous "Million Dollar Band" and earned Special Education Undergraduate, Masters, and Specialist degrees. "When I went through the Deaf Education program at the University of Alabama, I was the first and I was alone. I was the only one in the class."

Betty Carlan greets those who enter with "The coffee pot's in the kitchen. Make yourself at home." If there's a question, she either knows the answer or how to find it and, like many former teachers, she sets the rules. She's shown here with Rex White.

Betty taught at the School for the Deaf and later at the School for the Blind. Her specialty degrees were rare in those days and she was soon given offers she couldn't refuse. "I moved to Florida where I started a program for the hearing impaired in Brevard County and then agreed to return to Alabama to work with the State Department of Education in Montgomery."

Carlan's passion for teaching was matched by her passion for racing. An avid fan, she was known to frequent Alabama's dirt tracks where she loved the speed and the noise. Also known for thinking outside the box, when she was put in charge of coordinating a driver's training program for high-school-age mentally and physically handicapped youth, her two passions converged. "I had to do something spectacular with the program or I was going to lose my funding. The most spectacular thing in Alabama is the Speedway, so I called and asked to speak with Don Namon, who at that time was the general manager. I told him I wanted to bring five hundred kids to the speedway; I wanted to use the track for free; and I wanted Bobby Allison to talk with them."

Namon, who is also a creative thinker, decided to meet her demands, in exchange for publicity. "I arranged radio, newspaper and TV programs," says Carlan, "and had a proclamation made by the governor."

Soon afterwards, she took his publicity request even farther. Since her job required she drive all over the region, she offered to allow him to paint her brand new Camaro as a Talladega pace car to advertise races. "I told him if he gave me credentials, I'd take the car to Rockingham and drive in the parade lap. Later, when Don couldn't make racing events, he sometimes sent me. I was putting miles on my cars mighty fast and trading cars often. I'd trade a car, get the new one lettered and, after each race, have it lettered again. Ten years passed before I stopped lettering cars and before it was over, I was making speeches."

Carlan's "Driver Education Special Education Safety Day" at the Talladega Speedway was so successful, it became an annual event. Each year, the students were brought to the track where they met a popular motorsports personality who talked about racing and safety. The program encouraged the students to learn to drive and become more independent, while turning them into fans. "I was a State Department big shot during the week and would haul buggy to the races on weekends. Sometimes, I'd check my children out of class and tell school officials they had a fever. I didn't tell them it was racing fever and it was a lot of fun.

"Once when I went to Daytona, I got tired of walking through the pits so I wandered up on the scoring stand. Morris Metcalfe told me if I was going to sit, I was going to score. I loved scoring and being in the know about what was happening." Metcalfe was so pleased with his new protégé, he called Junior Johnson and told him he had a new scorer. Carlan kept her Department of Education day job and worked as Cale Yarborough's chief scorer on weekends.

Despite Carlan's accomplishments, she and State Department officials did not always see eye to eye. Finally, she decided enough was enough and moved to Randleman, North Carolina, where she rented a house from Richard and Linda Petty and taught in state and local school systems. Still involved with the track at Talladega, she made weekend trips back home.

"Don Namon had moved from general manager to executive director. One day, he called and told me the International Motorsports Hall of Fame was going to have a library and asked if I'd be the librarian. I couldn't get my application in fast enough."

In the beginning, the archives consisted of three cardboard boxes of books and materials. Today, the library contains almost three thousand books and thousands of files. Carlan has had to store much of the material on her computer and the library is outgrowing its space.

As the archives' overseer, she is concerned that so few visitors know about racing's heritage, and she makes sure everyone who researches the sport is aware of its past. "This is the only international motorsports library. I verify information and do research for people all over the world and for all the inductions. The main thing I try to teach is, there was racing before Jeff Gordon, because many of today's fans don't know. I take people through the museum and point out the cars and tell them their drivers and history."

Once married and now happily divorced, Carlan has two daughters, one granddaughter and, despite her father's fears, a sister named Helen. She lives near the speedway with her faithful dog Ralph and, never tiring of her job, remains a faithful fan. "Just think, they've put up with me for all these years. It has been a lot of fun, and I love what I do. I come early and stay late, take my chances, say what I darn well please and don't worry about it." The First Lady of Talladega is ready to help you with any questions, provide you with coffee, or settle in for good conversation. Just be sure to remember, you're at Talladeeeeeega.

CHAPTER 46

Larry Jendras:
Maryland Racing Historian

In real life, Larry Jendras is a Civil-Structural draftsman working on power plants with Bechtel. As a sideline, he has worked for many years to preserve Maryland's racing history, devoting himself to obtaining information on old drivers, races and speedways, acquiring a wealth of data and extensive photographic collections. He is known for the time and effort he puts into helping others with their research. Included are steps to take to obtain information on motorsports.

"Racing was more interesting in the old days," says Jendras, "because everything had

Historian Larry Jendras, Jr. He is fighting to preserve Maryland's racing past. (Courtesy Larry Jendras, Jr.)

Photographer Bob Williams at Dorsey Speedway in Maryland in 1985. Williams was one of the first black racing photographers. (Courtesy Larry Jendras, Jr.)

a personal touch. All of the cars worked differently and you could tell a Rex White car from a Jack Smith car. The creativity especially showed in the late models and modifieds. Those cars were special because most of them were built by their owners. We've lost that now because every car looks the same. We've lost that individuality."

To historians like Jendras, modern racing lacks the colorful characteristics of its past, times when you could tell which driver was rounding a corner by the sound of his car, when disputes were settled in the pits rather than in an office, and reporting was done in a press box, not a media center. Those times are gone forever, but if Jendras and others like him have anything to do with it, they won't be forgotten.

Born and raised in Baltimore, Maryland, Jendras became interested in motorsports history after looking through scrapbooks belonging to his father, Larry Sr. "There was plenty of racing activity around Baltimore in the fifties. My Dad owned a gas station and later drove trash trucks, and he also owned a stock car. I have a 1952 photo showing me sitting in a baby seat hanging off the roll bars protecting the radiator. I was probably at my first race. The first event I remember was at Westport Stadium in Baltimore when I was three and I have been going ever since.

"My Dad was a car owner at Maryland NASCAR tracks from 1952 to 1955 and in 1957. Although his driver was Lou Bee, my favorite was Johnny Roberts, 1953 NASCAR National Sportsman Champion, and 1960 and 1961 National Modified Champion. My favorite car was a 1937 Sportsman or Modified Ford." Jendras also had track preferences including the Beltsville Speedway asphalt track and the dirt track at Reading Fairgrounds.

This photo by Bob Williams preserves a moment in Maryland's racing history. Shown is the #10 with Elmo Langley at the wheel at Maryland's Hagerstown Raceway in 1959. (Courtesy Larry Jendras, Jr.)

Jendras' experiences with his father's racing taught him a lot about life and gave him empathy towards those who struggled against tough odds. "It takes hard work to get the job done. I hate when fans heckle or criticize a slow driver or a low-buck racecar, because it takes a tremendous amount of work just to get to the speedway. My father owned a stock car with one of the shortest racing careers. He built a 1940 Ford coupe around 1957 for racing at Westport. When he took it to race, the cars lined up for the heat with Dad's #240 mid-pack. Westport was a circular one-fourth mile dirt track built around a baseball diamond fenced with horizontal telephone poles. The tightly bunched field took the green flag, went through the first turn, slid around the second turn and got crossed up in the third. Dad's car was banged in the rear bumper, pushed into the inner rail and ended up on its nose. When it came down, it landed across one of the horizontal phone poles, breaking the frame. The new car had lasted only three-quarters of a lap."

The next year was more exciting because Jendras' father started selling go-karts. "Dad went into the business of selling them and I was a factory driver!" In 1975, Jendras and his wife were moving into their first house when he unpacked an old scrapbook with some photos of his father's car and his friends in racing. In looking through the scrapbook, Jendras thought about the times they'd spent together and how important his racing memories were. Determined to preserve the photos, he sought to put the pieces of the past together and find out more. When he began his research, he learned the Marlboro, Pomonkey, Beltsville, Westport and Lanham racetracks had been closed and many records were not available. Because of the sport's moonshine roots and early stigma, its part in

NASCAR writer Greg Fielden (right) is one of the most well-known of those who have preserved racing history. His outstanding and numerous works include the series *Forty Years of
Stock Car Racing* and have been acclaimed by sportswriters throughout the world. Rex White
and Greg Fielden are shown at the Living Legends of Auto Racing annual Daytona Beach
Parade.

America's past had not been valued. Realizing that much of his father's, and Maryland's,
racing history was fast being lost, he immediately set out to change that.

"I decided to look around for other photos and race results related to tracks. From
there, it built into a search for anything about Maryland's racing history. I began with
things from the area where I grew up and, as I got into it, decided to cover it all. I use
libraries as sources and search through their microfilms and find new information all the
time."

Jendras says there are several research avenues he has pursued. "Allan E. Brown's book
History of American Speedways has specific dates related to tracks, as do old newspapers
and racing programs. It's harder to come across things now because memorabilia has
become collectible and there's a lot of money involved. Inflated prices are an obstacle
because people want an exorbitant amount of money for a program or photograph. I have
found it best to talk with old drivers and their families. The worst words I hear are 'We
got rid of that stuff,' or 'It all got ruined in the basement.' There have been a few who
have thought I was trying to rob them, but most of the people have been helpful and are
usually happy to loan what they have so I can make copies."

Copying can be a problem if the person who is copying doesn't own the material's
rights and a photographer who takes a picture may retain the copyright. "Since scanning
came along on the Internet, it's been piracy out there. But, I can go to websites and find
a tremendous amount of information I couldn't have found ten years ago. I have to be
careful, but websites such as vintageracing.com and racing-reference.com are reliable."

Jendras has acquired the rights to several photographic collections so he can repro-
duce them, including those of Bob Williams, one of the first black race photographers.

"Williams was a resident of Washington, D.C. and worked as a photographer for the Department of Agriculture. The first racing photos he told me about were taken at Vista Raceway, around 1956 and were of midgets and motorcycles. He branched out to Marlboro Raceway, Dorsey Speedway and Westport Stadium. Those tracks were all in Maryland from the late fifties until the mid sixties. He started working at NASCAR in 1959 at Westport Stadium. He also made trips to Williams Grove, Lincoln, Reading, and Langhorne in Pennsylvania, and Southside and Fredericksburg in Virginia. When Westport closed in 1963, he began working at Dorsey and then in 1965 at the newly opened Beltsville Speedway, in Beltsville, Maryland. He was track photographer at Beltsville from 1965–1970. That was the last year of his racing photos, although he came out to Dorsey in 1985, which was the track's last year."

According to Jendras and other historians, one of their most valuable resources has been the research of author Greg Fielden. "His work is tremendous and he did a great job. He probably has more racing information than anyone and he combined it in such a way as to be interesting.

"Other sports are so well documented. I feel racing needs to catch up. It is important not to let its history be lost. Technology has drastically changed racing. Backyard engineering has given way to mass production and I miss the well plowed, tacky dirt tracks of my youth."

CHAPTER 47

Suzanne Wise: Librarian, Stock Car Racing Collection Archives, Appalachian State University

Stock car racing has been accorded little attention by scholars, and materials documenting its development have been largely overlooked by libraries. Much of its history is oral, residing in the memories of the sport's pioneers. The unprecedented growth and wide appeal of stock car racing, coupled with the recognition of its place in popular culture, underline the critical need to systematically document and preserve its history.

Mission

The Appalachian State University Stock Car Racing Collection is committed to becoming a comprehensive repository of stock car racing materials. In fulfilling its goal to document and preserve the history of the sport, it welcomes the public and assists them in their research. The collection is housed and organized according to professional archival standards of preservation and bibliographic cataloging, and trained staff provide reference assistance to both local and remote patrons. Information about resources in the Collection is made available internationally via the Internet.

—Appalachian State University Libraries,
Stock Car Racing Collection Newsletter, 2005

When Suzanne Wise made friends with members of the Classic City Sports Car Club, in Athens, Georgia, she had no idea they would change her life. "I'd accepted a job as a reference librarian at the University of Georgia in Athens and that's when I first came in contact with motorsports. The Club sponsored rallies and gymkhanas, and I got involved

Suzanne Wise is devoted to making Appalachian State University a premier repository of racing history. (Courtesy Suzanne Wise Photo Collection.)

with those activities. A friend and I won third place in a rally driving 'Sweet Baby James,' my little blue opal GT. Through the club, I began going to Road Atlanta to watch the SCCA Nationals and Can-Am Series races. I bought a stopwatch and kept a lap chart, just like the folks who knew what they were doing. I fondly recall seeing Paul Newman and Mark Donohue, and I loved the Super Vee races, with their souped-up Volkswagens, looking and sounding like bumblebees. Later, when I became a reference librarian at Appalachian State University, I saw my first stock car race at North Wilkesboro Speedway, which is just down the road. This was before the sport was widely televised and it was loud and exciting and I was entranced.

"For years, I was just a race fan. Then, I wrote several pieces on racing for the *International Encyclopedia of Women and Sports*. About the same time, Appalachian State offered a one-time course on the history of southern motorsports. When I checked to see what resources were available, there weren't many. When I conducted in-depth research on the topic, I found little scholarly work had been done and few institutions were committed to acquiring materials."

Wise also learned that whereas there were many general collections on motorsports, there had been little concentration in stock car racing. Records of its past were being lost. "Stock car racing has been a part of American culture since the first two automobiles were purchased and their owners competed to see who was fastest. It has since evolved into a major economic force that attracts a diverse national fan base."

Realizing the importance of the sport's history, Wise felt compelled to preserve it. "I visited the International Motor Racing Research Center at Watkins Glen and also spent several days with Betty Carlan at the McCaig-Welborn Research Library, International Motorsports Hall of Fame at Talladega. Betty was helpful and, in many ways, has been my role model."

When Wise finally taught her course, it was so successful, it attracted national attention and became regularly offered. This further fueled her determination to acquire materials. "I began purchasing books and films for the library collection and added subscriptions to racing magazines."

Soon, Wise became convinced Appalachian State University, with its location in the Blue Ridge Mountains, in the heart of stock car racing country, was ideally suited to become a repository for material documenting the sport. In 1998, with the help of her boss, University librarian Dr. Mary Reichel, Wise formally launched the university's Stock Car Racing Collection.

"The stock car racing community has been incredibly helpful and we have received many items from racing enthusiasts. Our most famous gift came from Linda Petty, who donated many materials documenting her husband's career. My personal goal is to see the Stock Car Racing Collection recognized as the preeminent collection on the sport by the time I retire."

With Wise's continuing efforts, Appalachian State University has acquired a wealth of resources and materials. The school also provides frequent programs and events related to stock car racing history. For more information, contact Suzanne Wise, Stock Car Racing Collection, Belk Library, Appalachian State University, Boone, NC 28608-2926; telephone (828) 262-2798; e-mail wisems@appstate.edu.

CHAPTER 48

Gerald Hodges:
Fan and Racing Reporter

Gerald Hodges' racing column is read by millions of race fans in hundreds of small town newspapers. According to Alabama District 35 Senator Gary Tanner, "Gerald Hodges has found his niche in the racing industry. He has been the voice for the Mobile International Speedway and has been in the forefront of the sport, caring not only for the drivers, but the families and communities that support them."

"I grew up with a need for speed," says Hodges, "but I wasn't destined to be a great racecar driver. They say in racing, you have to have 'big balls.' I only raced a year and a half. I had a lot of family responsibilities and didn't have the nerve to be really competitive. Some of us can follow our dreams, but some of us can't. I enjoyed the thrill of racing and writing stories is the next best thing. I'm still involved, and watching it is very exciting."

Hodges spent his childhood in Irvington, Alabama where boys who had cars, and men who thought they were boys, passed time by spinning dirt. He saw his first race, in the early fifties at age twelve, at Mobile's Lakeview Speedway, a quarter-mile dirt track with a lake in the middle. "Frank Mundy won. Two of the cars went into the lake and I thought that was the greatest thing in the world. One was in so deep, its hood was covered."

Hodges' fascination with the speedway stayed with him. After he married and completed a stint in the navy, he returned to Mobile and purchased a racecar. "By then, it was the mid-sixties. I bought a super modified, now called a sprint car, and ran it in a couple of races. A man named Wayne Hendrix and Leonard's Body Shop in Pensacola were my sponsors and Rat Lane drove it a couple of times. We raced quite a bit at Five Flags with Wayne furnishing parts from his junkyard. We didn't have a quick change rear end and we didn't have an expensive gear box, so we usually ran towards the back.

"Normally, we wouldn't start working on the car until about twelve o'clock on Saturday. Within an hour, somebody would come in with a six-pack and by the time we went to the track we were feeling good. One Saturday, we had a consequence. We paid a man twenty-five dollars to take the rear end out of a Crosley car and cut out one side of an axle and mount it onto the car for power steering. The man mounted the rear end wrong and

195

in order to turn right, the driver had to turn left. It had taken about three hours to put it in, so we weren't completely inebriated, but we spent the next half-hour wondering if the driver could adjust to the change. When we decided it wouldn't work, we spent the next four hours turning it around.

"When Red Farmer was running, he told people he didn't like to follow us and called our car a piss ant. I asked him what he meant by such a comment and he said, 'Your car goes down the track so erratically, it looks like an ant. You never know which way it's going to turn.' That was the kind of car I had because racing was so expensive. Super modifieds ran on alcohol methane and cam shafts cost seven hundred dollars. When I blew an engine and had to rebuild another one, my wife said, 'Gerald, you need to decide whether you want to race or have a family.' I sold the racecar and hauler the following week."

Looking back, Hodges sees his racing experience as a golden time when he drove by the seat of his pants and never knew what to expect. "In those days, if you bumped a local favorite you might have to fight at the end of the race. One night, there was a problem with a car at Five Flags and some of the fans didn't like the owner and started heckling. The man had been drinking and decided to climb the grandstand fence to get at them. Instead of being a chain link fence, it was made of chicken wire and when he reached the top it collapsed. He fell to the concrete walkway and, if it hadn't been for the police, the fans would have beaten him."

One of his favorite race stories relates to a "driver coming back from the dead." That driver was Joe Caspolich. "Joe was from Gulfport and raced in the area from Mobile to New Orleans. Once, after winning a race, Joe decided to give his trophy to a young boy who had been hanging around the track. The youngster was thrilled. Years passed and the boy grew up, but he never forgot the driver's generosity.

"During one of his later races, Caspolich became seriously injured and was transported to the local hospital where he was pronounced dead. As fate would have it, the young boy who had received the trophy had grown up to become a doctor in the hospital where Joe lay. Seeing his beloved racecar driver's name as deceased, he decided to pay his last respects and view the body. When he lifted the sheet, Joe's arm fell out. The startled doctor quickly realized that Joe was alive and began emergency life-saving treatment. Joe Caspolich lived for many more years."

Although Hodges got out of racing, the sport was still part of his heart. "I was in Dallas in 1986 when the famous psychologist Rollo May was appearing at Southern Methodist University. For twenty-five dollars, a person could have breakfast and talk with him. I was able to be with him for twenty minutes and he told me, 'If you're going the right way, doors will open. Things will happen in your life to further you along.'" Doors soon began opening in racing, in the field of writing.

"I worked in retail management for several years, before switching to marketing. In 1993, I was involved in market research and public relations when I became interested in racing again. That year, I bought a computer and was trying to find a way to pay for it so I went to Lee Fields, the promoter of Mobile International Speedway, and asked if I could put out a track program. I sold it for a dollar with little $5 weekly ads. When I began, I decided I better learn more about writing and took classes at a senior citizens' center. Within a month, I was making more money at the track than I was at my public relations job. A few weeks later, the track's public relations person was fired and the photographer left and I began to handle everything. At the same time, the *Mobile Press Register* needed someone to write racing stories."

Soon, Hodges found other newspapers wanted to pick up his articles. "NASCAR was putting out press releases on a fax machine so I could dial the machine and pick up highlights and race results within an hour and a half of the Sunday races. All I had to do was punch buttons and I could use their material to develop my stories."

Hodges could sell those stories weekly for five dollars apiece. When he found new markets, the money began adding up. "At the end of the year, I was furnishing stories for twenty newspapers and soliciting new business."

When the publishers began asking for photographs, he found another source of income. "In 1994, I bought a forty dollar camera from a pawn shop, took classes in photography at the University of South Alabama and began going to NASCAR tracks and taking pictures. I'd take fifteen or twenty rolls of film, including driver close-ups and head shots. Since this was before the Internet, I'd send the papers twenty-five or thirty photographs every two or three months. The pictures cost me about twenty cents apiece, but I increased my story fee to seven dollars. That meant two dollars a week more from each paper.

"Several publications wanted stories sent from Japan, so in 1996, 1997, and 1998, I took my laptop computer and went overseas. My publishers didn't think I could do it, but I did. I met some NASCAR officials who gave me a lot of new information. They told me NASCAR was changing to a youth movement and wanted to push out their older drivers, like Earnhardt and Elliott. I thought they were joking until a few years later when I found out it was true."

During his first trip to Japan, Hodges became friends with Mike Skinner and Richard Childress. "I have a lot of respect for Richard because he came into racing the hard way. He drove trucks when he first started and carried them back and forth on flatbed haulers. I've always respected individual effort. I don't like the total team effort we have now because it puts less emphasis on the driver."

One of Hodges' favorite drivers was Dale Earnhardt and he was deeply saddened when he died. "After his death, I received several hundred letters and e-mails. I knew there were a lot of people who liked him so in my column I offered to send a small photograph of Earnhardt to everyone who sent me a self-addressed envelope. I had to hire Kelly girls to open all the mail and we printed over three thousand. It was my way of contributing to his memory."

For Hodges, writing is rewarding, but the fun is not just in the product, but in the process. "I get a lot of satisfaction from my job and writing is something I love. When I first got into NASCAR, I had no formal training but I liked meeting and talking with people and I enjoyed learning. Now, I contact people for stories and never know who's going to be calling."

One of Hodges' more interesting projects is a book titled *King of the Modifieds* about Gene Tapia. "He was one of my heroes. I first met him in 1967 when we had a racecar. Ours was not a front-running car, but Gene was at the top of his game. One night, Gene came over to help us with our car and we remained friends."

When Tapia's family asked him to write a book about Gene, Hodges was amazed at what he learned. Tapia was known throughout the southeast as one of the best early racers, but he was also a World War II Marine hero and had struggled for years to locate his kidnapped first son. "Writing that book was one of the most enjoyable times of my life. I went to their house every morning, taped interviews and ate breakfast with them. By that time, he was 74 and his wife Francine was a wonderful cook. It was a great experience, even more satisfying than seeing the book finished. I'm going to follow the first book with one about the stolen baby."

Although he had to rush through it, Hodges was able to self-publish *King of the Modifieds* before Tapia's death. It quickly became popular among local drivers, and his columns increased in popularity, too. Now he sends columns to newspapers all over the nation. "Racing has been good to me and almost every day, I get a check. I take it to the bank and smile all the way."

Hodges has written about and documented races since the early nineties and has over fifty thousand photographic negatives. His work is the source of a vast amount of racing history, particularly in Alabama.

CHAPTER 49

Harlow Reynolds:
Sports Enthusiast Extraordinaire

A sports collector-fanatic, Harlow Reynolds is known not only for the vastness of his collection but also for his kindness and generosity. He has shared many pictures, souvenirs, and other memorabilia with drivers, crew members and car owners. If not for him, the tangible symbols of their treasured memories would not be preserved. Reynolds' collec-

Harlow Reynolds (right) is one of the most dedicated sports memorabilia collectors in the United States. Here, he is shown with one of his racing heroes, David Pearson. Pearson "drove" fans wild during the 1960s and '70s, earning the title of one of NASCAR's Top Fifty Drivers and the nickname, "The Cunning Silver Fox." (Courtesy Harlow Reynolds Photo Collection.)

tion ranges from the everyday to the bizarre, including anything related to NASCAR. He is involved with events at South Boston Speedway and participates in old-time driver reunions. A writer of racing articles for the *Lynchburg Legend*, he is an authority on NASCAR history.

Reynolds attended his first NASCAR event at Martinsville Speedway in 1957, when he was fourteen. "Glen Wood was the first driver I saw and he was in a convertible. He started on the outside pole, took the lead on the first lap and led for sixteen more before blowing his engine. It's been almost fifty years and I've been following the Wood brothers ever since."

To Reynolds, racing was as addictive as a drug, *and* as demanding. "I guess it's the same thing that happens to an alcoholic, or to a guy who gets hooked on playing poker or chasing women. I've been lucky over the years, getting stuff when other people weren't interested. Lots of times, drivers would talk with me and give me mementos. When people found out I was collecting, some of them said they had old stuff at home they didn't need and brought it to me and if I saw something I wanted, I'd offer to buy it. Glen Wood has really been good to me. He's given me some of his uniforms, racing pictures and quite a few shirts.

"The same thing happened in baseball. I was lucky enough to play baseball back in the old days, not as a professional, but I was able to follow the sport and meet lots of the players. I became friends with many of them and they gave me souvenirs. I've got over three hundred autographed baseballs and some of their uniforms. I've bought all kinds of autographed pictures and cards. I've saved letters they've sent and I still get a card at Christmas from Mickey Mantle's wife.

"I don't consider myself a historian, because collecting comes naturally to me. I think of a historian as someone who makes a living and really works at it. I just have fun, although I keep about twenty-five scrapbooks updated. I also collect guitars. I have five, plus a banjo, a 125-year-old fiddle, and a mandolin."

One year Reynolds' racing and baseball interests converged on the racetrack at Rockingham. "In 1977, Mickey Mantle was grand marshall for the race and I had my old Wood brothers lookalike car there for the parade. I always keep a baseball with me wherever I go, in case I see a player, and I had one under my car seat. I was going up pit row, when I saw Mickey walking. I stopped and held up the whole line, while I found it and had him sign it. It's the nicest part of my baseball collection."

Reynolds owned a succession of garages before retiring and going to work for Advance Auto Parts. In the mid-seventies, having had years of experience as a skilled mechanic, his passion for racing became so strong, he decided to drive. "In 1975, I drove a little on the dirt track at Natural Bridge Speedway. I had an old '67 six-cylinder Ford, painted red and white like the Woods brothers' #21 car. Another guy owned it, but I did the work. One week he'd drive it and the next week I drove. It lasted most of the '75 season. My driving talents weren't good and the car was slow, but we had a lot of fun with it."

Among Reynolds' collectables are hundreds of racing programs and photographs, thousands of driver autographs and cards, model cars, caps, shirts, books, banners, old speedway posters, pieces of cars, pieces of engines and tires. "I collect anything that has to do with NASCAR."

One of his most attention-getting mementos came from the front of the Wood brothers' garage and hangs on his wall. "It's a sign about twelve feet long and five feet high, made of plastic with inside lights."

He also has two classic cars, decorated like David Pearson's. "They're 1968 GT Ford Torinos and they're exactly alike. I did all of the work on them and built the first one in the seventies. When it reached 248,000 miles, I busted a piston and since it had some rust, I parked it. When the Wood brothers celebrated their fiftieth anniversary, I decided to build another one."

Reynolds' collection is interesting and historical, but to a visitor, it's overwhelming. "Everything is labeled and most of it's dated. I've written when I got it and who gave it or sold it to me. You have to watch where you walk, but it's organized, and I have a pathway. I'm single, so I live by myself. Recently, I asked a lady for a date and something came up and we stopped by my home. I invited her in and she began looking at the stuff on the walls and in the kitchen, my Richard Petty and Stacy Compton stand-ups and my Rex White souvenirs. I know she must have been joking, but she said, 'If anything comes of our relationship, all of this has to go.' I said, 'Wouldn't it be easier for you to go?' We laughed, but we never saw each other again."

CHAPTER 50

Greg Zyla: Journalist, Publisher, Racer and Broadcaster

In 1997, Greg Zyla was awarded the Eastern Motorsports Press Association's highest writing honor, the Frank Blunk *New York Times* Memorial Writer of the Year award. Highly respected as a journalist and columnist, Zyla has made a tremendous contribution to the auto and motorsports industry through his impact on his readership which numbers in the millions. His weekly columns "Racing," "Test Drive," "Crusin,'" and "Shop Talk" are published and syndicated throughout the United States and his monthly interviews in *Performance Racing Industry* magazine are considered among the best in the business. He also writes features for Times-Shamrock Communications (his parent company), National Speed Sport News, King Features Syndicate and others. He has numerous speaking engagements and is the publisher of *The News-Item*, a daily newspaper in Shamokin, Pennsylvania, owned by Times-Shamrock of Scranton.

Zyla is a graduate of Mt. St. Mary's College with a degree in psychology and a minor in business and marketing. He worked as a teacher for troubled boys in Mays Landing, New Jersey, before becoming a racecar driver, writer, track announcer and an auto racing radio and television show host. He and his father, Mike, produced and marketed a drag racing dice game that they sold through mail orders.

In 1980, Zyla established himself as a champion drag racer, dominating the NHRA Super Pro competition at Numidia Dragway in Pennsylvania. He appeared in nine final rounds out of eighteen races, winning six times and scoring three runner-ups. Giving up racing when his first of three children was born, he devoted himself to writing and broadcasting. He has been awarded two AARWRA and three Eastern Motorsports Press Association Broadcasting awards and has won over 60 writing awards.

"The first time I saw an automobile race on television," says Zyla, "I was mesmerized. It had to be back in 1955. I was born and raised in a little coal-mining town outside of Shamokin called Ranshaw in 1949. I lived there the first few years of my life and in 1957, my father took a new job at the *Times Journal* newspaper in advertising and moved us to Vineland, New Jersey. The town had a half-mile asphalt speedway, a quarter-mile dragstrip and a 1.7-mile road course. On Friday nights, they ran modified stock cars. On Saturday nights, they ran drag racing, and on every fourth Sunday, they held a Sports Car

Club of America competition. That was a big deal in the fifties and played a big part in my racing development.

"I saw my first race in person in 1957. It was a modified stock car race and I can still tell you the drivers who were in the field. Among them were Elton Hildreth, Wally Dallenbach, Frankie Schneider, Jimmie Delaney, Joe Kelly, Pete Freeze, Tommy Elliott, and Al Tasnady. I saw the cream of the crop in oval asphalt racing. I began going to the modified stock car races on Fridays and, on Saturdays, I saw all of the big names in drag racing. Super stock racers like Dave Strickler, Harold Ramsey, Ronnie Sox, Malcolm Durham and 'Dyno Don' Nicholson were there, as were drivers like Red Lang, Joe Jocono and Jack Kulp, all in their dragsters.

"I was at every Sunday sports car race and, in 1959 and 1960, I saw Roger Penske compete in his 'Birdcage' Maserati when he raced against Bob Holbert. Holbert was a highly favored Porsche driver and Penske just smoked him. The biggest surprise was a member of the Volvo team by the name of Walter Cronkite, who later achieved fame as our nation's most popular news anchor.

"Street racing was a really big thing in South Jersey and by the sixties the muscle cars were all over. I had a '67 GTX 440 and then a '68 Camaro SS 396–375 and also drove my friends' cars. We did a lot of serious street racing. I'm not proud of it, but that's a fact. We raced for five hundred to a thousand dollars and that was big money, but we paid a price. We lost a couple of guys in bad crashes."

While still a teenager, Zyla was influenced by NHRA two-time U.S. Nationals drag racing champion Pete Shadinger, who lived nearby in Vineland. When Zyla got his license, he drove his 1967 Plymouth 440 GTX over to see him and the two became friends. "I learned a lot from hanging around him and we built racecars in his garage. We had really fast cars, and Pete taught us to how make them faster.

"On Friday and Saturday nights, we'd go to the drive-in movies at the Delsea Drive-In on Rte. 47 with our dates, then go to Stewart's Root Beer for a burger. After the burger, we'd head to the street races. Hundreds of people came out and lit bon-fires all over the place.

"Pete and I had a system that worked many times. If the police came, we'd get in his old Ford Falcon station wagon. We kept a Bible on the seat and we'd put on white shirts and bow ties. I'd slick my hair down with Murray's pomade hair grease and we both looked like nerds. We'd sit there while everyone else was driving away and tell the police we were going to a family reunion or Sunday worship, and forced off the road because of the racing.

"During the sixties, I was a big fan of table games. I loved to play Easy Money, Clue and Monopoly. There was also a baseball game called Strat-O-Matic, which used dice and statistics to simulate professional players, who performed like they did in real life. I loved that game so much and played it so many times I learned dice probability and in 1963, I invented a drag racing game with cards and dice."

After attending Cumberland County College in Vineland and active duty with the Army National Guard in Columbia, South Carolina, Zyla graduated from Mt. St. Mary's College in Emmitsburg, Maryland, in 1973. He then worked with troubled boys who'd become gang members, but what he really wanted to do was to build his own racecar. "The drag racing game was in the back of my mind all those years and I decided to give it a shot. Using the game I'd invented in 1963, I developed it more and named it the Vallco Drag Racing Game. I did the work and my father helped me with the graphics. We used the names of professional drivers and advertised in *Super Stock Magazine* and *National Dragster*, hoping if we sold enough, I'd make enough money to build a car. We put the game out in 1976.

"One day I got a call from Woody Hatten at *Super Stock Magazine* and he asked to do a story on my game. Behold! The orders came rolling in and I had enough for my racecar. A 15-year-old boy named Ron Shurock lived with his mother above the garage I rented and I took him under wing as a 'partner.'

"We built a 1972 Vega funny car, and while we were working on it, I was involved in Sprint car and drag racing and was announcing drag racing in Pennsylvania. Nobody in Pennsylvania knew my background from New Jersey. They only knew I'd invented the game. When I finally finished building my car and got on the track, there were only three races left in the 1979 season. The drivers saw their announcer at Numidia come out of the press booth and enter Super Pro, which was the fastest class at the Dragway, and thought it was a joke. At the time, the cars were running in the nine second bracket at one hundred forty miles an hour and they assumed I was driving as a novelty."

Their thinking changed when Zyla won the last race of 1979 and the next year won the overall track championship. "I was married and my first child was on the way, so after the championship, I sold my racing equipment because of the cost. I'd always thought about being an announcer on radio and television and I saw a mention in *National Speed Sport News* about an opening for a radio race announcer for the 1981 NASCAR Winston Cup Mountain Dew 500 at Pocono Raceway. Publisher Chris Economaki suggested anyone interested should send a demo tape to the Motor Racing Network, which is owned by International Speedway Corporation and NASCAR. I didn't have a demo tape, but I had sound movies of Sprint car races. I set up a movie projector in my den and played the races and then turned on the microphone on my cassette recorder and made a voice-over. I gave a big rundown of the race and it sounded as if I were there. About a week after I sent it in, I received a letter from Mike Joy saying they'd picked me. I couldn't believe it. Motor Racing Network was on three hundred channels. Mike left a little note on the bottom of his letter saying he had purchased one of my Vallco Drag Racing games.

"I made it through the race, but I'll never forget what happened during the event. My spotter John Snyder and I were working the tunnel turn on top of a photo tower when, halfway through the race, a motorcycle gang climbed up with us. To make things worse, because I wore glasses, I couldn't see most of the race due to beer spray and rain. The motorcycle gang was rowdy, but somehow we got through it and I got help from Eli Gold, who was working turn one. John and I joke about it to this day because had it not been for him handing me notes I would never have made it. Darrell Waltrip won the race, which had to be stopped because of deer on the track. Eli later told us a bear came onto the track during another race, but I guess that's not surprising in the Pocono Mountains.

"Despite the hardship, something wonderful came from the experience. The week following my radio 'debut,' I was at a Sprint car race at Williams Grove Speedway in Pennsylvania, when a guy came up to me. He said, 'We heard you on MRN. Would you like to work on a Sprint car racing TV show? I worked from 1982 through 1990 in on-air television."

Zyla soon crossed paths with his old friend Woody Hatten. "He said I needed to start writing for magazines. I took his advice and submitted an article to *Super Stock* and *Drag Illustrated* and when I started writing for *Circle Track*, my career took off. I use a question-and-answer style and interview movers and doers. As part of my work, I also test-drive

Elton Hildreth, left, who drove the 16-J modified, with Greg Zyla. (Courtesy Greg Zyla.)

cars. The manufacturers bring them right to my house. I drive a brand new car every week and write a review on it.

"Being in the media allows me to call on the biggest names in racing and I feel very fortunate. I've had a wonderful career and the finest people I've met have been in motorsports. I thank God because without His blessings and the talents He's given me, I wouldn't have been able to do any of this."

CHAPTER 51

Rick Minter: Sportswriter

According to WSB talk show host and traffic reporter "Captain Herb" Emory, Rick Minter is the most dedicated reporter in NASCAR history. "Rick is a great friend of racing and to the early racers who paved the way for today. I'm happy he's my friend and often a part of our show. He is a supporter of racing history, not only in our state, but in others around our area. I don't know of anyone who does as much on the job as he does, reporting the news and upholding racing's heritage. He's number one on my list."

As dedicated to his family as he is to racing, Minter is known for his barbecue "socials" and annual Inman Heritage Days, an oldtime tractor show held on his farm. He is also an entrepreneur with a successful Christmas tree business. Rooted as firmly in southern soil as the trees he grows, he has a fondness for old equipment and enjoys making repairs. Friends describe him as a product of the early twentieth century because he tends to dwell in the past more than the present.

Minter was recently commended for his contributions to motorsports by the Georgia Automobile Racing Hall of Fame Association. He also received an award (Best Feature or Series-Non-Deadline—Pro Sports) from the Georgia Sportswriters Association.

As a child, Minter accompanied his sportswriter father Jim Minter to Atlanta International Raceway, sat in the press box while his dad worked, watched the race and met the winners. With so much exposure to the sport, he developed an interest at an early age.

Minter was raised in rural Georgia near a neighbor who raced and several short tracks. Mechanically inclined, he has served on pit crews for numerous drivers, including Bill Elliott who became a Winston Cup champion. Combining his passion for racing with a genetic talent for journalism, Minter followed in his father's footsteps, writing from a base of knowledge gained in blood, sweat, and grease. Drivers admire his no-holds-barred interviews and accuracy in quotes. Readers like his straightforward, "meet it head on" style. Known for finding the *real* story, Minter gives readers insights into racing behind the scenes, frequently championing the underdog.

"I enjoy writing about ordinary people who do extraordinary things with racecars," says Minter. "Everyday people impress me more than a Dale Earnhardt, Jr. or Tony Stewart. A guy who works in a body shop, takes all the money he can scrape up and goes to the track where he's a fierce competitor... I have to admire that. To me he's much more compelling."

"My Dad was a sportswriter and I've been following NASCAR and going to races forever. In 1962, Rex White won the first race I attended at Atlanta International Raceway. I went back several years later and sat in the press box. Richard Petty won the race and afterwards came to be interviewed. My Dad told me to sit in the corner so he could work. When Richard came in, he sat beside me. Someone told me to move but Richard said 'No.' Richard did his winner's interview sitting beside me. At the time, I was a Yarbrough fan, but after that I was sold."

In the old days, drivers got really hot and hours of grueling racing took their toll. His outstanding memory of Richard was an unusually sour smell which made Minter more aware that heroes are real.

"One time Mark Martin said something at Daytona that made a lot of sense to me. I asked him, 'Who is your favorite driver?' He said his heroes were always people who were within reach. Sometimes people have to tell you something about yourself for you to figure it out and he's exactly right. I used to go to races with Wesley Stubbs when I was a kid. Several years ago, I brought him to the speedway and we went into the garage. Nobody was there but Richard and a few officials. I told Richard the man with me had cancer and would like to meet him. Richard said he would be over in a little bit. I figured he wouldn't have time, figured he was blowing me off, but he sat with Wesley for forty-five minutes, just the two of them talking. Richard Petty became my hero because I was able to see him close-up."

When Minter was in his mid-teens, a guy named Don Patrick lived down the street. He owned a racecar and Tony Allison drove it. One day when Minter stopped by, Don invited him to go to the track and help on the car. He went with him for several years and then helped Ricky Williams, a driver who still runs dirt.

One of his most vivid memories is hanging out with friends on Saturdays at Leon Archer's shop. One Saturday when they were helping Leon, the University of Georgia was playing Auburn for the SEC Championship. Wanting to hear the game, the boys turned on the radio.

"Leon got mad, pitched a fit and turned the radio off. He said, 'If you're going to be football fans, be football fans, but if we're going to race, you have to give it one hundred percent.' He taught me if a person wants to compete, he can't be distracted. He's got to focus and stay after it. That's why Leon won all the time. When he arrived at the track, he was prepared and focused, and determined to win. He had tremendous driving ability, organizational skills, and a burning desire to succeed. He taught me about winning, working, and racing. I measure a lot of things against Leon and my Dad's work at the newspaper. My Dad had the same determination. You can't do things halfway and be proud. You can't take satisfaction without putting effort and passion into it."

Minter often writes about people striving to make it against all odds, and presenting their struggles and achievements are his specialty. "I never underestimate anybody and what they offer, even in writing news. It's foolish to look at people and judge them by their clothes, their cars or their houses. I reserve judgment until I find what they're made of and what they're about. The secret to being a good sportswriter is not discounting anyone. I respect people like Brad Teague, a talented driver still out there scuffling. He's compromised how he drives, but not his principles. I admire a guy like that and I like Tony Stewart, even though I've had difficulties covering him. I'd rather people be straightforward and mad at me than have them be insincere.

"I became interested in racing as a fan and then began working on racecars. That mechanical knowledge is important in motorsports writing. Understanding how cars work helps me in my job. Sportswriters should try to live in the real world and not let TV or their peers dictate what they write. They should find out for themselves what it's all about. Go to Daytona and sit in the grandstands in the fourth turn. Watch the cars jump around so fast and loud it scares you. Go to the garage at 6:00 in the morning. Go to Martinsville and sit in row one. Don't show up for the main event and sit in the press box. To know what it's like, you have to be there and experience it all."

Minter's experience includes good times, bad times, and times that are funny and strange. "One time when I was a teenager, I was at Dixie Speedway. Charlie Mincey was running wide open down the straightaway when the lights went out. He went half a lap around the track with it dark as midnight.

"During a race at Seven Flags Speedway in Douglasville, the promoter cut the purse and drivers decided to strike. When the green flag was thrown, they wouldn't race. They rode around in formation as if under caution. The promoter, deciding he wasn't going to put up with it, had a deputy block the track. When one of the guys went around his car, the deputy pulled out his pistol and shot out his tires.

"I saw a guy knocked out of his pants in a fight at Senoia. A crew member hit a car owner with an uppercut under his chin. He went up a foot and a half but his pants stayed still, then dropped all the way to his ankles. He undid his belt and unzipped his pants and pulled them back up.

"The most upsetting thing I've seen was Tiny Lund killed at Talladega. I was sitting in the backstretch and at the time I was a Tiny Lund fan. Several of us were standing by the fence when it happened at the start of the race. He slid to a stop and another driver piled into him, sending him on down the track. It took the fun out of going to races for a mighty long time."

Minter was also at Daytona during the race in which Dale Earnhardt was killed and it is ingrained in his memory forever. "From the time he wrecked until the time we left, it was like slow motion, seeing Dale, Jr. summoned to the hospital and Danny being summoned to go. It was weird watching Earnhardt's trailer leaving Daytona, knowing it would never come back in that form. I knew when it was happening the sport would change. Stock car racing would never be the same. I didn't lose a personal friend, but Earnhardt's death was a blow."

It's not unusual for Minter to form relationships with the people he writes about and he says conversations don't have to have a story in mind. He strives to build rapport and to be honest and forthcoming, traits he learned from his Dad. "An interview should be a two-way exchange because a one-way conversation is boring. My Dad is an incredibly good writer and one of the most underrated in the country. I'm not that good at writing because I don't have his command of the language. I compensate with knowledge and, with what I know and care about racing, I think it balances out.

"I try to be as conversational as I can, not use a lot of big words, and keep things simple. I think writing should have a ring to it, a cadence that flows. Today, you have to fit your writing to who you're writing for and it's hard to detect different writing styles in our newspaper. There are expectations and we have to meet them. Everybody self-edits, but four or five sets of eyes see our stories.

"When I prepare for interviews, I don't make a list of questions, but I make sure I have plenty of batteries in my recorder. The whole time I'm interviewing, I'm thinking about what I need, feeding off what people tell me, and milking it for all its worth. The

When he's not at the track, sportswriter Rick Minter (left, with Rex White, at his restored still) is usually farming or finding old things to fix. He has restored a gristmill, sorghum mill, saw mill and liquor still. He did such a good job on the still, it was recently stolen.

most difficult thing in writing is being fair and accurate. Being conscientious takes a lot out of you and I struggle with that all the time. I'm never satisfied until time goes by and nobody challenges me."

Minter says journalism is different from everyday writing. "As my father says, when a real estate agent sells land, they just fill in the blanks in the contract. Newspapers start from scratch every day. Reporting has more potential for making mistakes and the margin for error is slim.

"With sportswriting, I'm gone about twenty-eight weekends a year. I don't like that part of it, but I deal with it pretty well until the race is over. Once I get my stories written, the rest is miserable. I'd be a happy camper if I could beam myself home.

"My parents lived in Fayetteville for most of my life, then moved to Inman, the little community where I live. My wife Joanne is from Barcelona, Spain. We met when I was a hungry bachelor farmer and she managed a Pizza Hut. Our daughter Stephanie is in college and my stepdaughter, Tammy Watts, lives nearby. We live just down from my parents and, truthfully, my life's not different now than it's been. I've always liked old cars and trucks, tractors, farming and racing.

"I've never had any desire to race, not that I'm scared but because I don't have the ability. I learned that on the highway with Bill Elliott and my short track friends. They are more aware of their surroundings and I guess it's their vision. If something happens on the road, they can tell about it, frame by frame."

Minter first became interested in journalism when he was writing for his school's third grade paper. He majored in business administration at the University of Georgia and North Georgia College, and while he was at North Georgia he met Ernie Elliott.

"Ernie and I had classes together and I went to the Elliotts' garage. I helped them work every day for months at a time. Sometimes we worked on junk cars and sometimes we worked on the truck. I went to races with Bill, Ernie and Dan when Ernie was crew chief. I admire Bill for where he came from because he struggled so much."

When Minter graduated from college he returned to the family farm. "I farmed for ten years before my Dad bought part of a newspaper. In the early days, I went to short track races and called in results. They were just little paragraphs, without any real writing involved. When my Dad bought the *News Daily*, he decided the paper wasn't serving the racing market and made me editor of motorsports. I went to Senoia Raceway a couple of times a week and also sold ads and wrote for a racing paper." Later, he became a writer for the *Atlanta Journal-Constitution*, where he covered short tracks until switching to NASCAR.

Minter says being involved with racing is a comforting familiarity, like putting on a pair of old shoes. No matter how his life changes, the track stays the same. "I've come full circle since I was a teen. I like the same year and model cars, the same old tractors and Darlington is still my favorite track. Weekends off, I go to races with Dennis Schoenfeld and Andy Cash. I helped Andy last year at Senoia and watched him win."

Minter may be the same, but racing is not. "Drivers counted more at the old tracks. Equipment and aero issues weren't big and they had more control. Now, there are more people in the pits, more officials and more rules, and expectations of behavior are higher.

"When I first started going to races there were bad actors. Most were knowledgeable, but some got too drunk. In the past, people came to see. Now they come to be seen. People want to get autographs not for the signatures, but for their pictures made standing there getting them.

"I like short track racing because there's no worry about losing sponsorship. Cup drivers have to be polished and can't say what they think. You can't have million dollar lawsuits jeopardizing million dollar deals, but a lot of that is unnecessary. Sponsors don't mind drivers, once in awhile, saying what they think.

"I don't like putting drivers in cars when they don't qualify and it's hard to balance in the stories I write. It's always been a part of it, but it took me a long time to figure it out. I know somebody's got to pay for it and racing's become more of a business, but from the standpoint of loving the sport, it's disappointing."

When he's not at the track, Minter is usually farming or finding old things to fix. He has restored a gristmill, sorghum mill, saw mill and liquor still. He did such a good job on the still, it was recently stolen.

"Every tractor, every piece of equipment is different to me and even iron can have personality. Finding its characteristics is fun. If two racecars are built alike, one of them runs out front and one a lap down. My daughter Stephanie likes the same things I do and I think that's neat. I enjoy bringing back pieces of abandoned equipment and we work together. Nothing thrills me more than dragging out a junky locked-up tractor and cutting the bushes around it. I like to work on it, fire it up, and hear it running again. I've never gotten such a thrill out of writing a story as working on racecars and tractors. I've never written a story that's given me such an adrenaline rush."

CHAPTER 52

"Captain Herb" Emory: WSB Radio Racing Talk Show Host and Traffic Reporter

Herb Emory is one of the Atlanta, Georgia, metro area's most respected and beloved traffic reporters. A lifelong NASCAR fan, he writes a racing column for his website, www.captainherb.net, and hosts WSB's Allan Vigil Ford 120 racing talk show sponsored by Ford dealer Allan Vigil. Fondly referred to by his listeners as "Captain Herb," his knowledgeable insights and commentary have made him a popular broadcasting figure. Although Emory never had the desire to be a race driver, he has participated in many celebrity events, often competing in Legends cars where he has won almost every event he's run.

According to WSB Radio consumer advocate and talk show host Clark Howard, "Herb eats, sleeps, and lives stock car racing. His unparalleled enthusiasm has brought untold listeners to the sport. I have never been to a stock car race, but someday I might go just to see what brings the Captain so much joy."

Emory grew up loving the 3 Rs: radio, rock 'n' roll, and racing. As a child, he tagged along with his father whenever he could and one of their frequent destinations was the bowling alley. While the older Emory played in a league, Herb hung out at the radio station next door, talking with disk jockeys and watching the Associated Press teletype machines as they spit out the news. Appreciative of the opportunity to observe broadcasting firsthand, he swept the floors, took out the trash and did other chores. When he was in the sixth grade, he talked the announcers into letting him take the teletype news pages home where he practiced writing copy and reporting from his bedroom. The station's employees were so impressed by his enthusiasm that, when he reached high school, they put him on the air. Emory, who by then had decided to become a disc jockey, was spinning tunes for listeners by his senior year.

Today, Emory claims his career was influenced by the famous television personality Andy Griffith. "He was my hero because he was from North Carolina and grew up to be a TV star. He made me think there wasn't anything I couldn't do and that gave me motivation. My Granddaddy was a farmer and I grew up in the mountains in a place like

(Left to right) Georgia Governor Sonny Perdue, Karen Emory, Atlanta Mayor Shirley Franklin and "Cap'n" Herb Emory. According to Emory, in the old days, because fans had more access to drivers, many came to know each other. (Courtesy Herb Emory Photo Collection.)

Mayberry. When I watched Andy Griffith, I thought, 'I, too, can get away from the mills and farming and make a decent living.'"

Born and raised near Asheville, North Carolina, Emory's home was in the heart of NASCAR country where two of his cousins, Cecil and Lee Gordon, were drivers. Since both of his parents were die-hard race fans, they began taking him to the tracks when he was six months old.

"They put me in a little bassinet so I could sleep, before hauling me into the grand-stands. By the time I was seven, my Dad was parking cars on Friday nights at the track in Asheville to earn money to get in the races. The promoter paid him twenty dollars and let him in free. On Saturdays, we'd use what he earned to get in Greenville-Pickens and, on Sundays, we'd go to wherever Cecil or Ralph Earnhardt were running.

"My father was a good friend of Earnhardt and we'd go to races to see him. There was no training involved in being on a pit crew and whoever showed up volunteered. When Earnhardt was running, my father helped him while we watched the race. Now, nothing like that goes on in the pits. Today's fans don't have any idea how brave drivers were. Back then, the cars were like they'd come off the showroom floor and drivers took their lives in their hands. I remember one wild race in which a car went out of control and flew onto the guardrail and balanced there.

"You didn't have many pit stops in those days because the late model features were short and it took time to open the car's trunk and put in the fuel. Once when my Dad was helping him, Earnhardt wrecked his car in the heat race. Since he had a strong reputation for winning, a guy who had made it to the feature asked him if he'd drive his car. Earnhardt said yes, got in and shot down the track, then suddenly turned down pit road. My Dad hollered, 'What's the matter? What's the matter?' Earnhardt answered, 'I think I need gas.'

"My Dad ran out, threw open the trunk, looked inside and screamed, 'Where's the damn gas tank?' Earnhardt said, 'It's laying on the backstretch.' The car's owner had attached the gas tank with inner tubes and it had bounced back out on the track. Funny things were always happening in the old days."

According to Emory, because fans had more access to drivers, many came to know each other. "After races, Tiny Lund would give rides around the track to us kids and I've eaten sandwiches with Ralph and Dale Earnhardt. In the fifties and sixties, we could get two cents apiece for each Coke bottle we returned so picking up bottles in the infield was a regular routine. I'd be filling my trunk and see Dale out there gathering them, too."

After being dragged from race to race every Friday, Saturday and Sunday for years, Emory finally became burned out. When he reached junior high, he put racing aside and formed a rock 'n' roll band. "I told my Dad I'd had enough racing and refused to go back." From then until he completed high school, he balanced jobs at the radio station and bowling alley with playing in his band and football. After graduating, he headed for Atlanta where he worked part-time at metro stations while attending broadcasting school.

During his early radio years, Emory covered racing at WQXI, now Star 94. "I didn't have a show, but I'd do reports on the Friday before or the Monday after a racing event. I did whatever needed to be done at the stations, mostly playing records and announcing the news. In the beginning, I was strictly a stringer reporter, covering Cobb and Douglas Counties. The first year, I worked out of my house with a studio set up in my laundry room. I called the police and tracked down stories such as shootings, fires and floods. When they transferred me out of my utility room, I covered the capital, the Atlanta City Council and all the government news. I also filled in for traffic reporters.

"While I was working at WQXI, I was asked to drive a new car in the parade lap at Atlanta International Raceway. I thought about my Dad and his love of racing and invited him to join me. He had a great time riding around the track and by the end of the day I was hooked on racing again. Racing was back in my blood and I haven't missed an Atlanta race since."

Over the years, Emory has become increasingly interested in the sport and preserving its history. "I have strong feelings because I watched Fireball Roberts, Rex White, Junior Johnson, Billy Wade, the Pettys and Tiny Lund. I was fortunate and I treasure those memories."

When WQXI cut back on their news programs, Emory changed over to traffic and eventually accepted a job at WSB. Hovering above the interstates, his bird's-eye view reporting is a godsend for drivers. He helps them avoid delays by "riding along in a helicopter, running my mouth."

While in his early twenties, Emory joined a country band and performed around the metro area. He was involved with the band when he was invited on a blind date and met his future wife Karen. It took a while for her to share his appreciation for racing, but now she's a fan. "She had never been to the track and for the longest time wouldn't go. When she agreed, instead of paying attention to the race, she lay in the infield suntanning. She finally became involved in 1992 when we watched the Hooters' 500. It was a

Herb Emory and his Mayberry patrol car.

phenomenal event which included Jeff Gordon's first race and Richard Petty's last. There were 200,000 fans and it was very emotional. I hate to admit it but I even cried a few tears."

At the time, the WSB station executives were only concerned with baseball and football and didn't think racing was important. Emory covered the speedway as a few sound bites along with the news. The Hooters' race generated so much interest that station management took a hard look. "There were four times as many people at the speedway as at the University of Georgia football games and twenty times the people attending Braves games. I told my bosses a lot of fans would listen if we had a race program. Knowing my background they agreed and asked me to host it. I told my wife since it would air on Saturdays we'd have to make a family commitment. We never dreamed we'd still be doing it after twelve years. Karen answers the phone, screens the calls and produces the show. She contacts people, lines up our guests and keeps us on track."

Emory says there have been many changes in racing since his program began. The sport is growing fast and so is its number of fans. They identify with their drivers and, sometimes, that identification spills onto the interstate.

"Every day, I see cars running as if they're at Talladega. The speed is slower, but they dart in and out. I tell my listeners that as a captain I have three Cs: courtesy, caution, and common sense. The biggest problems are too little common sense and too many distractions, those in our vehicles and those around us. One day I was driving my truck and passed a car in which the driver had his cell phone propped on his shoulder held by his ear. He used his thumb to hold a manila folder on his steering wheel while he typed on a laptop computer in the passenger seat. He was cruising at sixty miles an hour on the interstate. That's too much to be doing while controlling 3500 pounds of machinery."

As a traffic reporter, Emory sees the results of multi-tasking much too often. Atlanta's I-75, I-85 and I-20 have wrecks every day. "Oh, my aching toe," he says to listeners, signaling everything will be stop and go.

Even though many years have passed and his job is far from his roots, Emory still recalls and looks up to his TV mentor. "Each year after Karen and I married, she asked me what I wanted for Christmas. Remembering my hero, Andy Griffith, I told her I wanted a Ford Galaxie from the early sixties to make into a Mayberry patrol car. Seven years ago, Karen was still asking and I was still answering the same. On Christmas Day, we went to her Mom and Dad's to open our gifts and have lunch. All of a sudden, my sister-in-law said the kids and I were making too much noise and sent us down to the basement. I was peeved at being sent into the basement to babysit, but I agreed to go. I was playing with the kids and their gifts when we were called back up and Karen said I'd missed opening one of my presents. Inside, I found a sheriff's department shirt and badge given to me years earlier by Douglas County Sheriff Earl Lee. As I pulled it from the box, the title for a Galaxie fell out. While I had been in the basement, they'd pulled up an old Ford Galaxie painted like a Mayberry patrol car. That car was the best Christmas surprise I've ever received."

CHAPTER 53

Chris Siebert:
Bandolero Bandit

Drivers are beginning to race at an earlier and earlier age. Chris Siebert represents many who, while still young, are developing their skills and becoming competitive.

According to twelve-year-old Bandolero driver Chris Siebert, "NASCAR gets more attention than baseball. It's a mind sport, a physical sport, and a hard work sport, not just turning left on a track. You have to have coordination and think ahead, know when to pass, hit the brake and hit the gas. You can't let the car drive you. You have to drive the car. If the car drives you, it's going to drive you into the wall."

In motorsports, drivers have to be strong to endure multi-lap races, and people who work on the cars have to stay in shape too. "I know why pit crew guys have muscles," says Chris. "They have to be able to jack up a car, run around it, and not make mistakes. Tire changers work fast and put lug nuts on tight." Chris has been racing since he was five years old, beginning on motorcycles. That was also when he began attending races.

"The first time we went to Atlanta Motor Speedway," says his father, Robert Siebert, "I sneaked him into pit row. He was wearing a Bill Elliott coat with Bill's autograph on it. He was standing on the pit wall wearing the coat when one of Bill's crew members saw him and talked with him. We thought that was cool.

"We walked over to the pit where a guy was taking wheels off and putting them on. Again, when he saw Chris' coat, he stopped to talk. He asked Chris if he'd like a souvenir, pulled the socket off of his air gun and gave it to him."

A couple of years ago, Chris, his father and his mother, Kim, started going to the summer Thursday Thunder races at Atlanta Motor Speedway. "Thursday Thunder is a big deal," says Robert. "It's the main show for kids in Georgia and a family affair. They have autograph sessions and entertainment for fans. It's five dollars for adults, a dollar for kids and you can take in a cooler. Drivers from eight to adult can race in their age category, in Bandoleros, Legends Cars and Thunder Roadsters. Bandoleros are tiny little cars with thirty horsepower Vanguard motors like V twin lawnmower engines. The motors are sealed so they go the same speed and everyone has a fair chance. Legends Cars are similar to cars of the thirties and forties and the Thunder Roadsters are open wheel racers."

Chris fell in love with the cars and wanted to race. "The secret was to go to racing events and learn by talking with other kids and parents, and then beg my parents for money!" He began racing Bandoleros last year.

"Before we jumped into buying a car, we put Chris in the Ride and Drive program for Bandoleros, Legends Cars and Roadsters, put on by the Atlanta Motor Speedway's Legends Car Shop," says Robert. "The shop is run by Pete Horne, who sells the cars and offers advice. The people there are really good and they have a website where they sell used cars. We got ours for $3200. Most used ones sell for $5000 and new ones for $7000."

The dollars for the car are just the initial investment. Because the engines are sealed, owners can't repair them and may have to send them off or buy a new one. "There's nothing you can do if an engine breaks," says Robert. "We've been lucky. That car had a year of racing on it when we bought it and it's hard when you don't have much money."

Chris gets sponsorship from his Dad's Meineke shop and Frank and White LLC Realty. "We use the money to buy parts, and put their name on the car," says Robert. "How much sponsors give determines the size of their ads. Our highest sponsor paid $1000, but every bit helps. We're looking for more sponsors and a back-up car so if one gets damaged we can still race. Kids with full sponsorship have back-up cars and NASCAR-type haulers."

The Sieberts say racing is expensive, but it's a family affair and involves the whole racing community. "You meet people in a big way," says Chris. "I know everybody who races in my class."

"These kids have a great time," adds Robert. "Chris' class is the Bandits and they're really tight. Younger kids are really what it's all about. They bump and bang on each other and don't take anything personally. They might be mad for a second, but ten minutes later they're out of their cars and playing. If somebody's car breaks down, we all jump on it and fix it. It keeps kids out of trouble. Families are together more and their kids are more disciplined."

Racing has become a part of the Sieberts' life, as a hobby for Chris and as a career opportunity. NASCAR drivers and pit crews begin as early as age eighteen. Chris' goal is to move up to Legends Cars and late models, attend Daytona's NASCAR Technical Institute and, eventually, become a Nextel Cup driver. He's already been to the Daytona speedway and taken the track tours. "It's a special thing. They pick people out of the crowd to participate in pit crew situations and I've done it twice as a tire carrier for Motorcraft. The Wood brothers have a little car without a motor and let us jack it up, take the tires off and put the tires they give you back on. They have the fastest times of the day and the fastest times overall. When I went up the second time, we beat the fastest time of the day for a one-tire stop."

He may be fast at tires, but Chris quickly learned a skill more important, how to avoid accidents. When Chris first started to race, his dad gave him good advice. He told him to let the pack fight it out and hold back. Chris learned to ride the track, be aware of his surroundings, and survive. "There have been some unbelievable crashes," says Robert. "Somehow he gets by them without hitting anybody. He won one race by being the only Bandolero Bandit to finish."

"Spinning out can scare you," says Chris. "When I see someone coming up the track in front of me sideways and I can see their number, I start to get out of the gas. When I start to spin, I hold the gas and hope I go back around. Once I was spun in the middle of a turn, when my friend hit me head on, but my seat and head restraint kept me from getting hurt."

"They actually have the same safety equipment as NASCAR uses," says Robert.

Racing has become a part of the Sieberts' life, as a hobby for Chris and as a career opportunity. NASCAR drivers and pit crews begin as early as age eighteen. Chris's goal is to move up to Legends Cars and late models, attend Daytona's NASCAR Technical Institute and, eventually, become a Nextel Cup driver. (Courtesy The Siebert Photo Collection.)

He says the most danger he's seen Chris involved in has been in the racing garage. "During a double feature, Chris started at number fourteen and fought his way to third. Suddenly he lost his brakes and spun to avoid other cars. He brought the car back to the garage because the brakes had locked. After the brakes were fixed, he went out on the track and made it back up to third. Having problems again, he started back to the garage, but was unable to stop and zoomed through it. People said they'd never seen anybody drive as well as that. He missed my toolbox, took out a trash can, missed three other tool boxes, and shot out the other side."

Chris recently graduated from Bandoleros to Legends Cars and his interest in racing is unfaltering.

Note for parents: According to the Sieberts, racing has its dangers, but Bandoleros and Legends Cars use the same safety technology as Nextel Cup cars. Kids wear fire retardant suits and race under roll bars.

CHAPTER 54

Joey Logano:
Fast Track to Fame

At sixteen years old, Joey Logano already has ten years of racing experience. Considered one of the most talented of the upcoming young drivers, he was signed at age fifteen by the Joe Gibbs racing team.

Logano won his first Eastern Grand National Championship in Jr. Stock Car Quarter Midgets at the age of seven. In 1998 and 1999, he won Grand National Championships in the Jr. Stock and Modified divisions. At age nine, he won the National Championship for Bandoleros. While racing Legends cars, he set a track record of fourteen consecutive wins at Atlanta Motor Speedway and won the Young Lions National Championship. At the age of twelve, he was the youngest in Legends history to win the Pro National Championship. In 2005, he became the youngest competitor in the Hooters Pro Cup Series, finishing the season with one win and six top fives.

Originally from Connecticut, the Logano family is and has always been into sports. "There are two stations always playing in our house," says Tom Logano, "ESPN and the Speed Channel. My daughter Danielle is a figure skater and Joey races. He was into hockey, but racing took over."

According to his father, Joey Logano's racing career began in Connecticut when he was a toddler. "I bought him an electric go-kart when he was three and a gas-powered one when he was four. I was in the garbage business and we had fourteen acres of dumpsters and trailers. On Saturdays, Joey accompanied me to work and drove around them. One of my employees raced quarter midgets and suggested I allow Joey to try them. When he turned six, we bought him a used one and he brought trophies home every week. He raced quarter midgets for three years and won three Grand Nationals.

"By the time Joey was nine, I was tired of the garbage business and Connecticut's cold winters so I sold the company, moved our family down south, and bought Joey a Bandolero. He raced his heart out but his car wasn't good so I took it to an expert to have it set up. After we got it back, Joey won fourteen straight races. When he was ten, we bought him a Legends car and he raced on an unsanctioned track. At age twelve, he won the Pro Nationals, the highest class Legends has."

Tom says veteran driver Ronnie Sanders and current Nextel Cup driver Mark

Sixteen-year-old Joey Logano poses in front of his #51 Joe Gibbs Racing Oil USAR Hooters Pro Cup Series car before a race at USA International Speedway in Lakeland, Florida. (Courtesy Jeremy Troiano, Speed51.com/51 Sports.)

Martin took an interest in Joey and worked with him, giving him advice on racing and promotion. When Joey won the Legends' Pro Nationals, Jim Gresham, a local Atlanta businessman, was so impressed with his talent he bought him a late model. Joey soon began racing ASAA and, at age fifteen, he competed in the Pro Cup Series.

Many who meet Joey are impressed with his driving and with his demeanor. Open and approachable, he projects a wholesome image and is fast becoming a favorite of fans.

"There are so many distractions that aren't good for kids," says Tom. "I think competition keeps them focused. Competing helps them understand about life as a whole, prepares them for its ups and downs, and I think it makes them each a better person. I've taught both of my children to honor the 'R' word. To get along in life, they've got to *respect* people. Whether they're racing, with friends, or with family, I want them to know the key is respect."

Joey says he's taken those lessons to heart and gained insight into the importance of treating people nicely, putting forth a good image, and the work ethic. "My Dad taught me the meaning of respect and he also taught me the meaning of hard work. I used to be very shy and I'm still a little shy, but I've started to open up as I've grown older. I've learned people skills and how to interact and be outgoing. There's more to racing now than there used to be. The media are important and drivers have a whole team to deal with. There are a lot more different types of people, including those with TV and newspapers. I've been on CNN and on *NBC Nightly News* and I think that's really helped me.

"There are also a bunch of things about cars a driver should know. I've learned to stay out of trouble, have patience, practice on the track and work on my car, even if it means coming to the shop when it's freezing."

Another thing he's learned is not to let a win make him over-confident. "Once when I won a race, I was making turns and hit the wall during burnout. I don't guess I'm the first to do that but I got it bad from the guys at the shop and it was really embarrassing."

Joey says that as the competition gets tougher, winning means more and he's looking forward to competing in the Nextel Cup Series. "It's cool to win. Racing means a lot to me. I really, really enjoy this and I have more fun now than I ever have." His Dad is solidly behind him and his mother Debbie and sister Danielle support him one hundred percent.

CHAPTER 55

Joe Gibbs and J.D. Gibbs: A Racing Legacy

One of the most admired team owners on the racing circuit, Joe Gibbs is the only man in history to lead both a football team and a racing team to victory. He first caught the nation's eye as an NFL coach when he took the Washington Redskins to four Superbowls with three wins, was named as "Coach of the Year" in 1982, 1983 and 1991, and became a 1996 inductee into the Pro Football Hall of Fame. Gibbs was still the Redskins' coach in 1991 when, with the help of his sons Coy and J.D., he formed Joe Gibbs Racing. In March of 1993, he retired from his position of head coach to apply his seemingly endless energy to motorsports and to spending more time with his family. Joe Gibbs has authored two books, *Racing to Win: Establish Your Game Plan for Success* and *Joe Gibbs: Fourth and One*. Although they remain involved in Joe Gibbs Racing, Joe and Coy are currently both on the Washington Redskins Coaching staff while J.D. oversees the race team as its president. The following is based on a 2006 interview with J.D.

"My Dad had a great love of cars, hot rods, street rods and drag cars. He spent his early years in Southern California where street rods were born. While he was in college playing football he built and raced dragsters. About the time he was graduating, his racecar blew up and since he didn't have the money to fix it, he went into full-time coaching. Coaching remains his bread and butter, even today."

Joe's passion for cars was passed on to his sons, but because of the family's commitment to football, decades passed before they had time to get involved. "We moved from California to Arkansas, where Dad coached the Razorbacks, and from there to St. Louis where he coached the Cardinals. Then, we moved down to Tampa and the Tampa Bay Buccaneers. After that, we were with the San Diego Chargers and from there, we went to Washington. He began coaching the Washington Redskins in 1981. Throughout that whole time, we watched the races and visited with Dad's friends in the drag racing community. By the nineties, we were also following NASCAR and thinking about getting involved and what we could do. We didn't have a nut, a bolt, or a racecar, but Rick Hendrick and Jimmie Johnson gave us guidance and we decided to take a shot."

Because they are a spiritually based family, the first thing the Gibbses did was to meet with Max Helton of Motor Racing Outreach to get his input. MRO is a non-profit organization, founded in 1988 to serve the NASCAR Nextel Cup (formerly Winston Cup) racing community. Now including other forms of racing, the organization's goal is to promote and nurture faith in Christ and Christlikeness throughout the world of motorsports. The organization, like the Gibbs family, is committed to using the principles found in God's Word to operate on a day-to-day basis while developing leadership skills.

"Years from now," says J.D., "people aren't going to know the scores in the Superbowl games my Dad won. Most people won't know the dates or the team members. The world sees money and fame, but those don't bring purpose and peace. Our racing team's purpose had to be what God wanted us to be. In order to be successful, we had to be where the Lord wanted us. When we are where He wants us, He opens doors."

After they met with Helton, the Gibbses felt secure in their decision. They then made a presentation to Interstate Batteries and met with Joe's personal business advisor, Don Meredith, and Jimmie Johnson. "They said 'Let's do it,' and we began building our team. We hired sixteen people on staff, the first of which was Jimmy Makar. Since my Dad was still coaching, Makar took charge of everything.

"In 1992, we began racing with Dale Jarrett as our driver and at the end of the year, my Dad officially retired as an NFL coach and moved to Charlotte for the '93 season. From the first, we wanted to win races and win championships in a way that honored the Lord. People have gifts in different areas and, whether in racing, football, or any other sport, I believe God matches people with their gifts and wants to be a part of what they love. One of my Dad's gifts from God is team building. With a team, everyone's gifts have to be molded together. We love team sports and that is what racing has become. The driver is like a quarterback; the crew chief is the coach; and members of the pit crew are the linemen. We like to maximize people's talents. Some guys, like Tony Stewart and Jeff Gordon, can drive a racecar and some guys are good at working on them. We try to match people with their God-given talents and use them on behalf of the team."

According to J.D., his father had several coaches who helped him maximize his talents and make him successful. They taught him to be a communicator and a motivator, two areas in which he has excelled. "The biggest obstacle we have to deal with is communication. All of the teams have good people and good equipment but unless they communicate and operate as a team they can't run well. The bigger you are, the harder it is and whoever is most effective is going to be ahead of the game. Communication makes us win and makes us a family."

J.D. says that three other crucial lessons motorsports teams must learn and put into practice are hard work, consistency, and humility. "Working hard and being humble aren't new but we lay it on the line because everyone is watching us. In racing, just like in life, teams go through hard times and good times. In most sports, people have jobs no matter what others think or whether anyone likes them, but in racing people appreciate our being the same in good times and bad.

"In football, if you get too close to a player you can be arrested so when I first went to racing, the closeness of fans was a shock. But race drivers know they don't get where they are by themselves. They realize they depend on their sponsors and fans. If they get cocky, they get knocked off their perch pretty quickly, and those who are successful are appreciative of what they have."

Today, Coy and Joe Gibbs work on the Washington Redskins coaching staff and, as president, J. D. continues to oversee Joe Gibbs Racing. "Sometimes I deal with corporate partners, sometimes with financial situations, and other times with issues that pop up at the shop. We help develop young drivers and I oversee all of that. Our job is to give them an opportunity and let them loose. They decide their future from there."

Joe Gibbs Racing now has three Cup teams and two and a half Busch teams. The organization has become one of the most respected in NASCAR, having won the 1993 Daytona 500 with Dale Jarrett, the 2000 Brickyard 400 with Bobby Labonte, the 2005 Brickyard 400 with Tony Stewart, over 50 Nextel Cup races and three Nextel Cup Championships. Their primary sponsors include Interstate Batteries, Home Depot and Federal Express. "We went from sixteen to four hundred people, from 10,000 to 250,000 square feet, and have our own engine program and ninety racecars. We've had a lot of good fortune, but we can't take credit for what the Lord is doing. Many doors have been opened and we've been blessed. Racing makes us happy, but we are trying to be what the Lord would have us to be, for all the right reasons."

CHAPTER 56

Chris Dilbeck:
Young and Restless

I see a lot of commitment in Chris. He's not scared of anything. He's focused and dedicated 100 percent. —Allan Vigil, Allan Vigil Ford

"He's hungry for it," says short track driver Ronnie Sanders' wife, Bobbie. "You can't fight that kind of ambition, drive, and want. He has the drive to succeed and nothing's been handed to him." The young driver she's describing is Atlanta Motor Speedway's Chris Dilbeck. Referred to by some as a "young gun," Dilbeck is determined to become a Nextel Cup driver. His driving record is commendable and his effort astounding. According to people who know him, Dilbeck has as much work power as he does horse power and he's willing to listen and learn.

Ronnie Sanders is one of the most respected drivers in the southeast, known not only for wins but for setting up cars. According to Bobbie, Dilbeck volunteered to help Ronnie at no charge, grateful to be with the car-building master. "He thanks Ronnie for letting him help. Ronnie needed somebody to assist him so it's like an answer to a prayer. Most boys, who say they'll help, just want to chat. Chris is serious."

Also serious about learning racetrack management, Dilbeck has in the last four years volunteered at Atlanta Motor Speedway as an intern in public relations. "I work in the media center and they give me a garage pass and a pit pass during Nextel Cup races. It enables me to walk through the garage when I'm on break and introduce myself."

He has found reading, as well as networking, to be an important resource in self-education. "Humpy Wheeler recommended I read *Born Fighting*, a book about how the legacy of the Scotch-Irish affected the southern racing world. I've also been reading a book about sales and marketing. It teaches you how to present yourself, how to brag on yourself without making it obvious. It doesn't matter how good a driver you are; you have to know how to network, speak well and talk. If you don't know how to network, you're not going to make it. You have to be able to represent a sponsor and be a combination of everything, plus know how to drive the wheels off a racecar. Being able to drive that racecar is most important, but you have to talk to the media.

"The ideal race driver needs to have a good attitude. You can't get your head down;

Chris Dilbeck—he does it all. (Courtesy Dilbeck Photo Collection.)

you have to keep digging. You have to do everything to your best ability. If a driver finishes last, or first, he should come out to the media center. If he has a bad day, he should say next week he'll do better. You have to be media savvy, give feedback and communicate. The media are the ones who got you where you are in the first place. The fans and the media make the sport. It's like a chain. Without the fans, you wouldn't need the media and without the media you wouldn't need racing. The fans are at the top of the pyramid.

"Being successful in racing is everything to me. I'm willing to work hard to be noticed and get where I want to go. I know everyone in NASCAR now. It's going to take awhile, but something should happen. After hearing my name over and over, somebody will eventually say, 'Hey! This kid can drive'"

Dilbeck credits a lot of his driving ability and his beginning knowledge of working on cars to Doug Stephens. "Doug puts the base setup on Legends cars and then watches a driver's style and helps him adapt. He can regulate the speed and make it go faster if he thinks a driver can handle it. He's taught me about shocks and springs and how to work on my car."

According to Dilbeck, Doug's always complaining that Chris' car is too loose and likely to fishtail and oversteer. Loose cars are more difficult to handle, but that's the way Dilbeck wants it. He says it provides the necessary preparation for Nextel Cup driving. "It's exactly what you need to be able to drive Cup cars. They depend so much on the right rear tire and there's so much down force on the front end. I've watched Doug drive and I've learned from him. In Legends cars on flat tracks, you do a lot of rubbing, pushing and bumping. If somebody's slow, it's crucial to know how to move them, to hit them without tearing anything up or spinning them out." He says the most important racing tactic he's learned is patience, as you're not going to win on the first lap anyway.

Raised in Hampton, Georgia, as a child, Dilbeck played baseball a short two minutes from the speedway. "You could see the racetrack condos over the baseball field. I could hear the Bandoleros and Legends cars practicing and my Dad took me to watch them. Every year, I'd hear the cars testing before the Cup races and my Dad would take me to see them on race weekend. We'd sit in the grandstands and watch and I liked it more and more. A lot of it had to do with Georgia driver Bill Elliott. My Dad was, and is always going to be, a Bill Elliott fan.

"My Dad and I finally started camping out in the infield and I sneaked into the pits and the garage. Much of the year the track is empty, but at Nextel Cup time stands are full. There are different rigs and souvenir trailers and cars in all different colors. I love the smell of rubber and oil and the sound of the engines and you can't get any better than a V8. When they first start, you hear the flywheel mesh and a little kink. When they come by behind the pace car, the hair on the back of my neck stands up.

"Racing is popular, because we're out here driving the cars we see in the races. They have sponsors with products, like Tide, we use everyday. People see McDonald's and think, 'I went there last night.'"

"One day Atlanta Motor Speedway had a Bandolero 'ride and drive.' My Dad paid Ken Ragan twenty dollars and I drove one and fell in love. I begged my Dad to buy me a racecar." After two years, when Chris was twelve, his Dad realized he was serious and did.

"Racing was my decision. Some people don't choose to race. Their parents choose for them. I chose to race and my parents have been very supportive. They said they'd find the money somewhere and they've been 100 percent behind every decision I've made.

"It started with the Bandoleros. One year, I was three points out of the championship lead when I was taken out in a heat race at Charlotte. I didn't have a backup car and we didn't have time to fix the car for the feature so I lost the championship. "My Mom said she was going to get me a back up car and she did. That carried over into Legends cars. I ran my Mom's car on short tracks and my Dad's on the big ones.

"We borrowed the money to buy our first Bandolero and, after nine weeks, I had my first plaque. When I started, I was racing with people who had been racing since they were five years old. During the first year that was a drawback. I struggled to finish in the top five. Now, all I want to do is win. I like the thrill of taking a car that shouldn't run up front and winning the race with it.

"About twelve weeks after my first win, we went to Shelbyville, Tennessee, for a Friday night race, then turned around the next morning and headed to Albany. I won my first race there and haven't stopped winning since."

Dilbeck continued to race Bandoleros for two seasons, winning the '99 Georgia Dirt Track Championship. In 2000, he ran second in the National Championship; in 2001 he ran second in the Charlotte Championship, and won the Georgia State Championship for the Bandolero and for the Legends cars, pulling "double duty." In 2002, he won the Georgia State Championship for Legends cars again, before moving up to Pro Division. He won the Pro Division Georgia State Championship in 2003.

With his efforts paying off, Dilbeck says his most difficult obstacle has been financial. "If I was a millionaire, I would get in a Cup car tomorrow. We're not a family that can afford to race, but we have a lot of friends and people who believe in me. People loan us money and say, 'Pay us back when you can.' Allan Vigil has been a sponsor, and he's been great. He knows a lot about racing and he challenges me to learn. He has been a key factor in my success in Legends cars and I've been proud to display his logo.

Vigil has been known to help many talented young drivers. "Mr. Vigil sponsored me in my Atlanta Motor Speedway Thursday Thunder Championship and in two wins on Nextel Cup weekends. It's neat winning on Cup weekends because you're in front of all the NASCAR fans. Those race weekend Legends races are advertised as opportunities to showcase our talent in front of the Nextel Cup boys. One year, I was going down the back straightaway when I saw Jeff Burton watching me.

"I found a nickel one day at Lanier National Speedway, up in Braselton. It was heads up on the ground and I thought, 'What the heck? I'll throw it in the seat of my Legends car.' I won seven races in a row and haven't taken it out since. It's still in my seat. I'm not a superstition nut but there's nothing wrong with thinking something's lucky. They say it's not good to eat peanuts on race day or have green on your car. I stay away from that because there's no reason to do it. My nickel's one of those deals where I thought it wouldn't hurt anything."

Tight finances have taught Dilbeck to improvise, to do for himself and to learn on his own. His Mom is an English teacher, and his Dad makes signs. By helping his father at work, he learned how to decal his car. To adapt to driving late models, he took a job with the Richard Petty Driving experience.

"I started at the bottom of the totem pole, just like you're supposed to, strapping people in cars, and worked my way up. Now, I'm trained to be an instructor.

"Racing has taught me everything," he continues. "I learned a lot in high school just like everybody else, but it's taught me how to handle people and how people handle me. It's a business, not just a sport, and it's opened a bunch of different doors."

After realizing the importance of driver looks, Dilbeck tackled self-improvement, losing weight and changing his hairstyle to a Hollywood "do." Hoping to attract a sponsor, he agreed to be filmed in the process by the Discovery Health Channel. "You have to have a good image. I needed to lose weight if I wanted to be serious so I dropped thirty pounds and learned how to work out. It's tough and it's hard to make time for it, but I go to a 24-hour gym, lift weights and run five miles, three times a week each. I used to be tired when I got out of a racecar, and now I'm not tired at all."

Dilbeck plans to major in sports managing or marketing, but believes first-hand experience is best. He's learned mechanical engineering through his work on cars and by helping mentors. He enjoys the work and the fellowship but especially likes its reward, the camaraderie with fans at speedways.

"Fans are funny. At Atlanta Motor Speedway's summer Thursday Thunder, they have a Legends Idol contest like *American Idol* and people come out of the grandstands to sing. Recently, I won five Legends races and one time, when I got out of the car at the finish line, the fans were just going nuts and had signs with my name on them. It was awesome. I never imagined seeing that in a Legends race. I like to do donuts when I win and my favorite sound is in Victory Lane, hearing the fans. There's no way to describe how you feel when you win, when everything you prepared for pays off. Your adrenaline builds on the last lap; then, at the sight of the checkered flag, it explodes."

Chris Dilbeck is currently racing late model in the Georgia Asphalt Series. "I'm driving the #4 Georgia Control Center Chevrolet and my car owner's name is Robby Chastain. He owns Chastain Racing Engines which supplies engines throughout the southeast. I drive, do all of the work on my car, work a full-time job in the engine shop and attend college courses at night. I'm hoping to catch the eye of a NASCAR team looking for a hungry and determined driver."

CHAPTER 57

The Greshams:
Racing Is a Family Affair

"Racing has brought our family together," says Tony Gresham, father of two Bandolero drivers, Charlie and Max. "It's a great opportunity for us to spend time together and has taught us how to communicate. We've had to learn a lot more about how each other thinks, what we see and feel, and it's taught us to respect one another.

"With this sport," says Gresham, "you develop a great deal of respect for people who make things happen—your crew, car owners, and fellow competitors. There's a lot of sportsmanship, humility, responsibility, discipline, and focus. Along with the drive to excel, you have to have a humble spirit. You can't win every race and you have to learn to concentrate."

Tony Gresham and his father Jim have been in the insurance business in Stockbridge, Georgia, for years. Gresham and Associates has been a successful enterprise, one that has provided the funds for exciting experiences. Their venture into racing is a three-generation affair.

"My family grew up within a couple of miles of Atlanta Motor Speedway," Tony continues. "We attended summer Thursday Thunder races every week before we became involved. When my oldest son Max turned eight, my father approached me and said, 'How about we put Max in a Bandolero and give him a shot at driving a racecar?' We all agreed it was a good idea so Max started practicing and learning skills. Now he is twelve and my youngest son Charlie turned eight and is racing a Bandolero as well. My Dad has a competitive side. He had never done any oval racing, but he'd drag-raced in his youth. He bought a couple of Legends cars and started driving one and let a friend drive the other. Now he's raised our number of cars to eleven, including four Bandoleros, three Legends cars, a Roadster, and a late model. We have a race shop in Sunnyside, Georgia, where we can put our cars and have a crew of four employees to work on them, including former ASA Champion Joey Clanton. We use a Renegade hauler with a double-decker trailer to transport the cars and also have a truck and trailer."

Both boys love the cars, but each in his own special way. "Max is more interested in how fast the cars go and who he can outrun," says Tony. "Charlie has an interest in what makes the car go, what the nuts and bolts do, and how the engine is made. The biggest obstacle they've faced is learning the mechanics of driving, and any time you operate equipment at high speed, it's going to be dangerous. We've seen our share of nasty

"With this sport," says Tony Gresham, "you develop a great deal of respect for people who make things happen—your crew, car owners, and fellow competitors." (Courtesy Gresham Photo Collection.)

collisions and had our share of wrecks, but never seen much in the way of injuries. The Bandoleros and Legends are made extremely well to protect the driver. They do a great job of putting them together and safety is paramount; plus, we own every piece of safety equipment there is. Our seats are custom-built and our drivers wear head and neck restraint harnesses, fire-proof suits, fire-proof shoes, and the best Simpson helmets we can find.

"Most of the tracks allow people to rent time. You can have private practices to learn how to get around and how the racecar operates. You can also attend open practices which may have five to fifty cars."

Many people question whether on-track racing leads to off-track speed. They wonder if it's a good idea for children.

"One of the most frequent questions I'm asked is what I expect when they turn sixteen, have a driver's license, and get out on the road. I don't expect them to be any different than other teen drivers. I expect them to have better training than most."

Although the family has shared great memories, there have been a few stressful incidents. One of their more harrowing experiences was at a nearby short track in Senoia.

"We were racing on Saturday," says Tony, "when Max came off of turn four. In an attempt to dodge two cars that were wrecking, he actually got upside down. He slid down the straightaway about one hundred feet, came to a stop, got out of the car, and was fine. We pulled the car to the pit area and as he was beginning to take his driving suit off and get back into his street clothes, he looked down and said, 'Well, it's still got four wheels on it. Are you sure I can't drive it?' I told him to sit out; his Dad had all he could take."

Last summer, Tony drove sixteen hours round trip from Myrtle Beach, South Carolina, to Atlanta so Max wouldn't miss a Thursday Thunder race. After they arrived, Max didn't get to the green flag before he'd already wrecked the car. They turned right around and made the trip back without skipping a beat.

"We gave the boys the opportunity to explore racing and they picked it up and fell in love with it. I raced once, but with two children in racecars, it takes time to make sure they have what they need. We haven't set any specific aspirations for winning races or championships, or trying to develop Max and Charlie into professional racecar drivers. If the opportunities present themselves and the boys learn enough skills, that may become a part of their future. Right now, we just want to go to the track as a family, have fun, enjoy ourselves, and become competitive."

The progression for those wanting to race is as follows: At eight they can run Bandoleros. They have to be twelve to be eligible for other classes, going from Legends to full-size Late Model cars. If they are successful, they may move on to ASA or Hooter's Pro Cup. From there they can go to NASCAR.

CHAPTER 58

Atlanta Motor Speedway President Ed Clark: The Other Side of the Tracks

Atlanta Motor Speedway dominates Hampton, Georgia's horizon with the presence of a giant movie set. The likeness is fitting. As in the world of cinema, the world of racing makes and breaks careers, produces big ticket celebrities, and lures millions of fans. Just as in the movie world, what is seen by the general public is only part of the story. Most of the action takes place behind the scenes.

In Hollywood, producers and directors are in charge. In racing, speedway owners and presidents make decisions, schedule events, and interact with local communities. In the case of Atlanta Motor Speedway, the most powerful man on the premises is its president, Ed Clark. Clark is a man who knows his field. His first experience with racing began when he was a toddler.

"There wasn't a lot to do in Keysville, Virginia, where I grew up. We had a black and white TV and our bikes, and that was it. My favorite uncle was a big race fan. When I was little and riding a tricycle, he called me Pancho. That's former NASCAR driver Marvin Panch's nickname."

As he grew older, Clark attended races, finally going into the pits at the age of nine. "I got autographs and it hooked me for life. Racing wasn't as big back then, but it was big to me and fans were as rabid as they are today."

Clark was interested in almost all sports and played football before high school and then played on the varsity baseball and basketball teams. "Baseball was a big part of my life. I followed the New York Yankees and Roger Maris was my favorite player. I liked him because he broke Babe Ruth's home run record and because, like me, he batted left-handed. My Dad's dream was for me to be a baseball player. My brother and I were both named after pro players. I was named after Edwin 'Duke' Snyder."

Still enthralled by racing when he was fifteen, Clark began covering races for a bi-weekly newspaper. "Later, I attended Virginia Tech and earned money working for a newspaper chain. I covered races and had a weekly motorsports column. That's how I made contacts in the industry."

Strangely, his enthusiasm for racing was matched by a passion for gardening. "I was a horticulture major in college. My grandmother was a big plant 'nut' and always had plants everywhere. I guess that rubbed off on my genes. I've always enjoyed working with landscaping and house plants and spend a lot of time doing it. One of the things I love to do on weekends is relax and work in my yard. I'd probably have gone into horticulture and had my own greenhouse if I'd had the money. If you don't have money to start a business, you look somewhere else. Racing was my big hobby. I loved it and saw opportunities.

"When I graduated from Virginia Tech, I started working at Bristol Raceway, which is Bristol Motor Speedway now. I worked there about two years, and then, when the guys I worked for bought the track in Nashville, I was transferred there. I was general manager in Nashville at age twenty-four.

"I stayed for almost two years before going to Charlotte, and came to Atlanta in 1992. Bruton Smith is the owner and primary shareholder of Atlanta Motor Speedway, and Humpy Wheeler, my former boss in Charlotte, is chief operational officer. They've given me a lot of support

"I try to make everything I do enjoyable. On this side of the business, the thing I'm passionate about is being able to go on the roof on race day, look down, and see the stands full." (Courtesy Ed Clark Photo Collection.)

and have both been real inspirations. They're good to work for and they're good friends. I've been with the company for twenty-two years.

"I try to make everything I do enjoyable. On this side of the business, the thing I'm passionate about is being able to go on the roof on race day, look down, and see the stands full. I love the color and excitement of the fans. No matter what they do for a living, or their background, everybody has a great time."

According to Clark, there are a lot of families attending racing events and one of the most interesting aspects is the speedway's geographical draw. "We draw strongly from within a 250-mile radius, but sell tickets in all fifty states and seventeen countries. People travel far to attend these events and they're great for our local economy and for our state."

Atlanta Motor Speedway's impact on Georgia is estimated at about $450,000,000 a year. These figures include advertising, promotional items, souvenirs, car rentals, gas tax, flights, and motel rooms. As in other NASCAR racetrack locations, the money helps save homeowners, and other community members, important tax dollars. "We try to be real community players and contribute in a positive way to the whole area."

Atlanta Motor Speedway photographer Howard Martin captures moments in racing history for posterity. (Courtesy Howard Martin Photo Collection.)

Clark lives in Peachtree City with his wife Teresa, whom he describes as the family director and a "domestic engineer." They have two children: daughter Nicki, a creative, artistic young lady who plays the guitar, and Collin, a "typical boy," who enjoys skateboarding, reading and video games.

"It's important to be involved in the community," says Clark. "I'm on the Board of Directors for the Atlanta Sports Council and the Atlanta Convention and Visitor's Bureau and on the local Boy Scouts' Council. Our Children's Charities Foundation contributes $350,000 or more, locally, each year. We work with drivers and local organizations to raise the funds and we've donated about $2 million dollars since we started."

One of the charities sponsored is A Friend's House, a shelter for abused and abandoned children in Henry County, begun with almost $300,000 from AMS in matching funds.

Another resource Atlanta Motor Speedway contributes is jobs. "We have sixty-three full-time employees and, during races, hire five-thousand. Many groups, such as civic and booster clubs, depend on us for their finances. They work hard, are good at what they do, and in turn, we depend on them."

The Speedway, with its size, garages, clubhouse and ballroom is also a venue for other local events. "We lease the track for car shows, concerts, dog shows and Scout shows, driving schools, and motorcycle races. We cater and accommodate proms, reunions, and weddings. We have every social function you can imagine. There aren't many activities we can't have here."

Atlanta Motor Speedway's impact on Georgia is estimated at about $450,000,000 a year. Speedway President Ed Clark points out those figures include advertising, promotional items, souvenirs, car rentals, gas tax, flights, and motel rooms. It's an important financial bonus, and tourism is a clean industry. (Courtesy the Atlanta Motor Speedway.)

During the months of "Summer Thunder," people come from throughout the region to race Legends cars. Recently, Ed Clark got involved, not as the speedway president, but as a driver. "I drove one race in 1980 at Rockingham, and until this, that's the only racing experience I'd had. It's the most fun I've had with a new activity in a long time, but I am way too serious, and I get reminded of that. I've thoroughly enjoyed it, getting to know the other people who race and their families. That's the neatest thing, whether you're in the stands or in the garage. There are a lot of families with kids and a lot of kids race."

Despite the wide variety of offerings, the Atlanta Motor Speedway's main focus remains on people attending NASCAR events. "Racing is really about fans," says Clark. "If the fans didn't come, all of this wouldn't mean anything."

Concern for fans and the community have led to progress and change. "We've had road improvement and NASCAR has helped us with rain dates. Now our races are drier and warmer. Traffic movement is better and we've added more spectator amenities. Our company's invested $100 million in rebuilding the Speedway and adding new facilities. Atlanta Motor Speedway has made a commitment. We want to have races for a long time to come."

Index

NCR

2/09